JOEY GREEN'S
ENCYCLOPEDIA
of Offbeat Uses for
Brand-Name Products

Also by Joey Green

Hellbent on Insanity

The Unofficial Gilligan's Island Handbook

The Get Smart Handbook

The Partridge Family Album

Polish Your Furniture with Panty Hose

Hi Bob!—A Self-Help Guide to the Bob Newhart Show

Selling Out: If Famous Authors Wrote Advertising

Paint Your House with Powdered Milk

Wash Your Hair with Whipped Cream

The Bubble Wrap Book

The Zen of Oz: Ten Spiritual Lessons from Over the Rainbow

JOEY GREEN'S
ENCYCLOPEDIA
of Offbeat Uses for Brand-Name Products

Hundreds of Handy Household Hints for
More than 120 Household Products—
from Alka-Seltzer® to Ziploc® Storage Bags

Joey Green

New York

Design by Joey Green

Library of Congress Cataloging-in-Publication Data

Green, Joey.
    [Encyclopedia of offbeat uses for brand-name products]
    Joey Green's encyclopedia of offbeat uses for brand-name products / Joey Green. — 1st ed.
        p.   cm.
    Includes bibliographical references and index.
    ISBN 0-7868-6354-4
    1. Home economics. 2. Brand name products—United States.
3. Medicine, Popular.   I. Title
TX158.G678   1998   97-30984
640'.41—dc21   CIP

First Edition
10 9 8 7 6 5 4 3 2 1

*For
Aunt Syl*

Ingredients

But First, a Word from Our Sponsor

I am constantly asked how I come up with all of these un-
usual ways to use brand-name products. The answer is
simple. I don't. Upstanding Americans just like you are
constantly discovering extraordinary ways to use ordinary
brand-name products they have around the house. They
might accidentally discover that Worcestershire Sauce shines
brass. They may polish silverware with Colgate Toothpaste.
Or they may figure out that Tidy Cat litter provides out-
standing traction for cars stuck in snow. Astounded by their
own ingenuity, they write enthusiastic letters to the manu-
facturers to share their discoveries. In return, they receive
polite thank you letters, explaining that the companies plan
to continue marketing Worcestershire Sauce as a condiment,
Colgate as a toothpaste, and Tidy Cat as a cat box litter. If
they're lucky, they'll also get a coupon for fifty cents off their
next purchase.

The companies do keep all these creative suggestions on
file, often compiling lists of the alternative uses, which are
then filed away, never to see the light of day again. The
companies should kiss the ground that their innovative,
think-outside-the-box customers walk on. After all, polishing silverware uses up a lot more toothpaste than simply

brushing your teeth does. Instead, hundreds of amazing uses for well-known products are foolishly kept secret from the American public.

So I contact the companies to obtain these secret lists. To me, it's like opening up the CIA's files. I also lock myself in the library for days at a time to research kitchen remedies, household hints, and folklore medicines. Then I test them all out at home. They're not only fun, but they actually work.

The result is—aside from a wild mess in my garage— this encyclopedia of hundreds of outrageous, economical, environmental, and convenient uses for the hundreds of products you probably have in your kitchen, bathroom, and workshop right now. It all adds up to a remarkable tribute to American ingenuity—and my wife's patience.

Make Play Dough
with Gold Medal Flour

Artwork

Make artwork with . . .

- **Hartz Parakeet Seed.** Paint a design in Elmer's Glue-All on construction paper, then cover the glue with Hartz Parakeet Seed and let dry.

Protect artwork with . . .

- **Alberto VO5 Hair Spray.** When sprayed on a chalk drawing, Alberto VO5 Hair Spray acts as a fixative, preventing artwork from fading.

Bank

Make a coin bank with . . .

- **Gerber Applesauce.** Use a screwdriver and a hammer to cut a slit in the lid of a clean, empty Gerber baby food jar.

Bath toy
Make a bath toy with . . .

- **Ivory Soap.** Carve a bar of Ivory Soap into the shape of a boat for a bath toy that floats and cleans.

Candlemaking
Dye candles with . . .

- **Crayola Crayons.** When making candles with paraffin wax, melt Crayola Crayons with the paraffin to make colored candles.

Remove homemade candles from molds easily with . . .

- **Crisco All-Vegetable Shortening.** Rub a thin coat of Crisco All-Vegetable Shortening on the inside of the candle mold before pouring in the hot wax.

Reduce ash and eliminate smoke problems from candle-wicks in homemade candles with . . .

- **20 Mule Team Borax.** Dissolve one tablespoon of table salt and three tablespoons 20 Mule Team Borax in one cup of warm water. Soak heavy twine in the solution for at least twenty-four hours. Allow the twine to dry thoroughly before using to make candles.

Crystal Paintings
Make crystal paintings with . . .

- **Epsom Salt.** Draw with crayons on construction paper. Then mix together equal parts of Epsom Salt and boiling water. Using a wide paintbrush, paint the picture with the salt mixture. When the picture dries, frosty crystals will appear.

Decorating
Hang pictures, sun catchers, or wind chimes with . . .

- **Oral-B Mint Waxed Floss.** Dental floss is stronger and more durable than ordinary string.

Dollhouses
Wallpaper the rooms of a dollhouse with . . .
- **Con-Tact Paper.** Con-Tact Paper makes excellent self-adhesive wallpaper for dollhouses.

Fingerpaints
Make fingerpaints with . . .
- **Barbasol Shaving Cream.** Let children paint with Barbasol on a kitchen table or vinyl tablecloth. For color, sprinkle in powdered tempera paint or add a drop of food coloring.
- **Kingsford's Corn Starch.** Mix one-quarter cup Kingsford's Corn Starch with two cups cold water, boil until thick, pour into small containers, and color with food coloring.
- **McCormick/Schilling Food Coloring.** Mix two cups soap flakes, two cups liquid laundry starch, and five drops food coloring in a large bowl. Blend with a wire whisk until the mixture has the consistency of whipped cream.

Flowers
Preserve flowers with . . .
- **20 Mule Team Borax.** Mix one part 20 Mule Team Borax and two parts cornmeal. Fill the bottom inch of an empty airtight canister with the mixture. Place the flower on the mixture, then gently cover the flower with

more mixture, being careful not to crush the flower or distort the petals. Flowers with a lot of overlapping petals, such as roses and carnations, are best treated by sprinkling mixture directly into the blossom before placing them into the box. Seal the canister and store at room temperature in a dry place for seven to ten days. When the flowers are dried, pour off the mixture and dust the flowers with a soft artist's brush. Borax removes the moisture from blossoms and leaves, preventing the wilting that would normally result.

Tint flowers with . . .

- **McCormick/Schilling Food Coloring.** Mix food coloring in warm water and place the flower stems in the solution overnight. The stems will absorb the colors by morning, revealing intriguing designs in different colors.

Flubber or Gak

Make flubber with . . .

- **Elmer's Glue-All, 20 Mule Team Borax,** and **McCormick/Schilling Food Coloring.** In a large bowl, mix two cups Elmer's Glue-All with one and a half cups water, and twenty drops McCormick/Schilling Food Coloring. In a second bowl, mix one teaspoon 20 Mule Team Borax with one-third cup water. Add the second bowl to the first bowl and mix until it clumps and set aside. Make another bowl of borax and water and again add it to the first bowl. Take out clump and set aside. Repeat this process until the glue solution in the first bowl is gone. Makes three to four small clumps. Store in an airtight container.

Glue

Apply glue with . . .

- **Forster Toothpicks.** Dip one end of a Forster Toothpick into the glue to apply small drops.
- **Q-Tips Cotton Swabs.** A Q-Tips Cotton Swab doubles as an excellent brush for dabbing on glue.

Make glue with . . .

- **Gold Medal Flour.** Mix Gold Medal Flour and water to a pancake batter consistency for use on paper, lightweight fabric, and cardboard.

Make a glue dispenser with . . .

- **SueBee Honey.** Fill a SueBee Honey bear with Elmer's Glue.

Make colorful glues with . . .

- **McCormick/Schilling Food Coloring.** Fill an empty SueBee Honey bear with Elmer's Glue and tint with a few drops of food coloring to make colorful glues.

Jewelry

Make colorful macaroni jewelry for kids with . . .

- **McCormick/Schilling Food Coloring.** Add a few drops of food coloring to a bowl of water. Dip dry macaroni in the water, drain, and dry. Then make necklaces by stringing the colored macaroni together.

Make colorful straw necklaces with . . .

- **Glad Flexible Straws.** Instead of using macaroni,

JELL-O-RAMA!

Every April Fool's Day in Eugene, Oregon, the Maude Kerns Art Gallery holds the Jell-O Art Show, better known as "Jell-O-Rama," featuring works of local artists using Jell-O as a medium.

let the kids cut up Glad Flexible Straws and run a string of yarn through them to make necklaces.

String beaded necklaces with . . .

- **Oral-B Mint Waxed Floss.** Oral-B Mint Waxed Floss is thin enough for small beads, yet stronger than thread.

Lava Lamp

Make a poor man's lava lamp with . . .

- **Canada Dry Club Soda.** Fill a glass with Canada Dry Club Soda and drop in two raisins. The carbonation will cause the raisins to repeatedly bob to the surface and then sink again.

Leaves

Preserve autumn leaves with . . .

- **Reynolds Cut-Rite Wax Paper.** Place the leaf between two sheets of Reynolds Cut-Rite Wax Paper, then place the wax paper between two sheets of brown paper. Press with a warm iron to seal, then trim the paper around the leaves.

Maracas

Make a maraca for children with . . .

- **Orville Redenbacher's Gourmet Popping Corn.** Put a handful of unpopped Orville Redenbacher's Gourmet Popping Corn inside a clean, empty milk carton, then seal the carton shut with Scotch Packaging Tape. Let the child decorate the milk carton with glitter, plastic jewels, and shapes cut from construction paper.
- **Uncle Ben's Converted Brand Rice.** If you don't have any Orville Redenbacher's Gourmet Popping Corn,

substitute a handful of Uncle Ben's Converted Brand Rice in the above hint.

Movie Making
Simulate blood in black-and-white movies with . . .

● **Bosco.** Bosco chocolate syrup looks just like blood on the silver screen and was commonly used as mock blood in early Hollywood productions.

Newspaper Clippings
Preserve newspaper clippings with . . .

● **Phillips' Milk of Magnesia** and **Canada Dry Club Soda.** Dissolve one Milk of Magnesia tablet in one quart Canada Dry Club Soda. Let the mixture stand overnight. The next day, stir the mixture well, then soak your clipping in the solution for one hour. Blot the newspaper clipping between two sheets of Viva Paper Towels and place on a screen to dry.

Paintbrushes
(See page 268)

Paint
Make black paint with . . .

● **Betty Crocker Potato Buds.** Bake Betty Crocker Potato Buds until they're black, grind thoroughly with a mortar and pestle, then add linseed oil until you achieve the consistency of paint.

● **Kiwi Shoe Polish.** Some artists use Kiwi Shoe Polish as paint in oil paintings.

Palettes

Make a disposable palette with . . .

● **Reynolds Wrap.** Mix paints on a piece of Reynolds Wrap.

Paper Dolls

Create paper dolls with . . .

● **Con-Tact Paper.** Cover magazine pictures with clear Con-Tact Paper and then cut them out.

Papier-Mâché

Enhance papier-mâché projects with . . .

● **Kleenex Tissue.** Use Kleenex Tissues as the paper for your papier-mâché projects to achieve different textures.

Make papier-mâché with . . .

● **Gold Medal Flour.** Mix one cup Gold Medal Flour with two-thirds cup water in a medium-size bowl to a thick glue consistency. To thicken, add more flour. Cut newspaper strips approximately one to two inches in width. Dip each strip into the paste, gently pull it between your fingers to remove excess paste, and apply it to any object (an empty bottle, carton, or canister). Continue until the base is completely covered. Let dry, then decorate with poster paint. After the paint dries, coat with shellac.

Color My World

● In 1903, Binney & Smith made the first box of Crayola Crayons, costing a nickel and containing eight colors: Red, Orange, Yellow, Green, Blue, Violet, Brown, and Black.

● In 1949, Binney & Smith introduced another forty colors: Apricot, Bittersweet, Blue Green, Blue Violet, Brick Red, Burnt Sienna, Carnation Pink, Cornflower, Flesh (renamed Peach in 1962, partly as a result of the civil rights movement), Gold, Gray, Green Blue, Green Yellow, Lemon Yellow, Magenta, Mahogany, Maize, Maroon, Melon, Olive Green, Orange Red, Orange Yellow, Orchid, Periwinkle, Pine Green, Prussian Blue (renamed Midnight Blue in 1958 in response to teachers' requests), Red Orange, Red Violet, Salmon, Sea Green, Silver, Spring Green, Tan, Thistle, Turquoise Blue, Violet Blue, Violet Red, White, Yellow Green, and Yellow Orange.

● The now-classic "64-box" of crayons, complete with built-in sharpener, was introduced in 1958. To bring the total number of colors to sixty-four, Binney & Smith added sixteen colors: Aquamarine, Blue Gray, Burnt Orange, Cadet Blue, Copper, Forest Green, Goldenrod, Indian Red, Lavender, Mulberry, Navy Blue, Plum, Raw Sienna, Raw Umber, Sepia, and Sky Blue.

● In 1972, Binney & Smith introduced eight fluorescent colors: Atomic Tangerine, Blizzard Blue, Hot Magenta, Laser Lemon, Outrageous Orange, Screamin' Green, Shocking Pink, and Wild Watermelon.

● In 1990, the company introduced eight more fluorescent colors: Electric Lime, Magic Mint, Purple Pizzazz, Radical Red, Razzle Dazzle Rose, Sunglow, Unmellow Yellow, and Neon Carrot.

● In 1990, Binney & Smith retired eight traditional colors from its sixty-four-crayon box (Green Blue, Orange Red, Orange Yellow, Violet Blue, Maize, Lemon Yellow, Blue Gray, and Raw Umber) and replaced them with such New Age hues as Cerulean, Vivid Tangerine, Jungle Green, Fuchsia, Dandelion, Teal Blue, Royal Purple, and Wild Strawberry. Retired colors were enshrined in the Crayola Hall of Fame. Protests from groups such as RUMPS (Raw Umber and Maize Preservation Society) and CRAYON (Committee to Reestablish All Your Old Norms) convinced Binney & Smith to release a million boxes of the "Crayola Eight" in 1991.

● In 1993, Binney & Smith celebrated Crayola brand's ninetieth birthday by introducing the biggest crayon box ever, with ninety-six colors, adding sixteen more colors, all named by consumers: Asparagus, Cerise, Denim, Granny Smith Apple, Macaroni and Cheese, Mauvelous, Pacific Blue, Purple Mountain's Majesty, Razzmatazz, Robin's Egg Blue, Shamrock, Tickle Me Pink, Timber Wolf, Tropical Rain Forest, Tumbleweed, and Wisteria.

Make a starch fabric stiffener with . . .

- **Elmer's Glue-All.** Mix water and Elmer's Glue-All in a bowl to desired consistency. Strips of newspaper or fabric dipped in the mixture can be shaped and dried in decorative forms and shapes.

Placemats

Make placemats from children's artwork with . . .

- **Con-Tact Paper.** Cover the child's drawing, painting, or construction paper collage with clear Con-Tact Paper and cut to size.

Play Dough

Make Play Dough with . . .

- **Gold Medal Flour.** Add five drops food coloring to two cups water. Then add two cups Gold Medal Flour, one cup salt, one teaspoon cream of tartar, and two tablespoons vegetable oil. Mix well. Cook and stir over medium heat for three minutes (or until the mixture holds together). Turn onto board or cookie sheet and knead to proper consistency. Store in an airtight container.

Make moldable dough that dries without baking with . . .

- **Elmer's Glue-All.** Mix equal parts Elmer's Glue-All, flour, and corn starch. Mix and knead well until blended. If too dry, add more glue. If too moist, add more flour and corn starch. Food coloring may be added if desired. Dough can be molded into any desired shape to create animals, figurines, ornaments, and jewelry. Dough keeps for weeks in a Ziploc Storage Bag.

Potpourri
Make potpourri with . . .
- **Ziploc Storage Bags.** Collect dried roses, juniper sprigs, tiny pinecones, strips of orange rind, bay leaves, cinnamon sticks, whole cloves, and allspice berries. Mix a few drops of rose, cinnamon, and balsam oils with orris root (available at your local crafts store). Add all ingredients and seal in a Ziploc Storage Bag for a few weeks to mellow, turning the bag occasionally.

Snow Globes
Make a snow-filled paperweight with . . .
- **Gerber Applesauce.** Glue a small plastic figurine to the inside bottom of a clean, empty Gerber baby food jar. When the glue dries, fill the jar three-quarters full with water, add a teaspoon of silver glitter, screw on the cap, and seal with clear Scotch Packaging Tape.

Spatter Painting
Make a spatter painting with . . .
- **Oral-B Toothbrushes.** Place a piece of paper inside a small cardboard box and place leaves, stencils, or flowers on the paper. Cover the opening of the box with a sheet of metal screening secured in place with rubber bands. Dip the Oral-B Toothbrush in paint and scrub it over the screen, allowing the paint to spatter over the paper. Remove the screen and various objects, and let the painting dry.

Storage

Store crafts with . . .

- **Huggies Baby Wipes.** Organize ribbons, beads, glues, or strings in empty Huggies Baby Wipes boxes.

- **Ziploc Storage Bags.** Buttons, beads, and various odds and ends store well in Ziploc Storage Bags.

THE WONDERFUL WORLD OF ART

In 1996, artist Michael Gonzalez's show at the Huntington Beach Art Center featured paintings incorporating Wonder Bread wrappers.

Stuffed Animals

Fill stuffed animals with . . .

- **Kleenex Tissue.** Use Kleenex Tissues to make stuffed animals when sewing.

Stuffing

Make waterproof stuffing for outdoor cushions and bathtub toys with . . .

- **Glad Trash Bags.** Cut a Glad Trash Bag into strips and use it as stuffing.

Sun Catcher

Make a crayon sun catcher with . . .

- **Reynolds Cut-Rite Wax Paper.** Using a small pencil sharpener, shave crayons onto a sheet of Cut-Rite Wax Paper. Fold the wax paper in half, covering all the shavings. Press with a warm iron until the crayon shavings melt. When cool, thread string through the top of the wax paper and hang in a window.

Telephone
Make a poor man's telephone with . . .
- **Dixie Cups.** Punch a small hole in the bottoms of two Dixie Cups. Then thread the ends of a long piece of string through the holes and tie each end to a button. You and a friend each take a cup and walk apart until the string is straight and taut. Speak into the open end of your cup. Your sound waves travel along the string and can be heard by your friend through the open end of the other cup.

Toy Parachute
Make a toy parachute with . . .
- **Kleenex Tissue.** Tie a piece of string (or Oral-B Dental Floss) to each of the four corners of a Kleenex Tissue and then secure the other ends of the string to a small weight or a toy soldier. Ball up the tissue and the weight and throw into the air.

Trays
Make decorative trays or holiday decorations with . . .
- **Reynolds Wrap.** Cut cardboard into desired shape and size and cover with Reynolds Wrap.

Weather Vanes
Make a weather vane with . . .
- **Dixie Cups.** Remove the bottom from a Dixie Cup and hang the cup horizontally from a string. The opening will tend to face into the wind.

Wrapping Paper
Make your own gift wrapping paper with . . .

● **Alberto VO5 Hair Spray.** Spray Alberto VO5 Hair Spray on the comics section from the Sunday paper to seal in the ink and give the paper a shiny gloss.

● **McCormick/Schilling Food Coloring.** Add five drops of food coloring to one cup water, making one cup for each one of the four colors. Stack several sheets of white tissue paper on top of each other, fold them in half, in half again, and in half again. Dip each one of the four corners into a different color solution without soaking the paper. Let the tissue dry on newspaper, unfold, then iron flat.

BACK IN THE U.S.S.R.

In 1988, at an erotic art exposition in Moscow, a woman was covered in whipped cream and men in the audience were invited to lick it off, according to *Time* magazine.

2

| Bathroom |

Clean Your Toilet

with *Coca-Cola*

Bath Toys
Hold bath toys with . . .

- **Glad Trash Bags.** Punch holes in a Glad Trash Bag and hang it on the shower nozzle to hold bath toys.

Bathtubs
Clean a bathtub with . . .

- **McCormick/Schilling Cream of Tartar.** Make a paste from Cream of Tartar and hydrogen peroxide, scrub with a brush, and rinse thoroughly.
- **Dr. Bronner's Peppermint Soap.** Mix one-half cup Dr. Bronner's Peppermint Soap, two cups Arm & Hammer Baking Soda, and two-thirds cup water in a squirt bottle. Then add two tablespoons Heinz White Vinegar, shake vigorously, squirt and sponge.

Clean bathtub rings with . . .

- **Cascade.** Sprinkle Cascade on a wet sponge and scrub.

Clean and refinish your bathtub with . . .

- **Turtle Wax.** Rub Turtle Wax into the tub, tiles, and faucets with a soft cloth, and polish immediately with a clean cloth or an electric buffer before the wax dries.

Eliminate bathtub rust stains with . . .

- **20 Mule Team Borax.** Scrub rust stains with a paste made from 20 Mule Team Borax and lemon juice.

Caulking

Clean caulking around bathtubs with . . .

- **Clorox.** Scrub with a solution of three-quarters cup Clorox Bleach to a gallon of water.

Cleanser

Clean soap scum, mildew, and grime from bathtub, tile, and shower curtains with . . .

- **Heinz Vinegar.** Simply wipe the surface with Heinz Vinegar and rinse with water.

Clean tight crevices with . . .

- **Forster Toothpicks.** Dip a Forster Toothpick in alcohol to clean tight spaces.

Clean the sink, bathtub, and bathroom tiles with . . .

- **L'eggs Sheer Energy.** Use a balled-up pair of L'eggs as a nonscratchy scouring pad.

Disinfectant

Kill germs on bathroom surfaces with . . .

- **Heinz Vinegar.** Use one part Heinz Vinegar to one

part water in a spray bottle. Spray the bathroom fixtures and floor, then wipe clean.

Drains
(See page 192)

Fiberglass
Clean a fiberglass bathtub or shower with . . .
- **Arm & Hammer Baking Soda.** Sprinkle Arm & Hammer Baking Soda on a damp sponge, scrub, and rinse clean.

Fixtures
Clean bathroom fixtures with . . .
- **Spray 'n Wash.** Spray generously with Spray 'n Wash, then shine with a cloth.

Grout
Camouflage stained grout with . . .
- **Liquid Paper.** Simply paint the grout with Liquid Paper.

Clean the grout between bathroom tiles with . . .
- **Oral-B Toothbrushes.** Use a clean, old Oral-B Toothbrush to scrub the grout clean.

Hairbrushes and Combs
Clean hairbrushes and combs with . . .
- **Clairol Herbal Essences.** Add a capful of Clairol Herbal Essences to warm water and soak brushes and combs for twenty minutes. Shampoo cuts through hair oils, leaving your brushes clean and fresh.

- **20 Mule Team Borax.** Mix a quarter cup 20 Mule Team Borax and a tablespoon of Dawn dishwashing detergent in a basin of warm water. Soak hairbrushes and combs in the solution, rinse clean, and dry.

Clean combs with . . .
- **Oral-B Toothbrushes.** Dip a clean, old Oral-B Toothbrush in alcohol and scrub the teeth of the comb.

Medicine Cabinets

Prevent sliding doors on a medicine cabinet from sticking with . . .
- **Alberto VO5 Conditioning Hairdressing.** Rub a little Alberto VO5 Conditioning Hairdressing onto the tracks.
- **Vaseline.** Rub a dab of Vaseline into the ridges so the doors glide smoothly over the lubricated runner.
- **WD-40.** A spritz of WD-40 along the tracks will help the doors slide easier.

Mildew

Clean mildew from shower curtains, shower caddies, bath mats, and plastic soap dishes with . . .
- **Clorox.** Place all the bathroom accessories into the bathtub, fill with two gallons water, and add one and a half cups Clorox Bleach. Rinse and drain. The Clorox Bleach also will have cleaned the bathtub, so sponge it down, too.

Clean mildew from grout with . . .
- **Clorox.** Mix three-quarters cup Clorox Bleach to one gallon of water, and use an old toothbrush.

Prevent mildew in the bathtub with . . .
- **Tidy Cat.** Pour unused Tidy Cat into a flat box and place the box in your bathtub when you leave your house

for a long time. (If you have cats, keep the bathroom door closed so they don't use the box.)

Mirrors

Dry steam off a fogged-up bathroom mirror with a . . .

- **Conair Pro Style 1600.** Simply use a Conair Pro Style 1600 to blow hot air at the mirror.

Keep your bathroom mirror from fogging up with . . .

- **Barbasol Shaving Cream.** Spread Barbasol on and wipe off. The effect can last two to three weeks.
- **SPAM.** SPAM can be used to keep the condensation off the bathroom mirror when showering, according to the *New York Times Magazine.*

Prescriptions

Protect labels on prescription medicines with . . .

- **Maybelline Crystal Clear Nail Polish.** Keep prescription labels clear and readable by painting them with Maybelline Crystal Clear Nail Polish.
- **Scotch Transparent Tape.** Cover the label with Scotch Transparent Tape.

Septic Tank

Maintain your septic tank with . . .

- **Arm & Hammer Baking Soda.** Flush one cup Arm & Hammer Baking Soda down the toilet once a week. Baking soda helps maintain proper pH and alkalinity, controlling sulfide odors.

SHOPLIFTERS BEWARE! Preparation H is one of the products most frequently shoplifted from drugstores, according to *New Times* magazine.

Shaving Cream Cans

Prevent the bottom edges of shaving cream cans from rusting with . . .

- **Maybelline Crystal Clear Nail Polish.** Paint the bottom edges of the can with Maybelline Crystal Clear Nail Polish.

Shower Curtains

Keep shower curtains gliding easily with . . .

- **Alberto VO5 Conditioning Hairdressing.** Apply a thin coat of Alberto VO5 Conditioning Hairdressing to the curtain rod.
- **Vaseline.** Apply a thin coat of Vaseline Petroleum Jelly to the curtain rod.

Remove wrinkles from shower curtains with a . . .

- **Conair Pro Style 1600.** Blow with a Conair Pro Style 1600 set on hot until the plastic softens.

Showers

Adjust the water in the bath or shower effortlessly with . . .

- **Cover Girl NailSlicks Classic Red.** Turn on the bathtub or shower faucets at the temperature you prefer, then mark the faucet(s) and the wall with a dot of Cover Girl NailSlicks Classic Red Nail Polish so they can be aligned immediately every time you bathe or shower.

Clean shower tiles and doors with . . .

- **Spray 'n Wash.** Spray with Spray 'n Wash, wait three minutes, then wipe clean with a sponge.

Unclog a shower head with . . .

- **Heinz Vinegar.** Unscrew the shower head, remove the rubber washer, place the head in a pot filled with

It's a Soft Drink.
It's a Toilet Bowl Cleaner.
No, It's Both!

- Coca-Cola stock went public in 1919 at $40 per share. In 1994, one of those shares was worth $118,192.76, including dividends.
- Rumor contends that a piece of meat left in a glass of Coca-Cola overnight will be completely dissolved by the following morning. It won't. A piece of meat soaked in Coca-Cola overnight will, however, be marinated and tender.

● During the 1960s, the Coca-Cola jingle was sung by Roy Orbison, the Supremes, the Moody Blues, Ray Charles (who sang the Diet Pepsi jingle in the 1990s), the Fifth Dimension, Aretha Franklin, and Gladys Knight and the Pips.

● Since 1893, the recipe for Coca-Cola has been changed only once. In 1985, when Pepsi-Cola outsold Coca-Cola in the United States for the first time in history, the Coca-Cola Company sweetened the product and renamed it New Coke. Within three months, consumers forced the company to bring back the old formula. It became known as Coca-Cola Classic, and New Coke, considered the marketing fiasco of the decade, soon disappeared from the marketplace.

● The World of Coca-Cola, a three-story pavilion in Atlanta, Georgia, features exhibits (including a thousand-piece memorabilia collection and John Pemberton's original handwritten formula book), soda fountains of the past and future, bottling exhibits, samples of Coca-Cola products from around the world, and films of Coca-Cola commercials.

● Coca-Cola outsells Pepsi worldwide by more than a two-to-one margin.

● The Coca-Cola Catalog, a mail-order catalog filled with Coca-Cola memorabilia from boxer shorts to O-gauge boxcars emblazoned with the Coca-Cola logo, is available for free by calling 1-800-872-6531.

equal parts Heinz Vinegar and water, bring to a boil, then simmer for five minutes.

● **Ziploc Storage Bags.** If a shower head cannot be removed for cleaning, fill a Ziploc Storage Bag with vinegar, wrap it around the shower head, and secure in place overnight with a rubber band.

Sinks
(Also see page 203)
Clean porcelain with . . .

● **Canada Dry Club Soda.** Pour Canada Dry Club Soda over the fixtures.

● **McCormick/Schilling Cream of Tartar.** Sprinkle Cream of Tartar on a damp cloth and rub.
Shine chrome faucets and handles with . . .

● **Alberto VO5 Conditioning Hairdressing.** Put a little Alberto VO5 Conditioning Hairdressing on a soft, dry cloth and buff lightly.
Whiten a porcelain sink with . . .

● **Clorox.** Fill the sink with a solution of three-quarters cup Clorox Bleach per gallon of water. Let sit for five minutes.

Soap
Turn soap slivers into liquid soap with . . .

● **Dixie Cups.** Place slivers of soap in a Dixie Cup with a little water, and wait a few days.

Soap Scum
Prevent water spots and soap scum on shower walls and doors with . . .

● **Endust.** Coat the tile walls with Endust and wipe clean.

Dissolve soap scum from shower doors with . . .

- **Baby Oil.** Apply baby oil with a damp cloth once a week.
- **Bounce.** Clean with a used sheet of Bounce.
- **Downy Fabric Softener.** Mix one capful of Downy Fabric Softener with a quart of warm water in a plastic bucket, and use a clean cloth to wipe the shower doors clean.
- **Pam No Stick Cooking Spray.** Spray Pam No Stick Cooking Spray on a soft cloth and wipe clean.

Tile

Clean bathroom tile with . . .

- **Arm & Hammer Baking Soda.** Sprinkle Arm & Hammer Baking Soda on a damp sponge, scrub, and rinse clean.
- **Dr. Bronner's Peppermint Soap.** Mix one-half cup Dr. Bronner's Peppermint Soap, two cups Arm & Hammer Baking Soda, and two-thirds cup water in a squirt bottle. Then add two tablespoons Heinz White Vinegar, shake vigorously, squirt and sponge.
- **Epsom Salt.** Mix equal parts of Epsom Salt and liquid dish detergent. Apply to grimy area and scrub with a brush. The Epsom Salt gives the detergent scrubbing action that dissolves and washes away as you clean.

Adhere plastic bathroom tiles with . . .

- **Wrigley's Spearmint Gum.** If a tile comes loose,

put a little piece of chewed Wrigley's Spearmint Gum on each corner and press back in place.

Toilets

Clean a toilet bowl with . . .

- **Alka-Seltzer.** Drop in two Akla-Seltzer tablets, wait twenty minutes, brush, and flush. The citric acid and effervescent action clean vitreous china.
- **Clorox.** Pour in one cup Clorox Bleach. Let it stand for ten minutes. Brush and flush.
- **Coca-Cola.** Pour a can of Coca-Cola into the toilet bowl. Let the real thing sit for one hour, then brush and flush clean. The citric acid in Coke removes stains from vitreous china, according to household-hints columnist Heloise.
- **Dr. Bronner's Peppermint Soap.** Mix one-half cup Dr. Bronner's Peppermint Soap and two cups Arm & Hammer Baking Soda with a fork. Add one-quarter cup water and two tablespoons vinegar, and one-half teaspoon tea tree oil. Pour the mixture into a squirt bottle, shake well, squirt inside the toilet, brush and flush. You can also use this mixture to clean the toilet seat with a sponge.

- **Efferdent.** Drop several Efferdent tablets into the toilet bowl, scrub, and flush.
- **Heinz Vinegar.** Pour in one cup of Heinz White

Vinegar, let it stand for five minutes, and flush.

● **Tang.** Put two tablespoons Tang in the toilet bowl, and let it sit for one hour. Brush and flush. The citric acid in Tang removes stains from porcelain.

Prevent rust on toilet seat screws with . . .

● **Maybelline Crystal Clear Nail Polish.** Paint the screws with Maybelline Crystal Clear Nail Polish.

Water Softener

Soften soap and rinse waters with . . .

● **20 Mule Team Borax.** Add one tablespoon of 20 Mule Team Borax per quart of water.

Windows

Make bathroom windows private with . . .

● **Con-Tact Paper.** Cover your bathroom window with frosted Con-Tact Paper for bright light and privacy.

Clean Your Car

with Canada Dry Club Soda

Air Freshener

Freshen the air in your car with . . .

- **Bounce.** Place a sheet of Bounce under the front seat.

Axle Grease

Grease a car or truck axle with . . .

- **Jif Peanut Butter.** George Washington Carver developed axle grease from peanuts.

Baby Seat

Clean baby car seats with . . .

- **Arm & Hammer Baking Soda.** Sprinkle Arm & Hammer Baking Soda on a damp sponge, wipe clean, and dry.

Battery

Prevent car battery corrosion with . . .

- **ChapStick.** Smear ChapStick on clean car battery terminals.
- **Vaseline.** Smear Vaseline Petroleum Jelly on clean car battery terminals.

Clean corrosion from car battery terminals with . . .

- **Coca-Cola.** Pour a can of carbonated Coca-Cola over the terminals to bubble away the corrosion, according to household-hints columnist Heloise.
- **Oral-B Toothbrushes** and **Arm & Hammer Baking Soda.** Use an old toothbrush to scrub encrusted battery terminals clean with a paste made from three parts baking soda to one part water.

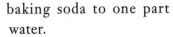

Revive a dead car battery with . . .

- **Bayer Aspirin.** Drop two Bayer aspirin tablets into the battery.

Bumper Stickers

Make your own bumper sticker with . . .

- **Con-Tact Paper.** Honk if you cut up Con-Tact Paper to make your own bumper sticker.

Make bumper stickers easy to remove with . . .

- **Turtle Wax.** Apply Turtle Wax to the spot before applying the bumper sticker, thus assuring that the bumper sticker will peel away with greater ease within a month.

Remove a bumper sticker with a . . .

- **Conair Pro Style 1600.** Blow it with a Conair Pro Style 1600 set on hot for a few minutes until the adhesive softens, then peel off.
- **Heinz Vinegar.** Soak a cloth in Heinz Vinegar and

cover the bumper sticker for several minutes until the vinegar soaks in. The bumper sticker should peel off easily.

Bumpers

Clean chrome bumpers with . . .

● **Arm & Hammer Baking Soda.** Sprinkle Arm & Hammer Baking Soda on a damp sponge, rub surface, and wipe clean with a dry cloth.

● **Coca-Cola** and **Reynolds Wrap.** Rubbing the bumper with a crumpled-up piece of Reynolds Wrap aluminum foil dipped in Coca-Cola will help remove rust spots, according to household-hints columnist Mary Ellen.

> ## The Truth About Turtle Wax
>
> Turtle Wax, Inc., is frequently offered supplies of turtles. Former company president Carl Schmid would refuse these offers politely and point out that the turtles in Turtle Wax are like the horses in horseradish.

● **S.O.S Steel Wool Soap Pads.** Scrub briskly with an S.O.S Steel Wool Soap Pad.

Shine car bumpers with . . .

● **Alberto VO5 Conditioning Hairdressing.** Put a little Alberto VO5 Conditioning Hairdressing on a soft, dry cloth and buff lightly.

Carpet

Deodorize carpeting in a car with . . .

● **Arm & Hammer Baking Soda.** Sprinkle Arm &

Hammer Baking Soda on the carpet, let sit for fifteen minutes, then vacuum up.

Clean Hands
Make cleaning up after doing a messy auto grease job easy with . . .
- **Alberto VO5 Conditioning Hairdressing.** Lightly coating your hands with Alberto VO5 Conditioning Hairdressing before fixing the car allows you to clean them off afterward without harsh solvents.

Clean hands after pumping gas or changing the oil with . . .
- **Huggies Baby Wipes.** Keep a box of Huggies Baby Wipes in the trunk of the car.

Decals
Remove decals with . . .
- **Heinz Vinegar.** Soak a cloth in Heinz Vinegar and cover the decal for several minutes until the vinegar soaks in. The decals should peel off easily.
- **Wesson Corn Oil.** Saturate the decal with Wesson Corn Oil.

Doors
Prevent car doors from freezing shut in winter with . . .
- **Pam No Stick Cooking Spray.** Spray the rubber gaskets with Pam No Stick Cooking Spray. The vegetable oil seals out water without harming the gasket.
- **Wesson Corn Oil.** Rub the gaskets with Wesson Corn Oil to seal out water without harming the gaskets.

Keep your car door open without wasting the battery with . . .
- **Wilson Tennis Balls.** Wedge a Wilson Tennis Ball into the door jamb to depress the interior light switch.

Driveway Stains
Clean oil and grease stains on driveways with . . .

- **Tidy Cat.** Tidy Cat works as an absorbent to pick up transmission leaks from garage floors. Pour a thick layer of unused Tidy Cat over the puddle, wait twenty-four hours, and sweep up with a broom. Scrub clean with a solution of detergent and hot water.
- **WD-40.** Spray with WD-40, wait, then blot. The mineral spirits and other petroleum distillates in WD-40 work as curing agents.

Emergency Lights
Make emergency lights with . . .

- **Maxwell House Coffee.** Wrap reflector tape around a couple of empty Maxwell House Coffee cans and store in the trunk of your car for emergencies.

Frozen Engine
Start a frozen car engine with a. . .

- **Conair Pro Style 1600.** Blow hot hair with a Conair Pro Style 1600 onto the carburetor.

Funnels
(See page 195)

Gas Tanks

Repair a leaking gas tank temporarily with . . .

● **Wrigley's Spearmint Gum.** Patch the leak with a piece of well-chewed Wrigley's Spearmint Gum.

Hubcaps

Clean chrome hubcaps with . . .

● **Arm & Hammer Baking Soda.** Sprinkle Arm & Hammer Baking Soda on a damp sponge, rub surface, and wipe clean with a dry cloth.

● **Efferdent.** Drop one Efferdent tablet into a glass of water, use a cloth to apply the fizzing solution to the hubcabs, and wash clean with water.

Ice

Prevent ice from forming on a car windshield overnight with . . .

● **Glad Trash Bags.** Cut open a Glad Trash Bag, place it over the entire windshield, and close the car doors over the edges of the bag to hold it in place. When you're ready to go, brush off any snow and peel off the plastic bag.

● **Heinz Vinegar.** Coat the window with a solution of

three parts Heinz White or Apple Cider Vinegar to one part water.

Insects

Prevent dead insects from sticking to the hood and grille with . . .

● **Pam No Stick Cooking Spray.** Spray with Pam No Stick Cooking Spray before driving. After the car trip, simply hose off the hood and grille.

● **WD-40.** Spray WD-40 on the hood and grille so you can wipe bugs off easily without damaging the finish.

Remove dead insects from the windshield with . . .

● **Arm & Hammer Baking Soda.** Sprinkle Arm & Hammer Baking Soda on a damp sponge, clean glass, and wipe clean with a dry cloth.

Remove dead insects from the hood with . . .

● **L'eggs Sheer Energy.** Use a damp, balled-up pair of L'eggs to clean the car without scratching the finish.

Locks

Thaw the frozen lock on a car door with a . . .

● **Conair Pro Style 1600.** Before you call the locksmith, use a Conair Pro Style 1600 to thaw the frozen lock.

Parking

Identify your car in a parking lot with . . .

● **Kleenex Tissue.** Attach a Kleenex Tissue to the aerial with a rubberband or string so you can easily find the paper flag blowing in the breeze.

Make parking cars in your garage easier with . . .

● **Wilson Tennis Balls.** Hang a Wilson Tennis Ball on

Four out of Five Dentists . . .

- A box of Arm & Hammer Baking Soda can be found in nine out of ten refrigerators. According to the *Los Angeles Times*, "More refrigerators are likely to have baking soda than working lightbulbs."
- Bounce fabric softener sheets can be found in more than one out of every four homes in the United States.
- Three out of four people surveyed in 1994 said Bob Barker is the TV game show host most likely to take Geritol.
- Virtually every woman in America knows who Betty Crocker is.
- According to *The First Really Important Survey of American Habits* by Mel Poretz and Barry Sinrod, 72 percent of Americans squeeze the toothpaste tube from the top.
- One out of every ten pea-

a string from the garage ceiling so it will hit the windshield at the spot where you should stop your car.

Price Tag Sheets

Remove the price tag sheet from an automobile with . . .

- **Wesson Corn Oil.** Apply Wesson Corn Oil. Let sit, then scrape away.

nuts grown in the United States for domestic consumption ends up in a jar of Jif.

● Listerine can be found in one out of every five homes in the United States.

● Reynolds Wrap can be found in three out of four American households.

● More than three out of four households in the United States own a barbecue grill.

● A jar of Vaseline Petroleum Jelly can be found in virtually every home in the United States.

● WD-40 can be found in four out of five American homes.

● Four our of five doctors who recommend baby food recommend Gerber.

● A box of Jell-O can be found in three out of four American pantries.

● Scotch Transparent Tape is found in virtually every home and office in the United States.

● The Crayola brand name is recognized by 99 percent of all Americans.

● One out of every two Americans has a MasterCard.

● According to the American Dental Association, four out of five Americans fail to replace their toothbrushes until after the bent bristles are no longer fit for cleaning teeth.

Radiators

Stop small leaks in a car radiator with . . .

● **McCormick/Schilling Black Pepper.** Add a teaspoon of McCormick/Schilling Black Pepper to your radiator. The pepper sinks to the bottom, finds its way into small holes, and expands, filling them.

Scratches

Repair a scratch on an automobile with . . .

● **Crayola Crayons.** Find a matching color Crayola Crayon and work it into the scratch.

Taillights

Repair a broken taillight with . . .

● **Scotch Packaging Tape.** Use Scotch Packaging Tape to hold the translucent red plastic in place.

Tar

Remove tar spots from your car without damaging the finish with . . .

● **Coppertone.** Apply Coppertone to a cloth and rub until the tar glides off.

Tires

Find a puncture in a tire with . . .

● **Palmolive.** Mix a few drops of Palmolive with water and brush on a leaky tire. The bubbles will indicate the exact location of the puncture.

Traction

Create emergency traction for automobiles with . . .

● **Tidy Cat.** Keep a bag of Tidy Cat in your car trunk in case you get stuck in the ice or snow. When poured under the tire, it provides excellent traction.

Store cat box filler in the trunk of your car for emergencies with . . .

● **Maxwell House Coffee.** Cat box filler, stored in empty Maxwell House Coffee cans, can be used for traction under the wheels of a car stuck in snow or ice.

Trailer Hitches

Prevent a chrome trailer hitch from getting scratched with . . .

- **Wilson Tennis Balls.** Slit a Wilson Tennis Ball and put it over the trailer hitch as a protective cover.

Upholstery

Lift dirt from car seats with . . .

- **Silly Putty.** Mold the Silly Putty into whatever shape will best fit into crevices.

Washing

Wash your car with . . .

- **Clairol Herbal Essences.** Add two capfuls of Clairol Herbal Essences to a bucket of water and soap up your car with the biodegradable suds.
- **Dr. Bronner's Peppermint Soap.** Add two teaspoons Dr. Bronner's Peppermint Soap to a bucket of water and wash your car or truck.
- **Palmolive.** Use one teaspoon of Palmolive per gallon of water.

Waxing

Shine your car with . . .

- **Kingsford's Corn Starch.** When buffing your car, sprinkle a tablespoon of Kingsford's Corn Starch on the wipe rag to remove excess polish easily.

Buff your car with . . .

- **L'eggs Sheer Energy.** Ball up

a pair of used panty hose and buff the car. The nylon in panty hose is a mild abrasive that polishes without scratching the finish.

Windshields

Remove grease from a car windshield with . . .
- **Canada Dry Club Soda.** Keep a bottle filled with Canada Dry Club Soda in the trunk of your car.

Repair a small dent in an automobile windshield with . . .
- **Maybelline Crystal Clear Nail Polish.** Fill hole with a few drops of Maybelline Crystal Clear Nail Polish, let it dry, then add a few more drops until full.

Clean Your Carpet

with Barbasol Shaving Cream

Cleaners
Clean carpets with . . .

- **Dr. Bronner's Peppermint Soap.** Mix one-quarter cup Dr. Bronner's Peppermint Soap and one-third cup water in a blender until foamy. Apply the foam on carpet spots, let sit for five minutes, brush, then blot dry with clean towels.
- **Kingsford's Corn Starch.** Sprinkle Kingsford's Corn Starch on the carpet, wait thirty minutes, then vacuum clean.

Deodorizers
Deodorize carpet with . . .

- **Arm & Hammer Baking Soda.** Sprinkle Arm & Hammer Baking Soda lightly over the dry carpet, let sit for fifteen minutes, then vacuum up.

Floors

Clean a varnished wood floor with . . .

- **Dr. Bronner's Peppermint Soap.** Add three tablespoons Dr. Bronner's Peppermint Soap to a bucket of water and mop.
- **L'eggs Sheer Energy.** Insert a folded bath towel into one leg of the stocking and hand buff the floor.
- **Lipton Tea Bags.** Cold Lipton Tea is a good cleaning agent for any kind of woodwork.
- **Nestea.** Cold Nestea makes an excellent cleaning agent for wood.

Clean and shine a floor between waxings with . . .

- **Reynolds Cut-Rite Wax Paper.** Put a piece of Reynolds Cut-Rite Wax Paper under the mop head and clean.

Cure a squeaky floorboard with . . .

- **Kingsford's Corn Starch.** Sprinkle Kingsford's Corn Starch into the crevices along the edges.

Repair a small dent in a wood floor with . . .

- **Maybelline Crystal Clear Nail Polish.** Fill hole with a few drops of Maybelline Crystal Clear Nail Polish, let it dry, then add a few more drops until full.

Remove scuff marks from floors with . . .

- **Pink Pearl Erasers.** Simply use a Pink Pearl Eraser.

Gum

Remove bubble gum from carpeting with . . .

- **WD-40.** Spray on WD-40, wait, and wipe.

Shaving Cream Versus Whipped Cream

In 1931, Charles Goetz, a senior chemistry major at the University of Illinois, worked part-time in the Dairy Bacteriology Department, improving milk sterilization techniques. Convinced that storing milk under high gas pressure might inhibit bacterial growth, Goetz began experimenting—only to discover that milk released from a pressurized vessel foamed. Realizing that cream would become whipped cream, Goetz began seeking a gas that would not saturate the cream with its own bad flavor. At the suggestion of a local dentist, Goetz succeeded in infusing cream with tasteless, odorless, nonflammable nitrous oxide, giving birth to aerosol whipped cream and aerosol shaving cream.

Pet Stains
(See page 303)

Silly Putty
Remove Silly Putty from carpeting with . . .
- **WD-40.** Spray on WD-40, wait, and wipe.

Stains

Remove spots from carpet with . . .

- **Barbasol Shaving Cream.** Squirt Barbasol on stain, scrub, and wash with water.

- **Dr. Bronner's Peppermint Soap.** Add one-quarter teaspoon of Dr. Bronner's Peppermint Soap to a quart of water, dip in scrub brush, scrub the stain, then blot with towels.

- **Murphy's Oil Soap.** Mix one-quarter cup Murphy's to one gallon of water. Spray the spot, then blot with a towel.

Remove spots from indoor-outdoor carpeting with . . .

- **Spray 'n Wash.** Spray spots generously with Spray 'n Wash, wait five minutes, then hose down.

Blot up spilled coffee from a rug or carpet with . . .

- **Huggies Baby Wipes.** Huggies Baby Wipes absorb coffee without leaving a stain.

Clean spills and stains on carpet with . . .

- **20 Mule Team Borax.** Blot up the spill, sprinkle 20 Mule Team Borax to cover the area, let dry, and vacuum. Before treating, make sure the carpet dye is colorfast by testing an unexposed area with a paste of 20 Mule Team Borax and water. For wine and alcohol stains, dissolve one cup 20 Mule Team Borax in one quart water. Sponge in the solution, wait thirty minutes, shampoo the spotted area, let dry, and vacuum.

Remove wine spills or other spots from carpet with . . .

The Name Game: Part 1

A. 1. Steak Sauce

Upon tasting the new sauce made by his royal chef, Brand, King George IV purportedly declared, "This sauce is A-one!" During George IV's reign (1820–1830), the phrase "A number one"—or "A-one" for short—became popular with the general public when Lloyds of London began rating ships for insurance purposes, with "A number 1" being the highest score.

Alberto VO5 Conditioning Hairdressing

Alberto VO5 is named after the chemist Alberto who invented Alberto VO5 Conditioning Hairdressing. VO5 stands for the five vital organic emollients in the hairdressing. Oddly, no one at Alberto-Culver knows Alberto's first name.

Barbasol Shaving Cream

Barbasol is a combination of the Roman word *barba* (meaning "beard," and the origin of the word *barber*) and the English word *solution*, denoting that the shaving cream is the same solution used by barbers. The stripes on the can evoke the familiarity of barbershop pole stripes.

Bayer Aspirin

Bayer was named after company founder Friedrich Bayer. The word *aspirin*, a trademark of Bayer, was derived from *Spiraea*, the genus containing the plant from which salicin, the active ingredient in aspirin, was isolated.

Campbell's Soup

The Campell Soup Company was named for company founder Joseph Campbell.

Canada Dry Club Soda

The word *Canada* denotes the country of the soft drink's origin, and the word *dry* suggests nonalcoholic beverages.

Carnation Nonfat Dry Milk

Legend holds that company founder Elbridge Amos Stuart noticed a box of Carnation cigars in the window of a Seattle tobacco shop and decided to use the name for his evaporated milk. The cigars were probably named Carnation to suggest opulence while simultaneously hinting at the word *Corona*.

Chun King Soy Sauce

Chun King is named after the Chinese city known in English as Chun King, according to the Wade-Giles system of writing Chinese using the Roman alphabet (developed by two British diplomats, Thomas Wade and Herbert Giles). In 1978, the Chinese government directed that Chinese names and words used in English be written in Pinyin, a more accurate system of writing Chinese using the Roman alphabet (developed by the Chinese government). According to that system, Chun King is Chongquing.

Clairol Herbal Essences

Clairol is apparently a combination of the French word *clair* (clear) with the suffix *-ol* (oil). Herbal Essence, the name of the original green shampoo, refers to the shampoo's herbal fragrance and seemed to imply that the shampoo was made from all natural ingredients, which it was not—until 1995, when Clairol reformulated the shampoo and renamed it Herbal Essences.

Coca-Cola

Bookkeeper Frank M. Robinson, one of Coca-Cola inventor Dr. John Styth Pemberton's four partners, suggested naming the elixir after two of the main ingredients: the coca leaf and the kola nut. He suggested spelling kola with a *c* for the sake of alliteration.

Cool Whip

Since General Foods could not legally refer to its nondairy topping as a whipped cream or milk product, the company's advertising agency generated hundreds of nebulous names, finally recommending Cool Whip as the noncrème de la noncrème.

Crayola Crayons

Alice Binney, wife of company co-owner Edwin Binney, coined the word *Crayola* by joining *craie*, from the French word meaning chalk, with *ola*, from *oleaginous*, meaning oily.

Cream of Tartar

Cream signifies the refining process used to procure the *Tartar* that adheres to the side of wine barrels.

Crisco All-Vegetable Shortening

The two suggested names for the vegetable shortening— Krispo (the word *crisp* combined with the then-popular suffix -*o*) and Cryst (an onomatopoeia for the hissing and crackling sound foods make while being fried)—were combined to form the unique hybrid Crisco.

Cutex

Company founder Northam Warren introduced the first liquid nail polish in the United States in 1916 and coined the name Cutex, taking the first syllable from the name of his liquid *Cut*icle Remover and adding -*ex*, a popular suffix at the time.

Dannon Yogurt

Dannon is an Americanized version of *Danone*, the Spanish yogurt manufacturing company founded by Dr. Isaac Carasso and named for his son Daniel. *Danone* means "Little Daniel."

Dixie Cups

Inventor Hugh Moore's paper cup factory was located next door to the Dixie Doll Company in the same downtown loft building. The word *Dixie* printed on the company's door reminded Moore of the story he had heard as a boy about "dixies," the ten-dollar banknotes printed with the French word *dix* in big letters across the face of the bill. They had been issued in the early 1800s by a New Orleans bank renowned for its strong currency. The "dixies," Moore decided, had the qualities he wanted people to associate with his paper cups, and with permission from his neighbor, he used the name.

Domino Sugar

Domino refers to the game played with a set of small, retangular, wood or plastic blocks, the face of each block divided into halves, each half being blank or marked by one to six dots resembling those on dice. Ironically, a domino is also a country expected to react politically to events as predicted by the domino theory, which derogatorily describes many sugar-producing countries.

Frisbee

Frisbee was inspired by the Frisbie Pie Company of Bridgeport, Connecticut, founded by William Russell Frisbie.

Geritol

Geritol is apparently a combination of the words *geriatric* and *tolerance*.

Glad Flexible Straws and Trash Bags

Glad apparently signifies the pleasure and joy consumers will experience when using these convenient flexible straws or when their trash is clad inside these pleasingly convenient trash bags.

- **Canada Dry Club Soda.** Apply Canada Dry Club Soda to the stain, rub it in, wait a few minutes, and sponge it off.

Static Electricity
Eliminate static shock on carpets with . . .
- **Downy Fabric Softener.** Mix one capful of Downy Fabric Softener into a spray bottle filled with water and spray the carpets.

Throw Rugs
Prevent throw rugs from skidding with . . .
- **Pink Pearl Erasers.** Glue thin slices of a Pink Pearl Eraser to the bottom of the rug at the four corners.

Wax
Remove candle wax from carpet or upholstery with . . .
- **Viva Paper Towels.** Place a sheet of Viva Paper Towels over the wax. Gently press the paper towel with a warm iron. The iron will melt the wax and the paper towel will absorb it.

5

CLEANING

Clean Your Piano Keys

with Colgate Toothpaste

Air Freshener

Freshen the air in your home with . . .

- **Bounce.** Place an individual sheet of Bounce in a drawer or hang one from a hanger in the closet.
- **Heinz Vinegar.** Heinz Vinegar is a natural air freshener when sprayed full-strength in a room.
- **Kingsford Charcoal Briquets.** Placing a coffee can filled with charcoal briquets in a closet or chest will absorb odors, according to *Reader's Digest*.
- **Lipton Tea Bags.** Mix one quart brewed Lipton Tea and four tablespoons ReaLemon, strain through a Mr. Coffee filter, and store in empty spray bottles.
- **Nestea.** Add two teaspoons Nestea into empty spray bottle, fill with sixteen ounces of water, and shake well.

Deodorize a closet with . . .

- **Arm & Hammer Baking Soda.** Place an open box of Arm & Hammer Baking Soda on a shelf.

Deodorize a room filled with cigarette smoke or paint fumes with . . .

- **Heinz Vinegar.** Place a small bowl of Heinz White Vinegar in the room.

Beds

Improvise a plastic sheet with . . .

- **Glad Trash Bags.** Cut a Glad Trash Bag down the sides and place it under the sheets.

Remove dust balls from under a bed with . . .

- **Scotch Packaging Tape.** Wrap Scotch Packaging Tape, adhesive side out, on the end of a broomstick and slide it under the furniture.

Warm cold bed sheets with a. . .

- **Conair Pro Style 1600.** Use a Conair Pro Style 1600 to make ice-cold sheets toasty warm.

Black Lacquer

Polish black lacquer with . . .

- **Lipton Tea Bags.** Wash black lacquer pieces with strong-brewed Lipton Tea, then wipe dry with a soft cloth.

Brass

Prevent tarnish on brass with . . .

- **Alberto VO5 Hair Spray.** After polishing decorative brass, spray with Alberto VO5 Hair Spray to add a protective coating.

Polish brass with . . .

- **Endust.** Use very fine steel wool sprayed with Endust.
- **Gold Medal Flour.** Mix equal parts Gold Medal Flour and Morton Salt and add one teaspoon Heinz

White Vinegar to make a paste. Spread a thick layer on the brass and let dry. Rinse and wipe off paste.

- **Hunt's Tomato Paste.** Rub brass with Hunt's Tomato Paste.
- **Morton Salt** and **ReaLemon.** Make a paste from ReaLemon and Morton Salt, scrub gently, then rinse with water.
- **Lea & Perrins Worcestershire Sauce.** Apply Worcestershire Sauce with a damp cloth.

Brooms
Prevent broom handles from falling over when leaning them against a wall with . . .
- **Playtex Living Gloves.** When your Playtex Living Gloves wear out, cut off the fingers and slip them onto broom handles.

Cables and Extension Cords
Organize cables and extensions cords with . . .
- **Scotch Packaging Tape.** Tape the cords together with Scotch Packaging Tape.

Candles
Discourage candle wax from sticking to candle holders with . . .
- **Vaseline.** Coat the insides of candle holders with Vaseline Petroleum Jelly so wax slides out.

Remove candle wax from a table or countertop with . . .
- **Conair Pro Style 1600.** Blow warm air an inch above the drips, then wipe away the wax with a paper towel.
- **Viva Paper Towels.** Use an old credit card to re-

> **MUNCHKINS FOR HIRE**
>
> McCormick/Schilling obtains its supply of Cream of Tartar from Italy, where very small people crawl through the very small holes in open wine casks to scrape out the residue left after the wine has been fermented and drained out.

move as much wax as possible. Then place a sheet of Viva Paper Towels over the wax and press gently with a warm iron to absorb the remaining wax. *Remove candle wax from other surfaces with . . .*

- **Coppertone.** Rub in a dollop of Coppertone to remove candle wax from furniture, carpeting, and clothing.

Remove candle wax drippings from candle stick holders with . . .

- **Alberto VO5 Conditioning Hairdressing.** Coat the candlestick holders with Alberto VO5 Conditioning Hairdressing before inserting the candles.

Revitalize dull candles with . . .

- **Endust.** Spray Endust on a cloth and wipe the candles.

Chrome

Polish chrome with . . .

- **Canada Dry Club Soda.** Use Canada Dry Club Soda in a spray bottle.
- **Reynolds Wrap.** Use a piece of crumpled-up Reynolds Wrap to polish the chrome on strollers, high chairs, and playpens.

Cleansers

Clean dirt, grime, and scuff marks from doors, stoves, laminated tabletops, linoleum floors, and tile with . . .

- **Arm & Hammer Baking Soda.** Sprinkle Arm &

Hammer Baking Soda on a damp sponge, wipe clean, and dry.

Make your own household cleanser for walls and floors with . . .

- **Dr. Bronner's Peppermint Soap.** Mix two tablespoons of Heinz White Vinegar, one teaspoon 20 Mule Team Borax, and sixteen ounces of purified water in a trigger spray-bottle. Shake vigorously to dissolve the borax. Then add one-quarter cup Dr. Bronner's Peppermint Soap. To scent, add ten drops of pure lemon oil. Simply spray and wipe clean.

- **20 Mule Team Borax.** Add one-half cup 20 Mule Team Borax, one-half teaspoon Dawn dishwashing liquid, and one teaspoon ammonia to two gallons warm water.

Clean dirt, grease, and grime from walls, glass, porcelain, wooden furniture, and the outsides of appliances with . . .

- **Cascade.** Dissolve one-quarter cup Cascade in one gallon of very hot water. Scrub, then wipe clean with a dry cloth. Cascade is spot-resistant and contains water-softening agents, so everything gets shiny clean without rinsing.

The Amazing Mr. Coffee

In the 1960s, Vince Marotta presided over North American Systems in Pepper Pike, Ohio, building shopping malls and housing developments. When business slowed in 1968, Marotta fell ill, and while recuperating in bed, he realized how fed up he was with percolated coffee and decided to develop a better way to make it. He contacted the Pan American Coffee Bureau and discovered that South American coffee growers believed that the best way to extract the oil from coffee beans was to pour water, heated to 200°F, over the ground beans. Marotta hired engineer Irv Schultze to devise a bimetal actuator to control the temperature of the water. Observing that restaurants used a white cloth in their large coffee percolators to capture

Cobwebs
Remove cobwebs from unreachable places with . . .
- **Wilson Tennis Balls.** Wrap a Wilson Tennis Ball inside a dust cloth secured with a few rubber bands, then toss at the distant cobweb.

Copper
Protect decorative copper from tarnish with . . .
- **Alberto VO5 Hair Spray.** After polishing decorative copper, spray with Alberto VO5 Hair Spray to add a protective coating.

Clean copper with . . .

loose grounds and eliminate sediment, Marotta decided to use a paper filter in his coffeemaker.

Marotta showed up at the 1970 Housewares Convention in Chicago with a prototype for Mr. Coffee. On the spot, he hired Bill Howe, a buyer with Hamilton Beach, to represent his product. Howe invited a hundred buyers up to Marotta's hotel room for coffee, and within two years, Mr. Coffee was selling 42,000 coffee machines a day. In 1972, Marotta single-handedly convinced Joe DiMaggio to be the spokesman for Mr. Coffee's television commercials, which DiMaggio did for the next fifteen years.

According to Marotta, the paper filters—"the blade to the razor"—were cut and fluted by a paper company from an existing paper stock. Marotta sold the Mr. Coffee Company in 1987, and the company went public in 1990. Today, Mr. Coffee is the best-selling coffeemaker in the world.

- **Gold Medal Flour.** Mix equal parts Gold Medal Flour and Morton Salt and add one teaspoon Heinz White Vinegar to make a paste. Spread a thick layer on the copper and let dry. Rinse and wipe off paste.
- **Morton Salt** and **ReaLemon.** Make a paste from ReaLemon and Morton Salt, scrub gently, then rinse with water.

Clean tarnish from copper with . . .

- **Hunt's Tomato Paste.** Rub copper pots with Hunt's Tomato Paste.

Crayon

Clean crayon from a chalkboard with . . .

● **Viva Paper Towels.** Place a sheet of Viva Paper Towels over the crayon marks and press the paper towel with a warm iron. The iron will melt the crayon wax and the paper towel will absorb it.

● **WD-40.** Spray WD-40 on the crayon marks, let soak for ten minutes, then blot clean with a cloth.

Remove crayon from wallpaper with . . .

● **Arm & Hammer Baking Soda.** Sprinkle Arm & Hammer Baking Soda on a damp sponge, scrub gently to avoid mussing the wallpaper, then wipe clean.

● **Conair Pro Style 1600.** Use a Conair Pro Style 1600 set on hot until the wax heats up, then wipe clean with a paper towel.

● **S.O.S Steel Wool Soap Pads.** Rub the crayon marks very gently with an S.O.S Steel Wool Soap Pad.

Remove crayon from most surfaces with . . .

● **WD-40.** Spray on WD-40, wait, and wipe.

Remove crayon from walls with . . .

● **Arm & Hammer Baking Soda.** Sprinkle Arm &

Hammer Baking Soda on a damp sponge, scrub gently to avoid mussing the paint or wallpaper, then wipe clean.

● **Colgate Toothpaste.** Brush the marks with Colgate on an old toothbrush.

Crevices

Clean tight crevices with . . .

● **Forster Toothpicks.** Dip a Forster Toothpick in alcohol to clean tight spaces.

● **Oral-B Toothbrushes.** Use a clean, old Oral-B Toothbrush with silver polish to remove tarnish from silver.

● **Q-Tips Cotton Swabs.** Dip a Q-Tips Cotton Swab in alcohol to clean the crevices between the push buttons on the telephone and on the blender, and the crevices in a camera, sewing machine, and shower door runners.

Curtains

Stiffen ruffled curtains with . . .

● **Alberto VO5 Hair Spray.** Hold the fabric taut and spray with Alberto VO5 Hair Spray.

Dampness

Prevent dampness in closets with . . .

● **Crayola Chalk.** Tie together a handful of Crayola Chalk and hang the bundle from the clothes rod to absorb moisture.

- **Maxwell House Coffee.** Fill an empty Maxwell House Coffee can with Kingsford Charcoal Briquets, punch holes in the plastic cover, and set on the floor in the back of the closet.

Prevent musty, damp odors in a closed summerhouse with . . .

- **Tidy Cat.** Fill several shallow boxes with unused Tidy Cat. Place one in each room before closing up the house to soak up musty, lingering odors.

Dust balls

Remove dust balls from under a couch with . . .

- **Scotch Packaging Tape.** Wrap Scotch Packaging Tape, adhesive side out, on the end of a broomstick and slide it under the furniture.

Dusting

Do your dusting with . . .

- **Conair Pro Style 1600.** Use a Conair Pro Style 1600 to blow cool air to clean dust off high shelves or out from under appliances, pleated lamp shades, carved furniture, crevices, and knickknacks.

Flowers

(See page 128)

Flowers, artificial

Clean artificial flowers and plants with . . .

- **Oral-B Toothbrushes.** Use a clean, old Oral-B Toothbrush and soapy water.

Clean dust off silk flowers with . . .

- **Morton Salt.** Put the flowers in a large paper bag, pour in two cups of Morton Salt, close the bag, and shake.

Salt knocks the dust off the flowers. Remove the flowers from the bag and shake off the excess salt.

Garbage Cans

Secure garbage bags inside your trash can with . . .

- **L'eggs Sheer Energy.** Cut off the elastic top of a pair of L'eggs Sheer Energy and use it like an extra-large rubber band around the rim of the trash can to hold the plastic garbage bag in place.

Deodorize a garbage can with . . .

- **Tidy Cat.** Cover the bottom of the garbage can with one inch of unused Tidy Cat to absorb grease and moisture.

Disinfect garbage cans with . . .

- **Clorox.** Wash the garbage cans with a solution made from three-quarters cup Clorox Bleach to one gallon water. Let stand for five minutes, then rinse clean.

Glass

Clean glass and Plexiglas tabletops with . . .

- **Downy Fabric Softener.** Mix one capful of Downy Fabric Softener in a gallon of water in a plastic bucket, and sponge the tabletops with this lint-free cleanser.

Clean cloudy glass with . . .

- **Betty Crocker Potato Buds.** Mix Betty Crocker Potato Buds with enough water to make a thick paste, cover the glass with the mixture, and let sit for twenty-four hours. Then rinse in cold water and dry.

Ink Stains

Clean ink from vinyl surfaces with . . .

- **Coppertone.** Apply Coppertone and wipe clean.

- **Crisco All-Vegetable Shortening.** Apply Crisco All-Vegetable Shortening and wipe clean.

Lint
Collect lint with . . .
- **Scotch Packaging Tape.** Wrap a strip of Scotch Packaging Tape around your hand, adhesive side out, and pat.
- **Silly Putty.** Flatten the Silly Putty into a pancake and pat the surface.

Marble and Metal
Polish marble and metal with . . .
- **Crayola Chalk.** Pulverize a few sticks of Crayola Chalk with a mortar and pestle until it is a fine powder. Dip a soft cloth in the powder, wipe the marble or metal, then rinse with clear water and dry thoroughly.

Mildew
Eliminate mildew odors with . . .
- **Listerine.** Wipe with full-strength Listerine.

Mirrors
Clean mirrors with . . .
- **Mr. Coffee Filters.** Mr. Coffee Filters are lint-free, so they'll leave your mirrors sparkling.

Mold and Mildew
Remove mold and mildew from outdoor

siding, tile, brick, stucco, and patios with . . .

● **Clorox.** Clean with a mixture of three-quarters cup Clorox Bleach per gallon of water.

Mops

Clean mops with . . .

● **Clorox.** Rinse mops in a bucket of sudsy water and three quarters cup Clorox Bleach per gallon of water.
Prevent mop handles from falling over when leaning them against a wall with . . .

● **Playtex Living Gloves.** Cut off the fingers of Playtex Living Gloves and slip them onto mop handles.

Pet Hair

(See page 300)

Pianos

Clean piano keys with . . .

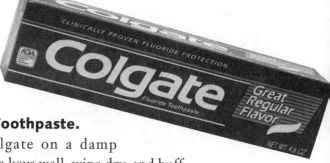

● **Colgate Toothpaste.** Squeeze Colgate on a damp cloth. Rub the keys well, wipe dry, and buff with a soft, dry cloth. After all, ivory is made from an elephant's tusk.

● **Pink Pearl Erasers.** Use a Pink Pearl Eraser to remove marks from the ivory keys.

Price Tags

Remove dried glue and gum left by price tags and labels peeled from glass, metals, and most plastics with . . .

● **Coppertone.** Apply Coppertone and wipe clean.

● **Crisco All-Vegetable Shortening.** Coat the area

The Stories Behind the Logos

The Arm & Hammer Symbol

The Arm & Hammer symbol was first used in the early 1860s by James A. Church, who ran a spice and mustard business called Vulcan Spice Mills. When Church joined his father in the baking soda business in 1867, he brought with him the trademark depicting the muscular arm of Vulcan, god of fire, with steel hammer in hand about to descend on an anvil. The Arm & Hammer logo ranks among the nation's most recognized product symbols.

Campbell's Soup Cans

The classic red-and-white soup cans, immortalized by Andy Warhol in his classic pop art painting, were inspried by the uniforms of the Cornell University football team. The circular seal on the can pictures a medal won by Campbell's Soup at the Paris Exposition of 1900.

The Canada Dry Shield

Company founder J. J. McLaughlin designed the original Canada Dry trademark—a map of Canada, emblems of the Canadian provinces, and a crouching beaver (the national animal) inside a shield capped with a crown to symbolize "kinglike quality."

Coca-Cola

Bookkeeper Frank M. Robinson came up with the Coca-Cola name and wrote it in his bookkeeper's Spencerian script, much the way it appears today.

The Johnson & Johnson Red Cross

Since 1888, Johnson & Johnson has used the same red Greek cross that the International Committee of the Red Cross has used since 1863. In 1905, U.S. law gave the American Red Cross exclusive use of the symbol, but vigorous lobbying by Johnson & Johnson and other companies resulted in an amendment in 1910 allowing companies that had used the trademark prior to 1905 to continue doing so. The Geneva Convention of 1929 forbids use of the trademark by any group other than the International Committee of the Red Cross. In 1945, the Senate passed a bill to fully implement the Geneva Convention on this issue, but it was defeated in the House of Representatives. Johnson & Johnson products still bear the red cross symbol, as do Red Cross shoes, Red Cross salt, and the Red Cross Nurse pump-spray disinfectant and deodorizer.

The Nabisco Double-Barred Cross

Nabisco's symbol, an oval topped by a double-barred cross, was used as a pressmark by Venetian printers Nicolas Jensen and Johannes de Colonia as early as 1480. In medieval times the mark symbolized the triumph of the spiritual world over the material world.

The Nestlé Bird Nest

The German word *nestle* means "little nest," and the Nestlé logo was inspired from this meaning.

The Reynolds Dragon

Reynolds' logo, used since 1935, was inspired by Raphael's version of the story of St. George and the Dragon. The legend of England's patron saint, depicted in several noted paintings, symbolizes the crusading spirit.

with Crisco All-Vegetable Shortening, let sit for ten minutes, then scrub clean.

- **Jif Peanut Butter.** Simply rub the dried glue with Jif Peanut Butter.
- **Pam No Stick Cooking Spray.** Spray with Pam No Stick Cooking Spray, then rub with a cloth.
- **Wesson Corn Oil.** Apply Wesson Corn Oil, let sit, and then scrape away.

Rubber Gloves
Dry the insides of rubber gloves with a . . .
- **Conair Pro Style 1600.** Insert the nozzle of a Conair Pro Style 1600 and blow warm air into the glove.

Sponges
Freshen old sponges with . . .
- **Clorox.** Soak sponges for five to ten minutes in a mixture of three-quarters cup Clorox Bleach per gallon of water, then rinse well.

Stainless Steel
Clean stainless steel with . . .
- **Canada Dry Club Soda.** Use club soda in a spray bottle.

Sweeping
Help dust and dirt slide off a dustpan with . . .
- **Turtle Wax.** Put a coat of Turtle Wax on the dustpan.

Sweep up dust and dirt with ease with . . .
- **Endust.** Spray the bristles of your broom or mop with Endust before sweeping.

Tape Decks

Clean the heads on a tape deck with . . .

● **Q-Tips Cotton Swabs.** Dip a Q-Tips Cotton Swab in alcohol and gently wipe the metal heads.

Television Screens

Eliminate static electricity from your television screen with . . .

● **Bounce.** Since Bounce is designed to help eliminate static cling, wipe your television screen with a sheet of Bounce to keep dust from resettling.

Upholstery

Clean cotton upholstery with . . .

● **Barbasol Shaving Cream.** Apply Barbasol sparingly to the stain and rub gently with a damp cloth.

● **Pink Pearl Erasers.** Rub lightly with a Pink Pearl Eraser.

Vases

Clean a vase with . . .

● **Alka-Seltzer.** To remove a stain from the bottom of a glass vase or cruet, fill with water and drop in two Alka-Seltzer tablets.

● **Cascade.** Place one teaspoon Cascade in a dirty glass vase, fill with water, and let sit overnight. The next morning, simply rinse clean.

● **Efferdent.** To remove a stain from the bottom of a glass vase or cruet, fill with water and drop in one Efferdent tablet.

VCRs

Clean the heads on a VCR with . . .

● **Q-Tips Cotton Swabs.** Dip a Q-Tips Cotton Swab in alcohol and gently wipe the metal heads.

Venetian Blinds

Eliminate static electricity from venetian blinds with . . .

● **Bounce.** Wipe the blinds with a sheet of Bounce to prevent dust from resetting.

Vomit

Neutralize vomit odor with . . .

● **Arm & Hammer Baking Soda.** Sprinkle Arm & Hammer Baking Soda generously on the stained area, let sit for an hour, then vacuum up.

Wallpaper

(Also see Crayon, page 58)
Clean wallpaper with . . .

● **Wonder Bread.** Use two-day-old crustless slices of Wonder Bread to rub down the wallpaper.

Walls

(Also see Crayon, page 58)
Clean grease from walls with . . .

The Miracle of Arm & Hammer Baking Soda

In 1846, John Dwight started making baking soda in the kitchen of his Massachusetts home. In 1847, he formed John Dwight and Company with his brother-in-law, Dr. Austin Church, introducing Cow Brand as the trademark for Dwight's Saleratus (aerated salt, as baking soda was then called). Church formed Church & Company to produce the baking soda, identifying his brand as Arm & Hammer. In 1896, the descendants of the founders of these two companies consolidated their interests under the name Church & Dwight Co., Inc.

● Arm & Hammer Baking Soda has been used to reduce air pollution in factory smokestacks. Arm & Hammer Baking Soda, when pulverized to an appropriate particle size, is, like other sodium sorbents, one of the most effective collectors of sulfur dioxide. Injecting Arm & Hammer brand sorbent-grade sodium bicarbonate directly into the flue gas ducts of coal-fired boiler systems desulfurizes flue gas. The baking soda reacts with sulfur dioxide to form sodium sulfate, and the cleaned flue gas exits through the stack.

● Arm & Hammer Baking Soda has been used to increase the effectiveness of sewage treatment plants. Baking soda helps maintain proper pH and alkalinity in biological digesters, fostering trouble-free operation of both anaerobic and aerobic treatment plants. Used in maintenance doses, baking soda boosts sludge compaction, alkalinity, and methane gas production while reducing biological oxygen demand and controlling sulfide odors. Plus, it's environmentally safe.

● Baking soda can restore lakes damaged by acid rain. In 1985, Cornell professor James Bisongi Jr. restored Wolf Pond, a virtually dead fifty-acre lake in the Adirondacks, by adding nearly twenty tons of baking soda to the water to dramatically reduce the acidity.

● The U.S. Environmental Protection Agency and the navy's Civil Engineering Lab have jointly developed an inexpensive method that uses baking soda to decontaminate soil laced with halogenated organic chemicals. The halogenated contaminates are decomposed by excavating, crushing, and screening the soil; mixing in baking soda at 10 percent of its weight; and then heating to 630°F for one hour. The treated soil can then be returned to its original location.

● Arm & Hammer Baking Soda has been used to increase the butterfat content of cow and goat milk. High-grain diets typically increase acid formation in the ruminant animals, interfering with the bacteria that aid digestion. Adding baking soda to cow and goat feed increases the pH in the animals' rumina, lowering the acidity, making for a more favorable environment for the microbacteria that aid digestion, elevating the rate of feed intake, and increasing milk production and the butterfat content of the milk.

- **Kingsford's Corn Starch.** Sprinkle Kingsford's Corn Starch on a soft cloth and rub the spot until the grease disappears.

Wastebaskets

Eliminate odors in wastebaskets with . . .

- **Bounce.** Place a sheet of Bounce at the bottom of the wastebasket.

Windows

Clean windows with . . .

- **Canada Dry Club Soda.** Fill a spray bottle with club soda, and use a soft, dry cloth.
- **Heinz Vinegar.** Use undiluted Heinz Vinegar in a spray bottle. Dry with a soft cloth.
- **Kingsford's Corn Starch.** Mix a little Kingsford's Corn Starch with ammonia and water.
- **L'eggs Sheer Energy.** Use a balled-up pair of L'eggs.
- **Mr. Coffee Filter.** Mr. Coffee Filters are lint-free, so they'll leave your windows sparkling.
- **20 Mule Team Borax.** Mix one-quarter cup 20 Mule Team Borax, one-half cup ammonia, and two gallons of water to add more sparkle when cleaning windows.

Clean hard water stains from windows with . . .

- **Downy Fabric Softener.** Cover the stain with full-strength Downy Fabric Softener, wait ten minutes, then rinse with a damp cloth.

Window Screens

Clean dust from window screens with . . .

- **L'eggs Sheer Energy.** Simply run a balled-up pair of L'eggs over the screen.

Wood Paneling

Prevent wood paneling from drying out with . . .

● **Alberto VO5 Conditioning Hairdressing.** Just rub on Alberto VO5 Conditioning Hairdressing with a clean, soft cloth and buff well, giving the paneling a warm glow.

Wooden Knickknacks

Clean wooden knickknacks and other wood objects with . . .

● **Alberto VO5 Conditioning Hairdressing.** Lightly coat the wood with Alberto VO5 Conditioning Hairdressing, then buff.

Woodwork

Erase fingerprints from woodwork with . . .

● **Pink Pearl Erasers.** Gently rub with a Pink Pearl Eraser.

Clean varnished woodwork with . . .

● **Lipton Tea Bags.** Cold Lipton Tea is a good cleaning agent for any kind of woodwork.

● **Nestea.** Cold Nestea makes an excellent cleaning agent for wood.

Polish wood surfaces with . . .

● **Coppertone.** Squeeze Coppertone onto a soft cloth to clean and polish natural wood.

6

CLOTHING AND SHOES

Lubricate a Zipper
with ChapStick

Belts
Keep belt buckles shiny with . . .
- **Maybelline Crystal Clear Nail Polish.** Paint Maybelline Crystal Clear Nail Polish on the buckle, allow to dry, repeat four times.

Bras
Prevent bra pads from slipping with . . .
- **Krazy Glue.** Use Krazy Glue to attach Velcro to the inside cups of the bra and the outside of the pads.

Prevent bra straps from showing with a wide neckline with . . .
- **Velcro.** Sew small strips of Velcro on the top of each bra strap and the inside of each shoulder seam of the dress or blouse.

Broken Heels
Reattach a broken heel with . . .

● **Krazy Glue.** Use a few drops of Krazy Glue and hold in place until secure.

Buttons
Protect shirt buttons with . . .
● **Maybelline Crystal Clear Nail Polish.** Dab the center of each button with Maybelline Crystal Clear Nail Polish to reinforce the threads so buttons stay on longer.

Deodorize
Deodorize shoes or sneakers with . . .
● **Arm & Hammer Baking Soda.** In the evening, sprinkle Arm & Hammer Baking Soda inside shoes to eliminate odors. Shake out in the morning.
● **Bounce.** Place a sheet of Bounce in your shoes or sneakers overnight so they'll smell great in the morning.
● **Tidy Cat.** Fill the feet of knee-high hose with unused Tidy Cat, tie the ends, and place inside shoes or sneakers overnight.

Drying Shoes
Keep shoes and sneakers dry and comfortable with . . .
● **Kingsford's Corn Starch.** Dust the insides with Kingsford's Corn Starch.
Dry wet boots or sneakers with a . . .
● **Conair Pro Style 1600.** Insert the nozzle of a Conair Pro Style 1600 into the boot and use on a low setting for five minutes.

Dustcovers
Make dustcovers for clothes with . . .
● **Glad Trash Bags.** Cut a small hole in the center of

the bottom of a Glad Trash Bag and slip the bag over the top of a suit or dress on a hanger.

Fuzz, Lint, and Pet Hair
Remove fuzz, lint, and pet hair from clothing with . . .
- **Scotch Packaging Tape.** Wrap a strip of Scotch Packaging Tape around your hand, adhesive side out, and pat.

Galoshes
Polish rubber galoshes with . . .
- **Crisco All-Vegetable Shortening.** Rub on Crisco All-Vegetable Shortening.

Garment Bags
Deodorize garment storage bags with . . .
- **Arm & Hammer Baking Soda.** Sprinkle Arm & Hammer Baking Soda into the bottom of the bag.

Gloves
Clean white kid gloves with . . .
- **Gold Medal Flour.** Rub Gold Medal Flour into the leather, then brush clean.

Protect white gloves with . . .
- **Scotchgard.** Spray with Scotchgard before you wear them.

Gum
Remove chewing gum from the bottom of a shoe or sneaker with . . .

- **WD-40.** Spray on WD-40, wait, and pull the gum free.

Hangers
Make hangers glide along a clothes rod with . . .
- **Reynolds Cut-Rite Wax Paper.** Rub a sheet of Reynolds Cut-Rite Wax Paper over the clothes rod, and hangers will glide back and forth more easily.
- **WD-40.** Spray WD-40 on the clothes rod.

Jeans
Soften a new pair of jeans with . . .
- **Morton Salt.** Add one-half cup Morton Salt to your detergent in the washing machine.
- **Downy Fabric Softener.** Fill your washing machine with water, add one capful of Downy Fabric Softener, soak the jeans overnight, then run through the rinse cycle and dry.

Leather
Condition leather with . . .
- **Alberto VO5 Conditioning Hairdressing.** If you're all out of mink oil, substitute Alberto VO5 Conditioning Hairdressing.

Lingerie
Prevent the knots of small ribbons on lingerie from coming

When Was It Invented?

1835	Lea & Perrins Worcestershire Sauce
1842	Kingsford's Corn Starch
1846	Arm & Hammer Baking Soda
1855	Miller High Life
1861	*THE CIVIL WAR BEGINS*
1862	Gulden's Mustard
1868	Tabasco Pepper Sauce
1876	*ALEXANDER GRAHAM BELL INVENTS TELEPHONE*
1877	Quaker Oats
1878	Ivory Soap
1879	*THOMAS EDISON INVENTS ELECTRIC LIGHT*
	Listerine
1880	Gold Medal Flour
	Heinz Vinegar
1886	Coca-Cola
1887	Forster Toothpicks

1887	Vaseline Petroleum Jelly
1890	McCormick/Schilling Food Coloring
	Lipton Flo-Thru Tea Bags
1891	20 Mule Team Borax
1892	Maxwell House Coffee
1893	Wrigley's Spearmint Gum
1896	Colgate Toothpaste
1897	Jell-O
1899	Wesson Corn Oil
1902	Crayola Chalk
1903	*WRIGHT BROTHERS INVENT THE AIR-PLANE*
	Crayola Crayons
	McCormick/Schilling Cream of Tartar
1906	Kiwi Shoe Polish
1908	Dixie Cups
1911	Crisco All-Vegetable Shortening
1912	Hellmann's Real Mayonnaise
	Morton Salt
1913	S.O.S Steel Wool Soap Pads
1914	*WORLD WAR I BEGINS*
	Wilson Tennis Balls
1916	Clorox Bleach
1919	Dannon Yogurt
1920	*PROHIBITION BEGINS*
	Barbasol
1921	Wonder Bread

1926	Hartz Parakeet Seed
	Hershey's Syrup
	Q-Tips Cotton Swabs
1927	Reynolds Cut-Rite Wax Paper
1929	*STOCK MARKET CRASHES*
	Scotch Transparent Tape
1930	Alka-Seltzer
	Canada Dry Club Soda
1932	*FDR ELECTED PRESIDENT*
1935	Avery Address Labels
1936	Windex
1937	SPAM
1938	Gerber Applesauce
1939	*WORLD WAR II BEGINS*
1943	Uncle Ben's Converted Brand Rice
1944	Coppertone
1945	Turtle Wax
1946	Lubriderm
1947	Elmer's Glue-All
	Reynolds Wrap
1948	Nestea
	Reddi-wip
1950	Geritol
1952	*EISENHOWER ELECTED PRESIDENT*
1953	Saran Wrap
	WD-40
1954	Carnation Nonfat Dry Milk
	Easy-Off Oven Cleaner
1955	Cascade
1956	Alberto VO5 Conditioning Hairdressing

When Was It Invented?

1956	Endust
	Jif Peanut Butter
	Scotchgard
1957	Frisbee
	Pam No Stick Cooking Spray
	Wishbone Thousand Island Dressing
1959	Tang
1961	Alberto VO5 Hair Spray
1962	*JOHN GLENN ORBITS THE EARTH*
1963	*JFK ASSASSINATED*
	Krazy Glue
1964	Aunt Jemima Original Syrup
1966	Efferdent
	MasterCard
1967	Viva Paper Towels
1968	Pringles
1969	*NEIL ARMSTRONG WALKS ON MOON*
1970	L'eggs Sheer Energy
	Spray 'n Wash
	Ziploc Storage Bags
1971	Clairol Herbal Essenses
	Conair Pro Style 1600
	Tidy Cat
1972	Bounce
	Mr. Coffee Filters
1974	*NIXON RESIGNS*
1985	Snuggle Fabric Softener
1990	Huggies Baby Wipes

untied with . . .

- **Maybelline Crystal Clear Nail Polish.** Dab the knots with Maybelline Crystal Clear Nail Polish.

Organizing

Separate lingerie, scarves, gloves, hosiery, and handkerchiefs with . . .

- **Ziploc Storage Bags.** Organize your smaller garments in Ziploc Storage Bags.

Panty Hose

Dry panty hose with a. . .

- **Conair Pro Style 1600.** Hang the wet panty hose on the shower rod and blow them dry.

Stop a run in panty hose with . . .

- **Maybelline Crystal Clear Nail Polish.** Paint the snag immediately with Maybelline Crystal Clear Nail Polish.
- **Scotch Transparent Tape.** In an emergency, place a piece of Scotch Transparent Tape over the snag.

Polish

Clean shoes with . . .

- **Huggies Baby Wipes.** Simply wipe the shoes with a Huggies Baby Wipe.

Shine leather shoes with . . .

- **Alberto VO5 Conditioning Hairdressing.** Rub in a little Alberto VO5 Conditioning Hairdressing, then buff.

- **ChapStick.** In a pinch, rub ChapStick over the leather and buff with a dry, clean cloth.
- **Endust.** Spray Endust on shoes and shine with a cloth.
- **Geritol.** In a pinch, you can shine your brown leather shoes with a few drops of Geritol on a soft cloth.
- **Lubriderm.** Rub a dab of Lubriderm on each shoe and buff thoroughly.
  - **Mr. Coffee Filter.** Ball up a lint-free Mr. Coffee Filter.
  - **Turtle Wax.** Dab on Turtle Wax and shine with a clean, soft cloth.
  - **Vaseline.** Rub Vaseline Petroleum Jelly over the leather and wipe off the excess with a towel.

Prevent shoe polish from smearing with . . .

- **Reynolds Cut-Rite Wax Paper.** Let the shoe polish dry, then rub with a sheet of Reynolds Cut-Rite Wax Paper to remove the excess polish. Use a second sheet of Cut-Rite Wax Paper as a work surface to prevent shoe polish from spattering the floor.

Protection

Protect leather shoes and boots from winter salt and ice with . . .

- **Alberto VO5 Conditioning Hairdressing.** Rub in Alberto VO5 Conditioning Hairdressing.

Raincoat

Improvise a raincoat with . . .

- **Glad Trash Bags.** Cut slits in a Glad Trash Bag for head and arms.

Scuff Marks

Cover up scuff marks on white shoes with . . .

- **Liquid Paper.** Touch up with Liquid Paper.

Remove scuff marks from patent leather shoes with . . .

- **Colgate Toothpaste.** Apply Colgate with a tissue, rub, and wipe off.
- **Coppertone.** Apply Coppertone to a soft cloth and rub into the patent leather.

Shoelaces

Prevent broken shoelaces from fraying with . . .

- **Elmer's Glue-All.** Dip the ends of the shoelaces into Elmer's Glue-All and let dry.

Fix a frayed shoelace tip with . . .

- **Scotch Transparent Tape.** Wrap the frayed end with a small strip of Scotch Transparent Tape.

Shoulder Pads

Create shoulder pads for dresses or shirts with . . .

- **Kleenex Tissue.** Fold a few Kleenex Tissues in quarters or eighths, tape in place with Scotch Tape, and place under your dress or shirt to create a shoulder pad.

Sneakers

Clean sneakers with . . .

- **S.O.S Steel Wool Soap Pads.** Use a wet S.O.S Steel Wool Soap Pad to gently clean dirty sneakers.

Squeaks

Take squeaks out of new shoes with . . .

- **Alberto VO5 Conditioning Hairdressing.** Give squeaky shoes a coat of Alberto VO5 Conditioning Hairdressing.
- **WD-40.** Spray WD-40 into the leather and shine.

Stains

Hide a stain on a white suit with . . .

- **Kingsford's Corn Starch.** Rub Kingsford's Corn Starch into the stain.

Static Cling

Eliminate static cling with . . .

- **Lubriderm.** Rub a dab of Lubriderm into your hands until it disappears, then rub your palms over your panty hose or slip.

Tassels

Reattach loose tassels with . . .

- **Krazy Glue.** Use a few drops of Krazy Glue and hold in place until secure.

Ties

Protect neckties from spills with . . .

- **Scotchgard.** Spray the tie with Scotchgard so spills roll right off.

Umbrellas

Waterproof an umbrella with . . .

- **Scotchgard.** Spray the fabric on an umbrella

with Scotchgard so water runs off with a quick shake, allowing the umbrella to dry faster.

White Suede
Cover spots on white suede with . . .
- **Crayola Chalk.** Rub with Crayola Chalk.

Windbreaker
Improvise a windbreaker with . . .
- **Glad Trash Bags.** Cut holes in a Glad Trash Bag for your head and arms and wear it under your coat.

Zippers
Lubricate a zipper with . . .
- **Alberto VO5 Conditioning Hairdressing.** Rub a little Alberto VO5 Conditioning Hairdressing into the teeth of the zipper.
- **ChapStick.** Rub ChapStick along the teeth of the zipper to make it zip smoothly.
- **Ivory Soap.** Rub the teeth of the zipper with a bar of Ivory Soap to make the zipper glide easier.
- **Reynolds Cut-Rite Wax Paper.** To make a metal zipper work smoothly, run a sheet of Reynolds Cut-Rite Wax Paper up and down the teeth.

Slice a Birthday Cake
with Oral-B Dental Floss

Baking Powder
Make tartrate baking powder with . . .
- **McCormick/Schilling Cream of Tartar.** Blend together one-half teaspoon Cream of Tartar, one-quarter teaspoon Arm & Hammer Baking Soda, and one-quarter teaspoon Kingsford's Corn Starch.

Bosco Fizz
Make a Bosco Fizz with . . .
- **Bosco.** Put a generous squirt of Bosco in a glass, add a splash of milk, and top off with cola, then stir well. To make a Bosco Fizz float, add a scoop of ice cream.

Bread
Bake bread with . . .
- **Miller High Life.** Sprinkle three to five tablespoons sugar over three cups self-rising flour, add one can Miller

High Life, and knead. Put the dough in a greased loaf pan, let stand for five minutes, then bake for forty-five minutes at 350ºF. Rub butter over the top and bake for an additional five minutes. Serve warm.

Broth Fat
Strain the fat from broth with . . .
- **Viva Paper Towels.** Strain the broth through a sheet of Viva Paper Towels.

A RECIPE FOR MIRACLES
The Miracle Whip Chocolate Cake, developed by consumers during World War II food rationing, has been the most requested recipe from the Kraft Kitchens.

Buttermilk Substitute
Cook with a buttermilk substitute with . . .
- **McCormick/Schilling Cream of Tartar.** Mix one cup milk with one and three-quarters tablespoons Cream of Tartar for use as a buttermilk substitute in recipes.

Cake
(Also see Frosting, page 96)
Prevent Saran Wrap from sticking to a cake with . . .
- **Pam No Stick Cooking Spray.** Spray the underside of the plastic wrap with Pam No Stick Cooking Spray.

Determine whether a cake is baked with . . .
- **Forster Toothpicks.** Insert a Forster Toothpick in the center of the cake and remove. If it comes out clean, the cake is ready.

Pipe icing on a cake with . . .

● **Ziploc Storage Bags.** Fill a pint-size Ziploc Storage Bag with icing, twist the bag to force icing to one corner, seal, and use scissors to snip a small bit off the corner. Squeeze out icing to make polka dots, squiggles, or write names. Use a separate bag for each color.

Prevent icing from running off the cake with . . .

● **Domino Sugar.** Douse the cake with Domino Sugar.

Never grease a cake pan again with . . .

● **Reynolds Cut-Rite Wax Paper.** Place each pan on a sheet of Cut-Rite Wax Paper, trace around the bottom of the pan, cut out the wax paper circle, and place it in the pan. After baking and cooling, loosen the sides of the cake with a knife. Invert the cake onto a cooling rack, remove the pan, and peel off the wax paper for a smooth surface that's ready to frost.

Cut cake with . . .

● **Oral-B Mint Waxed Floss.** Oral-B Dental Floss cuts cake into neat slices.

Spice up your baking with . . .

● **Tang.** Add Tang to your cake and cookie mixes for an "orange zest."

Caramel Corn

Make caramel corn with . . .

● **Orville Redenbacher's Gourmet Popping Corn.** Use popped Orville Redenbacher's Gourmet Popping Corn to make your own caramel corn. Just follow the recipe in any cookbook.

Cheese

Slice cheese with . . .

● **Oral-B Mint Waxed Floss.** Oral-B Mint Waxed Floss cuts neatly through cheese for clean slices.

Chicken

Make fried chicken golden brown with . . .

● **McCormick/Schilling Food Coloring.** Add a few drops of yellow food coloring to vegetable oil before frying. The chicken will absorb the food coloring and become a golden brown.

AEROSOL KETCHUP?

In the 1950s, after developing aerosol whipped cream, Reddi-wip, Inc. tried to develop aerosol mayonnaise, aerosol ketchup, aerosol shampoo, aerosol mustard, and aerosol iodine.

Coffee

Lighten coffee with . . .

● **Reddi-wip.** Use a tablespoon of Reddi-wip as a substitute for milk or cream in a cup of coffee.

Sweeten a cup of coffee with . . .

● **Aunt Jemima Original Syrup.** Substitute a teaspoon of Aunt Jemima Original Syrup for each teaspoon of sugar or honey.

Make an impromptu coffee filter with . . .

● **Viva Paper Towels.** Use a sheet of Viva Paper Towels in the coffeemaker.

Coffee Filter

Improvise a coffee filter with . . .

● **Kleenex Tissue.** Place three Kleenex Tissues in the coffee maker to filter the coffee.

Confectionery Sugar

Make confectionery sugar with . . .

- **Domino Sugar.** Grind up Domino Sugar in a food processor.

Cookies

Improvise a cookie tray with a . . .

- **Frisbee.** Turn the Frisbee upside down, line with Viva Paper Towels, and fill with cookies.

Lift cookies from a cooking sheet with . . .

- **Oral-B Mint Waxed Floss.** Slide a strand of Oral-B Mint Waxed Floss between fresh-baked cookies and the cookie sheet.

Wrap cookies and candies with . . .

- **Maxwell House Coffee.** Cover an empty Maxwell House Coffee can with wrapping paper, fill with cookies or candy, cover with the plastic lid, then wrap.

Corn

Desilk an ear of corn with . . .

- **Viva Paper Towels.** Shuck an ear of corn, then wipe it in a single stroke from top to bottom with a dampened sheet of Viva Paper Towels.

What's Shaking With Salt and Pepper

- In 80 B.C., Alexandria, Egypt, became the greatest spice trading port of the eastern Mediterranean, with one of its entrances known as "Pepper Gate."

- The first written reference to salt is found in the story of Lot's wife, who was turned into a pillar of salt when she disobeyed the angels and looked back at Sodom.

- In A.D. 410, Alaric the Visigoth demanded one and a half tons of pepper as ransom from Rome. Two years later, he started receiving three hundred pounds of pepper annually from the city.

- The expression "He is not worth his salt" originated in ancient Greece, where salt was traded for slaves.

- During the Middle Ages in Europe, pepper was counted

Dough

Prevent pastry dough from sticking to the cutting board and rolling pin with . . .

- **Kingsford's Corn Starch.** Sprinkle the cutting board and rolling pin with tasteless Kingsford's Corn Starch before rolling out the dough.

- **Pam No Stick Cooking Spray.** Spray the surface with Pam No Stick Cooking Spray.

out peppercorn by pepper-corn.

● Roman soldiers were paid "salt money," *salarium agentum,* the origin of the English word *salary.*

● In the eleventh century, many towns kept their accounts in pepper. Taxes and rents were assessed and paid in pepper. A sack of pepper was worth a man's life.

● The superstition that spilling salt brings bad luck may have its origins in Leonardo da Vinci's *The Last Supper,* which depicts an overturned salt cellar in front of Judas Iscariot. The French believed that throwing a pinch of salt over the shoulder would hit the devil in the eye, preventing any further foul play.

● Between 1784 and 1873, the pepper trade furnished a huge portion of the import duties collected in Salem, Massachusetts, at one point financing 5 percent of the entire United States government's expenses.

● At the turn of the century, unscrupulous spice dealers would cut shipments of peppercorns with mouse droppings.

● The Russians sprinkle pepper on vodka.

Eggs

Differentiate hard-boiled eggs from raw eggs in the refrigerator with . . .

● **Crayola Crayons.** Mark the hard-boiled eggs with a Crayola Crayon.

● **McCormick/Schilling Food Coloring.** Before hard-boiling eggs, add food coloring to the water to tint them.

Prevent cracked hard-boiled eggs with . . .

● **Heinz Vinegar.** Add two tablespoons of Heinz White

Vinegar per quart of water before boiling to prevent the eggs from cracking. The eggshells will also peel off faster and easier.

Fish
Thaw frozen fish with . . .
- **Carnation Nonfat Dry Milk.** Mix one and one-third cup Carnation Nonfat Dry Milk in three and three-quarters cup water. Place the frozen fish in a pan and cover with the milk solution. Milk eliminates the frozen taste, returning the fresh-caught flavor.

How They Drink Tang in France

On *Saturday Night Live*, Beldar Conehead (Dan Aykroyd) consumed mass quantities of the orange powder dry and straight from the jar.

Frosting
Decorate cake frosting with . . .
- **Forster Toothpicks.** Use a Forster Toothpick to draw your design on the cake, then squeeze the frosting over your lines.

Make Maple frosting with . . .
- **Aunt Jemima Original Syrup.** Combine one stick of margarine, one-third cup of Aunt Jemima Original Syrup, and three to four cups powdered sugar. Beat until desired thickness.

Set cake icing with a . . .
- **Conair Pro Style 1600.** Set a Conair Pro Style 1600 on warm and dry cake icing.

Fruits and Vegetables
Clean insecticide sprays off fruits and vegetables with . . .

- **Dr. Bronner's Peppermint Soap.** Three dashes of Dr. Bronner's Peppermint Soap in a sink full of water will wash most insecticides off fruits and vegetables.

Garlic

Make a garlic clove easy to handle with . . .

- **Forster Toothpicks.** Stick a Forster Toothpick into a clove of garlic before tossing it into a marinade, so you can remove it easily.

Store garlic cloves with . . .

- **Gerber Applesauce.** Peel garlic cloves, place them in clean, empty Gerber baby food jars, and store in the freezer.
- **L'eggs Sheer Energy.** Fill the foot of a pair of L'eggs Sheer Energy and hang it high to keep the contents dry.

Gelatin

Improvise a Jell-O mold with . . .

- **Maxwell House Coffee.** Use an empty Maxwell House Coffee can.

Ham

Bake a moist ham with . . .

- **Coca-Cola.** Empty a can of Coca-Cola into the baking pan, wrap the ham in aluminum foil, and bake. Thirty

OUR FRIEND, FOOD COLORING

An extensive survey conducted by the National Academy of Sciences in 1977 estimated that every day the average American consumes an average of 100 milligrams of FD&C Red Dye No. 40, 43 milligrams of FD&C Yellow Dye No. 5, and 37 milligrams of FD&C Yellow Dye No. 6.

minutes before the ham is finished, remove the foil, allowing the drippings to mix with the Coke for a sumptuous brown gravy.

Ice Cream

Enhance the flavor of ice cream with . . .

● **McCormick/Schilling Black Pepper.** *McCormick/Schilling's New Spice Cookbook* recommends softening one quart vanilla or chocolate ice cream just enough to stir (without allowing it to melt), spooning it into a large bowl, and adding one tablespoon crushed green peppercorns, one teaspoon coarse ground black pepper, and one-quarter teaspoon coconut extract. Then eat.

FRENCH FRIES ETIQUETTE

In Japan, the Japanese eat french fries with mayonnaise. In the United Kingdom, the British eat french fries with vinegar.

Jars

Open a stubborn jar with . . .

● **Playtex Living Gloves.** Put on a pair of Playtex Living Gloves to improve your grip to open a stubborn lid off a jar.

Ketchup

Unclog a freshly opened ketchup bottle with . . .

● **Glad Flexible Straws.** Insert a Glad Flexible Straw all the way into the bottle to add air and start the ketchup flowing.

Leftovers

Store leftovers with . . .

● **Ziploc Storage Bags.** Keep leftovers for single servings in Ziploc Storage Bags for quick meals.

Label frozen foods and leftovers with . . .

- **Avery Laser Labels.** Print information about the contents and the date you place the food in the refrigerator or freezer on Avery Laser Labels.

Liquor
Make a space-age screwdriver with . . .

- **Tang.** Mix Tang with vodka.

Make Wine Jell-O . . .

- **Jell-O.** *The Joy of Cooking* suggests boiling one cup water, mixing with gelatin powder in a bowl until dissolved, then adding one cup red wine. Stir well, then refrigerate for four hours or until mixture gels. Serves four.

Make a Bloody Mary with . . .

- **Tabasco Pepper Sauce.** Combine one quart tomato juice, one cup vodka, one tablespoon fresh lime or lemon juice, one tablespoon Worcestershire Sauce, one teaspoon salt, and one-quarter teaspoon Tabasco sauce in a two-quart pitcher. Stir well, chill, and serve over ice, garnished with a slice of lime.

Marshmallows
Make marshmallows with . . .

- **Jell-O.** Gelatin is the main ingredient in any recipe for marshmallows.

Matzah Balls
Make fluffy matzah balls with . . .

BANKING ON BOSCO

On the television sitcom *Seinfeld*, George Costanza's ATM password is Bosco.

POOR MAN'S VINEGAR

Vinegar can be made from virtually any sugary substance that can be fermented to ethyl alcohol, including molasses, sorghum syrup, fruits, berries, melons, coconut, honey, maple syrup, potatoes, beets, malt, grains, and whey. The oldest way to make vinegar is to leave wine made from fruit juice in an open container, allowing microorganisms in the air to convert the ethyl alcohol to acetic acid.

● **Canada Dry Club Soda.** Substitute Canada Dry Club Soda for the liquid called for in the recipes.

Measuring

Save ingredients when measuring with . . .

● **Reynolds Cut-Rite Wax Paper.** When measuring flour, sugar, baking mix, or other dry ingredients, crease a sheet of Cut-Rite Wax Paper down the middle, open it up, and place it on the kitchen countertop. Spoon the ingredient into a dry measuring cup, level off with a knife or spatula, letting the excess fall on the wax paper. Pick up the wax paper and pour the excess back into its canister.

Meats

Kill bacteria in meats with . . .

● **Heinz Vinegar.** Marinating meat in Heinz Vinegar kills bacteria and tenderizes the meat. Use one-quarter cup vinegar for a two- to three-pound roast, marinate overnight, then cook without draining or rinsing the meat. Add herbs to the vinegar when marinating as desired.

Marinate meats with . . .

● **Miller High Life.** Marinating inexpensive cuts of meat

in Miller High Life for approximately an hour before cooking increases the flavor and tenderness.

- **Ziploc Storage Bags.** Combine your food and marinade ingredients in a Ziploc Storage Bag and refrigerate.

Tenderize meat with . . .

- **Campbell's Tomato Juice.** Soak the meat in Campbell's Tomato Juice. The acids in tomatoes tenderize meat.

- **Lipton Tea Bags.** Add equal parts strong-brewed Lipton Tea and double-strength beef stock to a tough pot roast or stew. The tannin in tea is a natural meat tenderizer.

- **Nestea.** Mix Nestea and use one part tea to one part double-strength beef stock as the liquid when making a pot roast or stew.

Microwave Ovens

Cover bowls or dishes when cooking in the microwave with . . .

- **Mr. Coffee Filters.** Mr. Coffee Filters make excellent covers.

Oil

Recycle frying oil with . . .

- **Mr. Coffee Filters.** Line a sieve with a Mr. Coffee Filter to strain oil after deep-fat frying.

Onions

Store onions with . . .

- **L'eggs Sheer Energy.** Fill the foot of a pair of L'eggs Sheer Energy and hang it high to keep the contents dry.

Pancakes

Make fluffy pancakes with . . .

● **Canada Dry Club Soda.** Substitute Canada Dry Club Soda for the liquid used in the recipes.

Peanut Soup

Make peanut soup with . . .

● **Jif Peanut Butter.** Peanut butter is the main ingredient in any recipe for peanut soup.

Plastic Containers

Prevent tomato sauce stains on plastic containers with . . .

● **Pam No Stick Cooking Spray.** Spray the insides of the containers with Pam No Stick Cooking Spray before filling the containers with any food containing tomatoes.

Popcorn

Make spicy popcorn with . . .

● **Tabasco Pepper Sauce.** Add a few drops of Tabasco sauce to the cooking oil before adding the popcorn kernels.

Make salt stick to air-popped popcorn with . . .

● **Pam No Stick Cooking Spray.** Spray the popcorn with Pam No Stick Cooking Spray, then salt.

Poultry

Truss poultry for cooking with . . .

● **Oral-B Mint Waxed Floss.** Fill the cavity with stuffing, cross the two legs, and tie them together with dental floss. If necessary, sew the cavity closed.

Recipes

Cook with . . .

- **Coca-Cola.**
The Coca-Cola
Consumer Infor-
mation Center
offers a free
packet of reci-
pes—including
Mustard Herb
Dressing (an
Italian-style salad dressing
made with one-half cup of Coca-Cola), Twin
Cheese Dip (requiring three-quarters cup of Coca-Cola
and doubling as a sandwich filling), and Sweet-Sour Cab-
bage (using one-half cup of Coca-Cola and two tablespoons of bacon drippings). Just call 1-800-GET-COKE.

- **Miller High Life.** Will Anderson, author of *From Beer
to Eternity*, offers recipes for Beer Soup (requiring one
quart beer), Beer Sandwich (calling for three-quarters
cup beer), and Beer Omelet (made with one-half cup
beer). The Miller Brewing Company offers a free
recipe book, including recipes for Pot Roast with Beer
(calling for one cup of beer), Beer Burgers (needing
three-quarters cup beer), and Beer Cookies (requiring
one cup of beer).

- **Tabasco Pepper Sauce.** *The Tabasco Cookbook* by Paul
McIlhenny with Barbara Hunter contains such recipes
as Frog Legs Piquant, Cheese Scones, and Spiced
Peaches—all with Tabasco sauce.

- **Tang.** The Kraft Consumer Center offers a free packet
of recipes including Orangey Pancakes (made with one-

HONEY NEVER SPOILS

Crystallization does not affect the taste or purity of honey. If honey crystallizes, just pop the container into warm water or put the honey in a microwave-safe container and place it in the microwave on high for one to three minutes, stirring every thirty seconds.

half cup of Tang), Whipped Orange Butter (requiring two tablespoons of Tang), Oriental Barbecue Sauce (using one-third cup of Tang), and Herbed Orangey Dressing (made with three tablespoons Tang and one envelope of Good Seasons Classic Herb Salad Dressing Mix). Just call 1-800-431-1002.

Recipe Cards

Laminate recipe cards with . . .

- **Alberto VO5 Hair Spray.** Spray with Alberto VO5 Hair Spray to give the cards a protective gloss.

Save recipes clipped from magazines with . . .

- **Scotch Transparent Tape.** Simply use Scotch Transparent Tape to attach the clipped recipes to index cards.

Rice

Prevent rice from becoming sticky with . . .

- **Wesson Corn Oil.** Bring water to a boil, add one tablespoon Wesson Corn Oil, then add the rice.

Salad

Dry salad greens with a . . .

- **Conair Pro Style 1600.** Set a Conair Pro Style 1600 on cool, and dry wet leaves of lettuce.

Salt

Prevent moisture from clumping up salt with . . .

- **Uncle Ben's Converted Brand Rice.** Add a few grains of uncooked Uncle Ben's Converted Brand Rice to the salt shaker to absorb excess moisture.

Sausages

Cook sausages with ease with . . .

- **Forster Toothpicks.** Use two Forster Toothpicks to skewer two or three sausages together to make them easier to turn and brown evenly.

Snacks

Carry snacks with . . .

- **Gerber Applesauce.** Fill clean, empty Gerber baby food jars with raisins, nuts, or cereal for snacks on car trips.
- **Ziploc Storage Bags.** When traveling, pack snacks in Ziploc Storage Bags.

Keep healthy snacks in your kitchen with . . .

- **Orville Redenbacher's Gourmet Popping Corn.** Pop Orville Redenbacher's Gourmet Popping Corn and keep in airtight canisters. Unbuttered popcorn has fewer calories than most snack foods. You can also sprinkle it with chili pepper, paprika, or cayenne.

Soft Drinks

Make inexpensive soft drinks with . . .

- **Canada Dry Club Soda.** Add Canada Dry to fruit juice for a low-cost and healthy beverage.

Make a Cola Volcano with . . .

- **Tabasco Pepper Sauce.** Mix one or two drops Tabasco sauce to a glass of Coca-Cola, stir well, and add ice.

JELL-O OF OZ

In the movie *The Wizard of Oz*, to achieve the special effect of the Horse of a Different Color changing color in each successive shot, the horse was covered in different shades of Jell-O.

Soup

Thicken soup with . . .

- **Betty Crocker Potato Buds.** Instead of using flour to thicken soup, use Betty Crocker Potato Buds for a tastier thickener.

- **Kingsford's Corn Starch.** Corn starch has twice the thickening power of flour. When a gravy, sauce, soup, or stew recipe calls for flour, use half as much corn starch to thicken. One tablespoon of corn starch equals two tablespoons of flour.

Sour Cream Substitute

Make a sour cream substitute with . . .

- **Reddi-wip.** Mix three or four drops of lemon juice with one cup Reddi-wip and let sit for thirty minutes.

Spaghetti

Flavor spaghetti with . . .

- **Maxwell House Coffee.** Add one-quarter to one-half teaspoon of instant Maxwell House Coffee to spaghetti sauce. Coffee gives store-bought spaghetti sauce brown coloring and a less acidic flavor.

Strawberry Short Cup

Make a Strawberry Short Cup with . . .

● **Dixie Cups.** Place a spoonful of whipped topping in the bottom of six 9-ounce Dixie Cups. Alternate filling the cups with strawberries and cubed cake to one inch below the rim. Press down with a spoon to fill any air pockets. Complete with whipped topping and a single whole strawberry. Serves six.

Sugar

Prevent sugar from caking up with . . .

● **Sunshine Krispy Original Saltine Crackers.** Put a couple of Sunshine Krispy Original Saltine Crackers in the sugar canister.

Sugar Substitute

When cooking, substitute for sugar with . . .

● **Aunt Jemima Original Syrup.** Use three-quarters cup of Aunt Jemima Original Syrup for each cup of sugar.

● **SueBee Honey.** Use SueBee Honey in place of granulated sugar for up to half of the amount in the recipe. With experimentation, you will find that honey can be substituted for all the sugar in some recipes. For baked goods, add about one-half teaspoon baking soda for each cup of honey used, reduce the amount of liquid in the recipe by one-quarter cup for each cup of honey used, and reduce oven temperature by 25°F to prevent overbrowning. For easy removal, spray measuring cup with Pam No Stick Cooking Spray before adding honey.

Tacos

Hold tacos with . . .

● **Mr. Coffee Filters.** Mr. Coffee Filters make great holders for messy foods.

Tea

Sweeten a cup of tea with . . .

● **Aunt Jemima Original Syrup.** Substitute a teaspoon of Aunt Jemima Original Syrup for each teaspoon of sugar or honey.

Waffles

Make fluffy waffles with . . .

● **Canada Dry Club Soda.** Substitute Canada Dry Club Soda for the liquid used in the recipes.

Prevent waffles from sticking to a waffle iron with . . .

● **Pam No Stick Cooking Spray.** Spray Pam No Stick Cooking Spray on the waffle iron before heating it.

Weighing

Weigh chopped foods with . . .

● **Mr. Coffee Filters.** Place chopped ingredients in a Mr. Coffee Filter on a kitchen scale.

Who Invented Ketchup, Mustard, and Mayonnaise?

Ketchup

In the seventeenth century, English sailors whose ships were docked in Singapore discovered that local natives ate *kechap*—a Tangy sauce made from fish brine, herbs, and spices—with their fish and fowl dishes. Upon returning home to Britain, the sailors, yearning for the sauce, tried to recreate it, substituting mushrooms, walnuts, cucumbers, and, later, tomatoes for the ingredients they were missing. Ketchup, as the British called the surrogate sauce, became a national favorite.

Meanwhile, Maine sea captains acquired a taste for Singaporean *kechap* and for the exotic tomato, relished in Mexico and the Spanish West Indies. Maine families were soon growing tomatoes in their gardens and making *kechap*—which they called *"catsup"*—to use on codfish cakes, baked beans, and meat.

Making ketchup at home required that the tomatoes be parboiled and peeled. The puree had to be continually stirred on the stove to prevent the pulp from sticking to the cauldron and burning.

Fortunately for housewives, Henry J. Heinz introduced the first mass-produced, bottled ketchup in 1876. Today, ketchup is the best-known condiment in the world, and Heinz's Ketchup is America's favorite.

Mustard

Around 3000 B.C., mustard was first cultivated and used in India and China. The Romans turned mustard into a paste by adding grape juice, vinegar, oil, and honey, and they are credited with having brought mustard to Gaul (modern-day France). In the thirteenth century, the Provost of Paris granted the vinegar makers of Dijon the right to make mustard, paving the way for Dijon to become the French capital of mustard. Around 1720, in Durham, England, a Mrs. Clements developed a process for extracting the husk from mustard seeds and milling a smooth mustard powder, going into full production in 1729. In nineteenth-century France, Maurice Grey introduced new equipment to speed up the production and developed Grey Poupon Mustard, keeping his mustard recipe in a safe. Colman's, established in Norwich, became synonymous with mustard in Britain.

In 1880, fifty-seven-year-old Robert T. French founded a spice company in the hope of providing a livelihood for his three sons. By 1885 the company was operating out of an old flour mill in Rochester, New York, eventually manufacturing mustard. In 1904, the French family concocted a mild, bright yellow mustard that quickly became a national favorite. Most Americans think French's Mustard is named after the country.

Mayonnaise

In the eighteenth century, French Duc de Richelieu discovered a Spanish condiment made of raw egg yolk and olive oil in the port town of Mahón on the island of Minorca, one of the Balearic Islands. He brought the recipe for "Sauce of Mahón" back to France, where French chefs used it as a condiment for meats, renaming it *mayhonnaise*. When mayonnaise arrived in the United States in the early 1800s, it was considered a haute French sauce, too difficult to prepare. The invention of the electric blender and the advent of bottled dressings catapulted mayonnaise into the mainstream as a sandwich spread. In 1912, Richard Hellmann, a German immigrant who owned a delicatessen in Manhattan, began selling his premixed mayonnaise in one-pound wooden "boats," graduating to glass jars the following year. Hellmann's eventually extended its distribution from the East Coast to the Rocky Mountains.

Meanwhile, Best Foods, Inc., had introduced mayonnaise in California, calling it Best Foods Real Mayonnaise and expanding distribution throughout the West. Eventually the two companies merged under the Best Foods, Inc., banner, but since both brands of mayonnaise had developed strong followings, neither name was changed.

To this day, Hellman's Real Mayonnaise is distributed east of the Rocky Mountains, and Best Foods Real Mayonnaise is distributed west of the Rocky Mountains. The two are essentially the same, although some people find Hellmann's mayonnaise slightly more tangy.

Whipped Cream

Substitute whipped cream with . . .

- **Carnation Nonfat Dry Milk.** Whip one cup Carnation Nonfat Dry Milk in a cup of ice water for five minutes. Use immediately.

Prevent a mess when whipping cream with an electric beater with . . .

- **Reynolds Cut-Rite Wax Paper.** Cut two small holes in the middle of a sheet of Reynolds Cut-Rite Wax Paper, slip the stems of the beaters through the holes, and attach the beaters to the machine. Lower the beaters into the mixing bowl, keeping wax paper over the bowl, and turn on the machine.

Yogurt

Make a Maple Yogurt Smoothie with . . .

- **Aunt Jemima Original Syrup.** Combine one cup ice cubes, one cup plain yogurt, one-half cup low-fat milk, one-third cup Aunt Jemima Original Syrup, and one peeled banana in a blender. Cover and blend on high speed until smooth and thick.

Yogurt Cheese

Make yogurt cheese with . . .

- **Dannon Yogurt.** Yogurt cheese has the same consistency as cream cheese but is much lower in fat. It can be used as a spread for bagels, toast, and crackers, or as a low-calorie, low-fat, low-cholesterol substitute for cream cheese in traditional cheesecake recipes. To make yogurt cheese, empty a pint of yogurt into a large, fine-meshed strainer or colander lined with a double thickness of cheesecloth, a coffee filter, or a yogurt strainer. Place a bowl under the strainer to catch the liquid (whey) that drains from the yogurt. Cover the remaining yogurt and refrigerate for eight to twenty-four hours (texture will vary depending on how long it drains). Save the calcium-rich whey to use in soups and gravies. Makes about one cup of yogurt cheese.

8

FURNITURE

Polish Your Furniture

with SPAM

Clean

Remove fuzz, lint, and pet hair from furniture with . . .

- **Scotch Packaging Tape.** Wrap a strip of Scotch Packaging Tape around your hand, adhesive side out, and pat.

Clean varnished furniture with . . .

- **Lipton Tea Bags.** Cold Lipton Tea is a good cleaning agent for any kind of woodwork.
- **Nestea.** Dampen a cloth with cold Nestea and polish the wood.

Formica

Hide scratches on furniture and Formica with . . .

- **Crayola Crayons.** Rub the nick with a matching Crayola Crayon.

Glue

Remove airplane glue or cement glue from furniture with . . .

- **Jif Peanut Butter.** Simply rub the dried glue with Jif.
- **Wesson Corn Oil.** Apply a dab of Wesson Corn Oil and rub.

Knickknacks

Prevent knickknacks from scratching highly polished tabletops with . . .

- **Scotch Transparent Tape.** Cover the bottoms of the objects with Scotch Transparent Tape.

Knobs

Tighten loose dresser drawer knobs with . . .

- **Maybelline Crystal Clear Nail Polish.** Dip the end of the screw in Maybelline Crystal Clear Nail Polish and replace the knob in the hole to dry snugly.

Lamps

Decorate bedroom lamps with . . .

- **Con-Tact Paper.** Adorn the lamp shades with Con-Tact cut-outs.

Lubricate Drawers

Lubricate furniture drawers with . . .

- **Alberto VO5 Conditioning Hairdressing.** Rub in a little Alberto VO5 Conditioning Hairdressing on the casters.
- **ChapStick.** Rub ChapStick on the casters of drawers so they slide open and shut easily.
- **Ivory Soap.** Rub Ivory Soap on the casters of drawers and windows so they slide open and shut easily.

Polish

Polish furniture with . . .

- **Kingsford's Corn Starch.** After polishing furniture, sprinkle on a little Kingsford's Corn Starch and rub wood with a soft cloth.
- **L'eggs Sheer Energy.** Ball up your used panty hose and buff the furniture. The nylon in panty hose is a mild abrasive that polishes without scracthing.
- **Nestea.** Cold Nestea makes an excellent cleaning agent for wood.
- **SPAM.** SPAM purportedly makes good furniture polish, according to the *New York Times Magazine*.
- **Turtle Wax.** A coat of Turtle Wax rejuvenates dulled plastic tabletops and Formica counters.
- **WD-40.** Spray WD-40 on a cloth and wipe.

Scratches

Repair scratches on wood furniture with . . .

- **Alberto VO5 Conditioning Hairdressing.** Put a dab of Alberto VO5 Conditioning Hairdressing on a clean, soft cloth, then buff the spot.
- **Chun King Soy Sauce.** Use a cotton ball to dab Chun King Soy Sauce on the scratch until achieving the right tone of brown.
- **Crayola Crayons.** Rub the nick with a matching Crayola Crayon.
- **Forster Toothpicks.** Dip a Forster Toothpick in paint to retouch fine scratches or to reach small nooks and crannies.

- **Kiwi Shoe Polish.** Cover up small scratches or discolorations on furniture or woodwork.
- **Lea & Perrins Worcestershire Sauce.** Use a cotton ball to apply Worcestershire Sauce to the scratched surface.
- **Q-Tips Cotton Swabs.** Dip a Q-Tips Cotton Swab in paint to retouch fine scratches. Fill scratches on cherry or mahogany by applying iodine.

Stains

Remove stains, rings, and minor scratches from wood furniture with . . .

- **Geritol.** Apply Geritol to the wood with a cotton ball, wipe away excess, and polish as usual.

Upholstery

Clean cotton upholstery with . . .

- **Barbasol Shaving Cream.** Apply Barbasol sparingly to the stain and rub gently with a damp cloth.
- **Pink Pearl Erasers.** Rub lightly with a Pink Pearl Eraser.

Remove stubborn stains from furniture upholstery and clothes with . . .

- **Heinz Vinegar.** Apply Heinz White Vinegar directly to the stain, then wash as directed by the manufacturer's instructions.
- **20 Mule Team Borax.** Blot up the spill, sprinkle 20 Mule Team Borax to cover the area, let dry, and vacuum. Before treating, make sure the fabric dye is colorfast by testing an unexposed area with a paste of 20 Mule Team Borax and water. For wine and alcohol stains, dissolve one cup 20 Mule Team Borax in one quart water. Sponge

on the solution, wait thirty minutes, shampoo the spotted area, let dry, and vacuum.

Remove chewing gum, crayon, tar, and Silly Putty from most surfaces with . . .

- **WD-40.** Spray on WD-40, wait, and wipe.

White Rings

Remove white rings and spots from wood furniture with . . .

- **Baby Oil.** Gently rubbing baby oil may remove stubborn spots.
- **Miracle Whip.** Wipe on Miracle Whip, let stand for an hour, wipe off, and polish the furniture.
- **Turtle Wax.** Apply Turtle Wax to the ring with your finger.
- **Vaseline.** Cover each scratch with a liberal coat of Vaseline Petroleum Jelly, let sit for twenty-four hours, rub into wood, wipe away excess, and polish as usual.
- **Wesson Corn Oil.** Dip a cloth in Wesson Corn Oil, then into cigar or cigarette ashes. Rub with the grain, across the spot, until it disappears.

Wobbly Tables

Fix a wobbly table with . . .

- **Pink Pearl Erasers.** Cut a Pink Pearl Eraser to fit the bottoms of the table legs and affix with nails or glue.
- **Silly Putty.** Place a piece of Silly Putty under a leg.

Everything You Always Wanted to Know About SPAM

Jay C. Hormel, son of the Hormel company's founder, was determined to find a use for several thousand pounds of surplus pork shoulder. He developed a distinctive canned blend of chopped pork and ham known as Hormel spiced ham that didn't require refrigeration. SPAM luncheon meat was hailed as the "miracle meat," and its shelf-stable attributes attracted the attention of the United States military during World War II. By 1940, 70 percent of Americans had tried it, and Hormel hired George Burns and Gracie Allen to advertise SPAM on their radio show. On March 22, 1994, Hormel Foods Corporation celebrated the production of its five billionth can of SPAM.

● 100 million pounds of SPAM were issued as a Lend-Lease staple in the rations to American, Russian, and European troops during World War II, fueling the Normandy Invasion. GIs called SPAM "ham that failed the physical." General Dwight D. Eisenhower confessed to "a few unkind words about it—uttered during the strain of battle."

● Former British Prime Minister Margaret Thatcher, as a young woman of eighteen working in her family's grocery store, remembers SPAM as a "wartime delicacy."

● In *Khrushchev Remembers*, Nikita Khrushchev credited SPAM for keeping the Soviet army alive during World War II: "We had lost our most fertile, food-bearing lands—the Ukraine and the Northern Caucasians. Without SPAM, we wouldn't have been able to feed our army."

● In the 1980s, David Letterman suggested SPAM-on-a-Rope for his *Late Night* audience "in case you get hungry in the shower."

● When Vernon Tejas made his solo winter ascent of Mount McKinley in 1988, he took a picture of himself with a can of SPAM at the summit.

● Hormel Foods Board Chairman R. L. Knowlton presented a can of SPAM to Mikhail Gorbachev in June 1990 and another can of SPAM to Boris Yeltsin in June 1992.

● The Pentagon sent approximately $2 million worth of SPAM to United States troops during the Gulf War.

● South Koreans consider SPAM an upscale food. The *Wall Street Journal* reported that a Seoul executive in search of the perfect present bought SPAM, explaining, "It is an impressive gift."

● Anthropologist Jane Goodall and her mother once made

two thousand SPAM sandwiches for Belgian troops fleeing from their African colony.

● SPAM can be grilled, pan-fried, broiled, sautéed, and baked—or added to ethnic dishes, sandwiches, pasta salads, pizzas, casseroles, stir-fry dishes, appetizers, and soups.

● The Ala Moana Poi Bow in Honolulu serves SPAM musubi and SPAM, eggs, and rice.

● The Green Midget Café, created by Monty Python's Flying Circus, serves "egg and SPAM; egg, bacon, and SPAM; egg, bacon, sausage, and SPAM; SPAM, bacon, sausage, and SPAM; SPAM, egg, SPAM, SPAM, bacon, and SPAM; SPAM, SPAM, SPAM, egg, and SPAM; SPAM, SPAM, SPAM, SPAM, SPAM, SPAM, baked beans, SPAM, SPAM, SPAM, and SPAM; or lobster thermidor aux crevettes with a mornay sauce garnished with truffle paté, brandy and a fried egg on top, and SPAM."

● Mr. Whitekeys' Fly By Night Club in Spenard, Alaska, offers Cajun SPAM, SPAM nachos, and pasta with SPAM and sun-dried tomatoes in cream sauce.

● The winning recipes from the 1992 State Fair Best of SPAM Recipe Competition included SPAM Mousse, SPAM Golden Harvest Clam Chowder, and SPAM Cheesecake.

● A SPAMBURGER, "the only hamburger actually made with ham," can be made by grilling, pan-frying, or broiling a slice of SPAM, and then layering the slice with lettuce, tomato, mayonnaise, and cheese on a hamburger bun.

● Hormel Foods' cookbook, *The Great Taste of SPAM*, includes recipes for SPAM Stew with Buttermilk Topping, SPAM Fajitas, and SPAM Strudels with Mustard Sauce.

● Sixty-eight state and regional fairs hold Hormel Foods–sanctioned SPAM recipe contests each year.

● In Hawaii, Maui Mall hosts an annual SPAM cook-off.

● Austin, Texas, has been home to the SPAMorama barbecue and cooking contest since 1974.

● Seattle, Washington, hosts a yearly SPAM luncheon meat celebration.

● The SPAM Jamboree, held every Fourth of July weekend in Austin, Minnesota, is the only SPAM event Hormel officially sponsors.

● At the 1983 SPAMposium, thirty-three self-proclaimed SPAMophiles gathered from across the nation to deliver scholarly papers and demonstrations, including making explosives from SPAM.

Everything You Always Wanted to Know About **SPAM**

Fertilize Your Lawn

with Maxwell House Coffee

African Violets
Kill plant lice on African violets with . . .

● **Alberto VO5 Hair Spray.** Spray Alberto VO5 Hair Spray into a plastic bag (not directly onto the plant), place the bag over the plant, secure shut with a twist tie, and let sit overnight.

Azaleas
Grow beautiful azaleas with . . .

● **Heinz Vinegar.** Occasionally water plants with a mixture of two tablespoons Heinz Vinegar to one quart water. Azaleas love acidic soil.

Bees, Wasps, and Yellow Jackets
Kill bees, wasps, and yellow jackets with . . .

● **Miller High Life.** Fill a clean, empty jar with a can of Miller High Life, punch three-eighth inch holes in the lid, cover tightly, and place near plants where the insects pollinate. Bees, wasps, and yellow jackets love beer and drown in it.

Bulbs
Store plant bulbs with . . .
- **L'eggs Sheer Energy.** Fill the foot of a pair of L'eggs Sheer Energy and hang it high to keep the contents dry.

Cleaning
Clean plant leaves with . . .
- **Alberto VO5 Conditioning Hairdressing.** Apply a small dab of Alberto VO5 Conditioning Hairdressing to the leaves with a soft cloth.
- **Carnation Nonfat Dry Milk.** Mix one and one-third cup Carnation Nonfat Dry Milk with seven and three-quarters cups water, and using a soft cloth, wipe the leaves.
- **Dr. Bronner's Peppermint Soap.** Add a teaspoon of Dr. Bronner's Peppermint Soap to a gallon of water and spray your flowers and fruit trees.

Cuttings
Secure plant cuttings with . . .
- **Reynolds Wrap.** Place Reynolds Wrap across the top of a glass jar filled with water. Poke holes in the foil and insert the cuttings securely in place. The foil also prevents the water from evaporating too quickly.

Fertilizer
Fertilize ferns with . . .
- **Star Olive Oil.** Add two tablespoons Star Olive Oil at the base of the plant once a month.

Rejuvenate a palm with . . .

- **Star Olive Oil.** Add two tablespoons Star Olive Oil at the base of the plant once a month.

Fertilize a garden or houseplants with . . .

- **Maxwell House Coffee.** Work Maxwell House Coffee grounds into the topsoil.

Spread fertilizer with . . .

- **Maxwell House Coffee.** Punch holes in the bottom of an empty can of Maxwell House Coffee, fill with fertilizer, cover with the plastic lid, and shake the can as you walk through your garden.

Fertilize a lawn with . . .

- **Listerine** and **Miller High Life.** Jerry Baker, author of *The Impatient Gardener*, suggests mixing one cup Listerine, one cup Epsom Salt, one cup liquid soap, and one cup ammonia in a one-quart jar, filling the rest of the jar with beer. Spray this on up to 2,500 square feet of lawn with a hose-attached sprayer in May and again in late June.

Revive an ailing houseplant with . . .

- **Aunt Jemima Original Syrup.** Add two tablespoons Aunt Jemima Original Syrup at the base of the plant once a month.

- **Geritol.** Give the plant two tablespoons Geritol twice a week for three months. New leaves should begin to grow within the first month.

Flowers

Keep long-stemmed flowers standing upright in a vase with . . .

- **Scotch Transparent Tape.** Crisscross Scotch Transparent Tape across the mouth of the vase.

Prolong the life of flowers in a vase with . . .

- **Bayer Aspirin.** Drop in two Bayer Aspirin tablets per quart of water.
- **Clorox.** Add one-quarter teaspoon (twenty drops) of Clorox Bleach to each quart of water used in your vase.
- **Domino Sugar, Heinz Vinegar, Listerine,** and **Palmolive.** Add one tablespoon Domino Sugar, one teaspoon Heinz Vinegar, one teaspoon Listerine, and three drops Palmolive per quart of water.
- **Heinz Vinegar.** Add two tablespoons Heinz White Vinegar plus three tablespoons sugar per quart of warm water. Stems should be in three to four inches of water.

Preserve floral arrangements with . . .

- **Alberto VO5 Hair Spray.** Spray Alberto VO5 Hair Spray on baby's breath, broom grass, and cattails to help preserve them.

Elongate flower stems that are too short for a vase with . . .

- **Glad Flexible Straws.** Insert the flower stem into a Glad Flexible Straw cut to whatever length you need.

Germinating

Sprout seeds before planting with ...

- **Dixie Cups.** Turn a Dixie Cup upside down and use a pencil to poke a hole in the center of the bottom. Then fill half of the cup with soil. Place seed inside and cover with more soil. Follow directions on seed package for proper care. Write plant name on cup with marker.
- **Saran Wrap.** Lay a sheet of Saran Wrap over four Popsicle sticks inserted into a seed tray. The Saran Wrap creates a tiny greenhouse, providing enough humidity to keep the growing medium moist for germination. If too much moisture collects on the inside of the plastic, remove it for a few hours.
- **Viva Paper Towels.** Cut a three-inch strip from a Viva Paper Towel, dampen it, and lay it on top of a strip of Saran Wrap. Place the seeds on top of the paper towel at the intervals recommended on the seed packet. Cover with another strip of damp Viva Paper Towel, then roll the paper and plastic together, place in a Baggie, and store in a warm place. When the roots begin to sprout, remove the Baggie, unroll the Saran Wrap, plant the strip of Viva Paper Towels in a well-tilled garden bed, cover with a fine layer of soil, and water thoroughly. The Viva Paper Towels act as a mulch to inhibit dehydration and soon dissolve, ensuring a perfectly spaced row of seedlings.

Accelerate the germination of grass seeds with . . .

● **Lipton Tea Bags.** Mix two tablespoons of cold, strong-brewed Lipton Tea into each pound of seed, cover, and set in the refrigerator for five days. Before sowing, spread the seed to dry for a day or two on newspapers on the garage or basement floor.

RENT-A-BEE

Many commercial beekeepers rent their colonies during the year to pollinate crops for farmers. The U.S. Department of Agriculture estimates that about 2.8 million acres of almonds, apples, melons, plums, avocados, blueberries, cherries, cucumbers, pears, cranberries, kiwi, and other major crops in the United States depend on insect pollination from honeybees.

Gloves
Garden with . . .

● **Playtex Living Gloves.** When Playtex Living Gloves wear out for work in the house, use them for gardening outdoors. Cut off the fingertips of the gloves to improve dexterity.

Harvesting
Make a hip bucket for harvesting fruits or berries with . . .

● **Clorox.** Cut a large hole in the side of an empty, clean Clorox Bleach bottle opposite the handle, then string your belt through the handle.

Hoses
Find the end of a hose easily with . . .

● **Con-Tact Paper.** Wrap the last six inches of your garden hose with Con-Tact Paper in a contrasting color so you can always find the end of the hose.

Hot Caps

Make a hot cap with . . .

● **Clorox.** Cut off the bottom of an empty, clean Clorox Bleach jug and place the jug over the seedlings. Take off the cap during the day and replace the cap at night. To anchor these hot caps, simply cut off the top of the handle, insert a sharp stick, and drive the stick into the ground.

Insects

Kill insects on plant leaves with . . .

● **Dawn.** Mix one-half cup Dawn dishwashing detergent to one pint water. Spray on both sides of plant leaves, let sit for one hour, then spray clean with water.

Control spider mites, whiteflies, aphids, and thrips on houseplants with . . .

● **Tabasco Pepper Sauce.** Purée two teaspoons Tabasco sauce and three cloves garlic in a blender, add three cups water and two tablespoons biodegradable liquid detergent, then strain into a spray bottle and coat the leaves of the plant.

Labels

Label your vegetable garden with . . .

● **Con-Tact Paper.** Tape a Popsicle stick to the center of an empty seed packet, so about an inch of the stick can be used as a stake. Cover the packet with clear Con-Tact Paper and use to identify garden rows of seedlings.

Lawns

Prevent grass from growing in crevices with . . .

● **Heinz Vinegar.** Pour Heinz White Vinegar in crevices and between bricks.

● **Morton Salt.** Sprinkle Morton Salt in the cracks. Salt is a corrosive that kills plants.

Lawn Mowers

Prevent cut grass from sticking to the blades of a lawn mower with . . .

● **Pam No Stick Cooking Spray.** Spray the cutting blade of the lawn mower with Pam No Stick Cooking Spray before cutting the lawn.

● **WD-40.** Spray WD-40 on the underside of the lawn mower housing and blade before cutting the grass.

Melons

Grow better melons with . . .

● **Maxwell House Coffee.** Raise melons off the ground by resting them on the tops of upside-down empty Maxwell House Coffee cans pushed into the soil. The metal cans accumulate heat, making the fruit ripen earlier, and repel insects.

Plants

Seal plants with . . .

● **Elmer's Glue-All.** Gardeners use Elmer's Glue-All

to seal ends of pruned stems and branches against insects and excessive moisture loss.

Potatoes and Avocados
Root a potato or avocado with . . .

- **Forster Toothpicks.** Securely insert four Forster Toothpicks equidistantly around the equator of the potato or avocado. (You can use a nail to punch starter holes in the avocado.) Fill a glass with water, and set the potato or avocado in the glass so the toothpicks allow only the bottom half of the potato or avocado to sit in the water. Place the glass on a windowsill to get sunlight. When roots and shoots appear, pot the plant in soil.

Potted Plants
Prevent the soil from leaking out of a potted plant with . . .

- **L'eggs Sheer Energy.** Place a pair of L'eggs Sheer Energy in the bottom of a plant pot to provide drainage.

CUTTING THE MUSTARD
The Mount Horeb Mustard Museum in Mount Horeb, Wisconsin, houses the largest collection of mustards in the world, with over two thousand different types of mustard. Subscribe to the museum's newsletter, *The Proper Mustard*, by calling 1-800-438-6878.

- **Mr. Coffee Filters.** Line a plant pot with a Mr. Coffee Filter to keep the soil from leaking through the drainage holes.

Sap
Clean sap from gardening equipment with . . .

- **WD-40.** Spray with WD-40, wait, and wipe clean.

ATTACK OF THE KILLER TOMATOES

The leaves of tomato plants are toxic if eaten.

Scarecrows

Make a scarecrow with . . .

● **Glad Trash Bags.** Cut a Glad Trash Bag into long strips, staple to the lip of a Dixie Cup, and then nail the cup to a tree or a pole in your garden. The plastic strips blowing in the wind will scare birds away.

Seed Markers

Keep seed markers in the garden legible with . . .

● **Scotch Transparent Tape.** Cover the seed markers with Scotch Transparent Tape.

Seeding

Spread grass seed with . . .

● **Maxwell House Coffee.** Punch holes in the bottom of an empty can of Maxwell House Coffee, fill with grass seed, cover with the plastic lid, and shake the can as you walk through your garden.

Slugs

Kill slugs with . . .

● **Miller High Life.** Fill jar lids with a half inch of Miller High Life. Slugs love beer and drown in it.

Soil Sifting

Sift soil with . . .

● **Clorox.** Cut the bottom off an empty, clean Clorox Bleach bottle at an angle to make a scooper. Insert a six-inch-diameter piece of one-quarter-inch hardware cloth to rest above the handle hole. Scoop up dirt, sift through the narrow opening, and stones will be caught by the hardware cloth.

Staking Plants
Stake up small plants with . . .
- **Oral-B Toothbrushes.** Use the handles from old Oral-B Toothbrushes.

Straighten bent stems in your garden with . . .
- **Forster Toothpicks.** Make a splint with a Forster Toothpick and Scotch Transparent Tape.
- **Q-Tips Cotton Swabs.** Make a splint with a Q-Tips Cotton Swab and Scotch Transparent Tape.
- **Scotch Transparent Tape.** Make a splint with a Popsicle stick and Scotch Transparent Tape.

Storing Seeds
Store leftover garden seeds with . . .
- **Ziploc Storage Bags.** Seal seeds in the bag and put them in a cool, dry place until ready for planting.

Coffee, Tea, or Me?

● Coffee, native to Ethiopia and cultivated and brewed in Arab countries for centuries, was not introduced in Europe until the seventeenth century.

● According to an ancient Chinese legend, the first cup of tea was brewed by Emperor Shennong in 2737 B.C. when a few leaves from a tea plant accidentally fell into water he was boiling.

● The most flavorful coffee beans are grown between three thousand and six thousand feet above sea level, especially on volcanic soil.

● Since tea plants grow more slowly in cooler air, yielding a better-flavored leaf, the best teas are grown at altitudes between three thousand and seven thousand feet. Tea connoisseurs consider the tea grown on the slopes of the Himalayan Mountains near Darjeeling, India, to be among the world's finest.

● The average coffee tree, grown from seed, bears its first fruit after five to eight years and yields approximately one pound of coffee beans each year.

● Although tea is often considered a British custom steeped in tradition, tea was not introduced to England (or the American colonies) until British merchants formed the East India Company in 1600.

● While the coffee plant has many varieties, two species, *Coffea arabica* and *Coffea robusta*, provide 99 percent of the world's coffee.

● During the Boston Tea Party on December 16, 1773, American colonists disguised as Indians and protesting British taxes on imported tea boarded three ships in Boston harbor and dumped into the water 342 chests of tea valued at nine thousand British pounds, leading to the Revolutionary War.

● Coffee trees grow fifteen feet high and have fragrant, white flowers that give way to pulpy "cherries" containing the beans. The cherries must be harvested by hand, and, after the pulp is removed, the beans are dried and shipped to be roasted, ground, and packaged.

● Tea is the most popular beverage in the world, and Lipton is the best-selling tea in America.

● Instant coffee accounts for approximately one-fifth of all coffee sold. To produce instant coffee, an atomized spray of coffee extract is either freeze-dried or forced through a jet of hot air to evaporate the water and leave dried coffee particles.

● India produces one third of the world's tea, followed by China and Sri Lanka.

● Coffee is decaffeinated by processing the bean in a bath of methylene chloride to remove the caffeine, followed by steam to remove the methylene chloride. Newer, more environmentally sound methods require using steam only.

Tomatoes

Protect baby tomato plants with . . .

● **Dixie Cups.** Remove the bottoms of Dixie Cups and push the cups into the soil to encircle young plants.

● **Maxwell House Coffee.** Remove the tops and bottoms from Maxwell House Coffee cans, place a can over each plant, and step on the can to set it firmly in the soil. Remove cans when plants are a few weeks old.

Tie tomato plants to stakes with . . .

● **L'eggs Sheer Energy.** The soft nylon of L'eggs Sheer Energy secures tomato stalks without causing any damage to the plant.

Watering

Water your plants with . . .

● **Canada Dry Club Soda.** Feed flat Canada Dry Club Soda to your houseplants or outdoor plants. The minerals in club soda are beneficial to green plants.

Invigorate houseplants with . . .

● **Lipton Tea Bags.** Water ferns and other houseplants once a week with a weak, tepid-brewed Lipton Tea.

Prolong the Life of a Christmas Tree

with Aunt Jemima Original Syrup

Birthdays

Cut birthday cake with . . .
- **Oral-B Mint Waxed Floss.** Oral-B Dental Floss cuts cake into neat slices.

Make streamers with . . .
- **Glad Trash Bags.** Cut a Glad Trash Bag into strips, starting from the open end and stopping two inches before you reach the bottom, then hang in a doorway.

Christmas

Prolong the life of a Christmas tree with . . .
- **Aunt Jemima Original Syrup.** Cut an extra inch off the bottom of the tree, stand the tree in a bucket of cold water to which one cup of Aunt Jemima Original Syrup has been

added, and let the tree soak for two or three days before decorating.

Clean artificial snow from windows with . . .

- **Pam No Stick Cooking Spray.** Before decorating windows with artificial snow, spray the glass lightly with Pam No Stick Cooking Spray.
- **WD-40.** Spray windows with WD-40 before spraying with artificial snow so the decorative spray will wipe off easier.

Clean the sap from a Christmas tree from your hands with . . .

- **Wesson Corn Oil.** Rub your hands with Wesson Corn Oil and wipe clean with Viva Paper Towels.

Decorate a Christmas tree with . . .

- **Orville Redenbacher's Gourmet Popping Corn.** Use a needle and thread to string popped Orville Redenbacher's Gourmet Popping Corn together. (Hint: Stale popcorn is easier to string than freshly popped popcorn.)

Decorate windows with snow with . . .

- **Con-Tact Paper.** Cut snowflakes from white Con-Tact Paper.

Frost a window with . . .

- **Epsom Salt.** Mix Epsom Salt with stale beer until the beer can hold no more. Then apply the mixture to the glass with a sponge. When it dries, the window will be frosted.

Halloween

Label Halloween candy with . . .

- **Avery Laser Labels.** Print your name, address, and phone number on Avery Laser Labels and adhere them to the wrappers of the candy you give out for Halloween so parents will know whom the candy came from.

Make white clown makeup with . . .

- **Crisco All-Vegetable Shortening** and **Kingsford's Corn Starch.** Mix two tablespoons Kingsford's Corn Starch with one tablespoon Crisco All-Vegetable Shortening. For colored makeup, add a few drops of food coloring.

Glitter your face for a holiday party with . . .

- **Alberto VO5 Conditioning Hairdressing.** Rub a little Alberto VO5 Conditioning Hairdressing onto your cheeks, then dust lightly with glitter.

Make a Hawaiian grass skirt with . . .

- **Glad Trash Bags.** Cut off the bottom of a Glad Trash Bag and cut long one-inch strips to within three inches of the pull cord.

Passover

Make fluffy matzah balls with . . .

- **Canada Dry Club Soda.** Substitute Canada Dry Club Soda for the liquid used in the recipes.

Weddings

Substitute rice at weddings with . . .

- **Hartz Parakeet Seed.** Instead of throwing rice, which is difficult to clean up and dangerous for birds, give your guests packets of Hartz Parakeet Seed instead. When the wedding is over and the guests have all gone home, the birds and squirrels will clean up the birdseed.

Gold Medal Flour

Gold Medal Flour is cleverly named after the gold medal this flour won at an 1880 exhibition.

Gulden's Mustard

In the fourteenth century, Dijon's mustard makers adopted Duke Philip the Bold's motto, *Mout me Tarde* ("I ardently desire"). Legend holds that this motto was shortened to *Moustarde*—the French name for the condiment. Gulden's Mustard is named after company founder Charles Gulden.

Hartz Parakeet Seed

Company founder Max Stern named the Hartz Mountain Corporation after the Harz Mountains of Germany, his native country.

Heinz Vinegar

Heinz is named for company founder H. J. Heinz. *Vinegar* is derived from two French words: *vin* (wine) and *aigre* (sour).

Ivory Soap

Harley Procter, considering a long list of new names for his white soap, was inspired one Sunday morning in church when the pastor read Psalm 45: "All thy garments smell of myrrh, and aloes, and cassia, out of the ivory palaces, whereby they have made thee glad."

Jell-O

Mary Wait, the inventor's wife, came up with a name for the fruit-flavored gelatin by combining the word *jelly* with *-o*, a popular suffix added to the end of a slew of food products at the time.

Jif Peanut Butter

Jif is short for *jiffy*, the amount of time it takes to make a peanut butter sandwich.

Kiwi Shoe Polish

Inventor William Ramsay named the shoe polish Kiwi in honor of his wife, Annie Elizabeth Meek Ramsay, a native of Oamaru, New Zealand. The kiwi is the national bird of New Zealand, and "Kiwi" is also a nickname for a New Zealander, just as "Yankee" is a nickname for a citizen of the United States.

Land O'Lakes Butter

In 1921, a group of small, farmer-owned dairy cooperatives banded together to form the Minnesota Cooperative Dairy Association in Arden Hills, Minnesota, to distribute butter produced by the cooperatives. In 1924, the association decided to package the butter under one brand name and asked farmers in the member cooperatives to send in their suggestions for a name. One of those suggested was Land O'Lakes, a nickname for the state of Minnesota, which is famous for having over 15,000 lakes.

Lea & Perrins Worcestershire Sauce

Worcestershire sauce was named for the town of Worcester, England, which is in the shire (county) of Worcester.

L'eggs Sheer Energy

A clever combination of the words *legs* and *eggs*, with an apostrophe added to make the wordplay idiot-proof.

Listerine

Listerine was named in honor of Sir Joseph Lister, the nineteenth-century British surgeon who pioneered sanitary operating room procedures.

Maybelline

T. L. Williams named his company in honor of his oldest sister, Mabel, who inspired him to produce an easy-to-use mascara, combining her name with the popular suffix -*line*. The letter *Y* was apparently added to make the spelling and pronunciation of the company name phonetic.

Maxwell House Coffee

Maxwell House Coffee is named after the Maxwell House Hotel in Nashville, Tennessee.

Miller High Life Beer

Miller Beer was named after the company founder, Frederick Miller. In 1903, when Miller's son, Carl, sought a new name for the light-colored pilsner, his wife's uncle, Ernst Miller, chanced upon a building in New Orleans called High Life Cigars. The Miller Brewing Company paid $25,000 for the factory and the right to use the name. The word *beer* is believed to come from the Celtic word *beor*, used to describe the malt brew produced in the monasteries of north Gaul.

Miracle Whip

The word *miracle* presumably refers to the whip's endless uses rather than to any supernatural properties.

Mr. Coffee Filters

Inventor Vince Marotta, determined to give his coffeemaker a simple, catchy name, came up with the name Mr. Coffee off the top of his head.

Oral-B Dental Floss

Oral-B is a combination of *oral* hygiene and the letter *B*, which stands for the word *better*. Dental floss is a simple combination of the words *dental* and *floss*, stemming from the Latin word *dentalis* and the Danish word *vlos*.

Orville Redenbacher's Gourmet Popping Corn

The famous popping corn is named after company founder Orville Redenbacher. Redenbacher originally called his popcorn "Red Bow," after the first syllable of his last name and the first syllable of the last name of his partner, Charlie Bowman. The name was also a nod to Redenbacher's trademark bow ties. A Chicago advertising agency consultant recommended that the product would sell better if it was called Orville Redenbacher's Gourmet Popping Corn.

Repel Ants

with Crayola Chalk

Ants

Eliminate ant nests with . . .

● **Dr. Bronner's Peppermint Soap.** Add one cup Dr. Bronner's Peppermint Soap to a bucket of boiling water, and—being careful not to burn yourself—pour the water directly on the nest.

Kill ants with . . .

● **Dr. Bronner's Peppermint Soap.** Mix three tablespoons Dr. Bronner's Peppermint Soap with 16 ounces of water in a trigger spray-bottle and spray directly on the ants. In seconds, the soap kills the ants in their tracks.

● **Scotch Packaging Tape.** Use a strip of Scotch Packaging Tape to pick up an advancing line of ants.

Repel ants with . . .

● **Crayola Chalk.** Draw a line of Crayola Chalk around windows and doors outside your home and around water pipes inside your home. Ants will not cross a chalk line.

The Facts of Life About Bees

The queen bee is the only sexually developed female in the hive. Worker bees (sexually undeveloped females) select a two-day-old larva to be the queen. She emerges from her cell eleven days later to mate in flight with approximately eighteen drone bees (males), receiving several million sperm cells, which last her two-year life span. The queen starts to lay eggs about ten days after mating. A productive queen can lay three thousand eggs in a single day.

- **Gold Medal Flour.** Fill cracks and make a line with Gold Medal Flour where ants enter. Ants will not cross through flour.
- **Heinz Vinegar.** Use a spray bottle or mister filled with a solution of equal parts Heinz Vinegar and water around doorjambs, windowsills, water pipes, and foundation cracks.
- **Maxwell House Coffee.** Sprinkle dried Maxwell House Coffee grounds outside doors and cracks. Coffee deters ants.
- **McCormick/Schilling Black Pepper.** Sprinkle McCormick/Schilling Black Pepper in cracks and crevices.
- **McCormick/Schilling Cream of Tartar.** Sprinkle Cream of Tartar around entrances to ant nests and into cracks and crevices.

Bees, Wasps, and Yellow Jackets

Lure insects away from an outdoor party or barbecue with . . .

- **Aunt Jemima Original Syrup.** Coat a few small pieces of cardboard with Aunt Jemima Original Syrup and place around the perimeter of the yard. Stinging insects, like wasps, bees, and yellow jackets, will be attracted to the syrup instead of your guests.

Kill bees, wasps, and yellow jackets with . . .

- **Miller High Life.** Fill a clean, empty jar with a can of Miller High Life, punch three-eighth inch holes in the lid, cover tightly, and place near plants where the insects pollinate. Bees, wasps, and yellow jackets love beer and drown in it.

Cockroaches

Kill cockroaches with . . .

- **Domino Sugar.** Mix one tablespoon Domino Sugar and one-half cup baking soda. Sprinkle mixture in corners and crevices. Roaches will walk through the mixture, lick it off their feet, and, unable to digest the baking soda, explode.
- **Kingsford's Corn Starch.** Mix equal parts Kingsford's Corn Starch and plaster of Paris. Sprinkle the mixture in cracks and crevices. Cockroaches will eat the mixture and "petrify."
- **McCormick/Schilling Alum.** Mix equal parts McCormick/Schilling Alum and peppermint oil. Place in a saucer and set on the floor. The peppermint oil attracts the roaches, and the alum kills them.

Earwigs

Kill earwigs with . . .

- **Wesson Corn Oil.** Fill a saucer with Wesson Oil and set it out in your backyard. Earwigs love oil, crawl into the saucer, and drown.

Flies

Shoo flies away from a screen door with . . .

- **Kleenex Tissue.** Hang a Kleenex Tissue on a string on a screen door.

Garbage Cans

Keep dogs, maggots, and flies out of trash cans with . . .

- **WD-40.** Coat the trash cans with a thin layer of WD-40.

Garden Pests

Keep dogs, raccoons, cats, and other animals away from your garden with . . .

- **McCormick/Schilling Black Pepper.** Sprinkle McCormick/Schilling Black Pepper around your hedges and flower beds.

Repel raccoons and woodchucks with . . .

- **Epsom Salt.** Sprinkle a few tablespoons of Epsom Salt around your garden and garbage cans. Raccoons and woodchucks dislike the taste of salt. Repeat after rain. Epsom Salt is good for your plants and will not harm rodents.

Insect Repellent

Repel insects with . . .

- **Baby Oil.** Rubbing a thin coat of baby oil on exposed

skin forms a barrier against gnat bites.

- **Coppertone.** Slather on Coppertone to keep insects away.
- **Vicks VaporRub.** Apply Vicks VaporRub to your skin to repel insects, including mosquitoes.

Insecticide

Immobilize flying insects with . . .

- **Alberto VO5 Hair Spray.** Spray Alberto VO5 Hair Spray on a flying insect to stiffen its wings, bringing the pest spiraling to the ground.

Mealworms

Keep mealworms and other pests away from pasta with . . .

- **Wrigley's Spearmint Gum.** Place a few sticks of wrapped Wrigley's Spearmint Gum on the shelf near open packages of noodles, macaroni, or spaghetti. Spearmint repels these household pests.

Mice and Rats

Trap mice or rats with . . .

- **Jif Peanut Butter.** Bait a mouse or rat trap with Jif Peanut Butter.

Plug up mouse holes with . . .

- **S.O.S Steel Wool Soap Pads.** Plug small cracks and holes with S.O.S Steel Wool Soap Pads.

Too Hot to Handle

● Tabasco Pepper Sauce is made from a variety of pepper called *Capsicum frutescens*, known for centuries in Latin America and first recorded by Dr. Chauca, the physician on Columbus's voyage, in 1493.

● In 1898, Lord Horatio Herbert Kitchener' troops brought Tabasco Pepper Sauce on their invasion of Khartoum, in the Sudan.

● In the 1920s, Fernand Petiot, an American working at Harry's Bar in Paris, created the Bloody Mary. Tabasco Pepper Sauce was added to the recipe in the 1930s at the King Cole Bar in New York's St. Regis Hotel.

● During the Vietnam War, the McIlhenny Company sent thousands of copies of the *Charley Ration Cookbook*—filled with recipes for spicing up C-rations with Tabasco Pepper Sauce—

Moles
Repell moles with . . .
> ● **Star Olive Oil.** Soak a rag in Star Olive Oil and shove it into the tunnel. Moles hate the smell of olive oil.

Mosquitoes
(Also see Insect Repellent, page 150)
Repel mosquitoes with . . .
> ● **Bounce.** Tie a sheet of Bounce through a belt loop when you're outdoors during mosquito season.

wrapped around two-ounce bottles of Tabasco Pepper Sauce in waterproof canisters. The United States military now packs Tabasco Pepper Sauce in every ration kit.

● President George Bush is a Tabasco Pepper Sauce devotee, sprinkling the pepper sauce on tuna fish sandwiches, eggs, and fried pork rinds. After receiving the Republican nomination for president in 1988, Bush handed out personalized bottles of Tabasco Pepper Sauce as presents for members of his family who dined with him at Arnaud's Restaurant in New Orleans. "I love hot sauce," Bush told *Time* magazine in 1992. "I splash Tabasco all over."

● Tabasco Pepper Sauce bottles are labeled in fifteen languages and are shipped to more than a hundred countries.

● Americans use more Tabasco Pepper Sauce than any other nation, followed by the Japanese, who sprinkle it on pizza and spaghetti.

● Food critic Craig Claiborne claims, "Tabasco sauce is as basic as mother's milk."

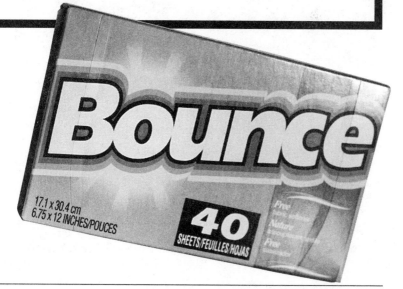

Moths

Repel moths with . . .

- **McCormick/Schilling Black Pepper.** Use McCormick/Schilling Black Pepper as an alternative to mothballs. Fill a cheesecloth bag or the foot of a nylon stocking with pepper and use it as a sachet.

THE BEEHIVE STATE?

Utah is known as the beehive state—despite the fact that, in 1994, North Dakota led the nation in honey production with more than 32 million pounds, followed by South Dakota, California, and Florida with more than 19 million pounds each.

Skunk

Eliminate skunk odor with . . .

- **Campbell's Tomato Juice.** Pour several cups of Campbell's Tomato Juice into your bathwater and soak for fifteen minutes, sponging it over your face.

Slugs

Repel slugs with . . .

- **Crayola Chalk.** Slugs will not cross a chalk line.
- **Miller High Life.** Fill jar lids with a half inch of Miller High Life. Slugs love beer and drown in it.
- **Morton Salt.** Sprinkle Morton Salt on the sidewalk close to the grass. When slugs try to approach your house, the salt will kill them by reverse osmosis. This works well in keeping slugs away from pet food, too.

Spider Mites

Control spider mites, white-flies, aphids, and thrips on houseplants with . . .

- **Tabasco Pepper Sauce.** Purée two teaspoons

Tabasco sauce and three cloves garlic in a blender, add three cups water and two tablespoons biodegradable liquid detergent, then strain into a spray bottle and coat the leaves of the plant.

Squirrels

Prevent squirrels from climbing into a birdhouse with . . .

- **Slinky.** Secure the Slinky to the bottom of the birdhouse and let it hang down over the pole, making it nearly impossible for squirrels to climb up.
- **WD-40.** Spray WD-40 on the metal pole or wires.

JEWELRY

Polish Your Diamonds

with Efferdent

<u>Gems</u>

Clean diamonds, rubies, sapphires, and emeralds with . . .

- **Canada Dry Club Soda.** Simply soak the gems in Canada Dry Club Soda.

Polish diamonds with . . .

- **Efferdent.** Drop one Efferdent tablet into a glass of water and immerse diamonds for two minutes.

Polish jewelry with . . .

- **Alka-Seltzer.** Drop two Alka-Seltzer tablets into a glass of water and immerse the jewelry for two minutes.

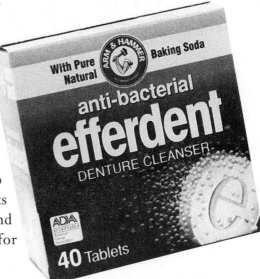

Gold

Clean gold with . . .

- **Colgate Toothpaste.** Colgate will shine up silver and gold. Rinse thoroughly.
- **Pink Pearl Erasers.** A Pink Pearl Eraser will gently scour gold-plated items such as pens and jewelry without damaging the material.

Pearls

Clean pearls with . . .

- **Star Olive Oil.** Rub a dab of Star Olive Oil over pearls, cleaning each pearl individually. Wipe dry with a chamois cloth.

Restringing

Restring a necklace of beads of graduated sizes with . . .

- **Scotch Transparent Tape.** Tape a strip of Scotch Transparent Tape, adhesive side up, on a desktop. Arrange beads in order on the tape, then restring.

Silver

Clean silver with . . .

- **Colgate Toothpaste.** Colgate will shine up silver and gold. Squeeze toothpaste on to a soft, clean cloth, rub silver, then rinse thoroughly.

Storing

Keep jewelry together with . . .

- **Ziploc Storage Bags.** Organize rings, earrings, necklaces, and brooches in Ziploc Storage Bags.

In Space, No One Can Hear You Endorse a Product

- In 1964, John Glenn circled the earth in *Friendship VII*, which was covered with WD-40 from top to bottom.
- In 1965, Tang accompanied the astronauts on the *Gemini* spaceflights and all United States spaceflights through to the *Apollo 11* moon landing in 1969, helping Tang garner a reputation as a nutritionally balanced futuristic food.
- The astronauts on *Apollo 8* played with Silly Putty during their flight and used it to keep tools from floating around in zero gravity.

Protect jewelry with . . .

- **Kleenex Tissue.** Wrap delicate jewelry in one or more Kleenex Tissues for safekeeping in your jewelry box or in your luggage while traveling.

An Average Day for the Average American

- On the average day in 1993, consumers drank 705 million servings of Coca-Cola and other Coca-Cola soft drinks worldwide.
- According to *Americana* magazine, the average high school graduate has eaten 1,500 peanut-butter-and-jelly sandwiches.
- The average jar of peanut butter is consumed in less than thirty days.
- While the average fad lasts six months, demand for Silly Putty has surpassed forty years.
- The average Hawaiian eats twelve cans of SPAM a year, followed by the average Alaskan with six cans, and then Texans, Alabamians, and Arkansans with three cans apiece.
- On average, children between the ages of two and

Tangles

Prevent tangles in fine chain jewelry with . . .
- **Glad Flexible Straws.** Run the chain through a length of Glad Flexible Straw and fasten the catch.

Untangle a chain necklace with . . .
- **Kingsford's Corn Starch.** Dusting the chain with

seven color for twenty-eight minutes every day.

● The average child in the United States will wear down 730 crayons by his or her tenth birthday.

● According to the United States Department of Agriculture, in 1991 the average American consumed 2.8 gallons of tea, 6.5 gallons of coffee, 7.3 gallons of juice, 25.7 gallons of milk, and 43.2 gallons of soft drinks.

● Americans now drink an average of 1.75 cups of coffee a day, nearly half what they drank in 1962.

● An average of 200 million credit cards are used every day in the United States. The typical American credit card holder carries nine credit cards and owes over $2,000.

● The average American drinks approximately 23 gallons of beer every year.

● Every year the average American consumes 1.1 pounds of honey. To make a pound of honey, a hive of bees must tap 2 million flowers, flying over 55,000 miles. The average worker honeybee makes one-twelfth of a teaspoon of honey in her lifetime, flying about 15 miles per hour and visiting between 50 and 100 flowers in each collection trip.

● The average American chews 168 sticks of gum each year.

● On an average day, Americans eat more than 690,000 boxes of Jell-O.

Kingsford's Corn Starch will make it easier to untangle.

Tarnish

Prevent costume jewelry from tarnishing with . . .

● **Crayola Chalk.** Place a piece of Crayola Chalk in your jewelry box.

Prevent Diaper Rash

with Crisco All-Vegetable Shortening

Bangs

Trim bangs with . . .

● **Scotch Transparent Tape.** Place a piece of Scotch Transparent Tape across the bangs and cut the hair just above the tape.

Bath Toys

Make a bath toy with . . .

● **SueBee Honey.** Use an empty SueBee Honey bear in the bathtub.

Bathroom

Decorate shower doors with . . .

● **Con-Tact Paper.** Decals cut from Con-Tact Paper can brighten up shower doors.

Bed Wetting

Protect mattresses from bed wetters with . . .

- **Scotchgard.** Spray the mattress with Scotchgard to resist moisture.

Neutralize urine odors from mattresses and mattress covers with . . .

- **20 Mule Team Borax.** Dampen the spot, rub in 20 Mule Team Borax, let dry, then vacuum or brush clean.

Bottles

Clean baby bottles, nipples, and bottle brushes with . . .

- **Arm & Hammer Baking Soda.** Soak in a solution of warm water and Arm & Hammer Baking Soda, then sterilize before use.

Deodorize "sour" baby bottles with . . .

- **Colgate Toothpaste.** Scrub with Colgate and a bottle brush.

    Make the raised gradation marks on plastic baby bottles clearly visible with . . .

    - **Cover Girl NailSlicks Classic Red.** Paint the gradation marks with Cover Girl NailSlicks Classic Red Nail Polish.

Bubble Bath
(See page 275)

Bubbles

Blow bubbles with . . .

- **Glad Flexible Straws.** Diagonally cut the end of a Glad Flexible Straw, dip into bubble soap, and blow.

Make bubble solution with . . .

- **Palmolive.** Mix three parts Palmolive to one part water.

Building Blocks

Make building blocks for kids with . . .

- **Con-Tact Paper.** Cover empty shoe boxes with Con-Tact Paper to create building bricks.

Change of Clothes

Carry a change of baby clothes with . . .

- **Ziploc Storage Bags.** Pack a change of clothes for a baby in a Ziploc Storage Bag. In separate bags, store a pacifier, cotton balls, and medication. Place all the items in a jumbo zippered storage bag and keep it in the baby bag.

Changing Pad

Improvise a diaper changing pad with . . .

- **Reynolds Cut-Rite Wax Paper.** A sheet of Reynolds Cut-Rite Wax Paper can be used as a disposable changing mat.
- **Ziploc Storage Bags.** In an emergency, a jumbo Ziploc Storage Bag can be used as an easy-to-tote changing mat.

Childproofing

Prevent small children from poking objects into electrical outlets with . . .

WHAT IS BABY OIL?

Used topically to treat dry skin or diaper rash, baby oil is made primarily from mineral oil, a clear, colorless, oily liquid with little odor or taste. Distilled from petroleum, mineral oil is used medicinally as a lubricant and laxative, as an oil base in cosmetics and hair tonics, and as an ingredient of paints and varnishes.

- **Scotch Transparent Tape.** Cover the sockets with Scotch Transparent Tape.

Childproof the sharp corners of furniture with . . .

- **Wilson Tennis Balls.** Cut old Wilson Tennis Balls in halves or quarters and use Scotch Packaging Tape to tape the sections over sharp corners of coffee tables, end tables, cabinets, dining room tables, and other pieces of furniture that might be dangerous to a small child.

Crayons

Store crayons with . . .

- **Huggies Baby Wipes.** Keep crayons in an empty Huggies Baby Wipes box.
- **Kleenex Tissue.** A decorative Kleenex Tissue box, when empty, makes an excellent container for storing crayons.
- **Ziploc Storage Bags.** Keep a few crayons in a Ziploc Storage Bag for trips so kids always have something to do in restaurants.

Diaper Pails

Deodorize a disposable diaper pail with . . .

- **Arm & Hammer Baking Soda.** Sprinkle liberally with Arm & Hammer Baking Soda.

Diaper Rash

Prevent diaper rash with . . .

- **Crisco All-Vegetable Shortening.** Use Crisco All-Vegetable Shortening as a balm on a baby's behind.
- **Vaseline.** Apply a thin coat of Vaseline Petroleum Jelly to a baby's clean bottom before putting a fresh diaper on the tyke.

Diapers

Carry dirty diapers in a baby bag without any offending odors with . . .

- **Ziploc Storage Bags.** Keep extra Ziploc Storage Bags in your baby bag so you can seal dirty diapers inside a plastic bag until you can dispose of them properly. This is especially considerate when visiting friends' homes.

Repair a disposable diaper with . . .

- **Scotch Packaging Tape.** If the adhesive tab doesn't stick, tape the diaper together with Scotch Packaging Tape.

Emergencies

Teach your child to push the red button on the phone in an emergency with . . .

- **Cover Girl Nail-Slicks Classic Red.** Paint a red dot with Cover Girl Nail-Slicks Classic Red Nail Polish in the middle of the *0* on your telephone so young children can always call for help.

Flame-Retardant Clothes

Make children's clothing flame retardant with . . .

- **20 Mule Team Borax.** Mix together nine ounces of 20 Mule Team Borax and four ounces boric acid in one gallon water. If the article is washable, soak in the solution after final rinsing, then dry. If the garment is not washable, spray with the solution. This solution, recommended by fire departments, may wash out of clothing and should be used after each washing or dry cleaning.

Fun Experiments
Turn a chicken bone into rubber with . . .
- **Heinz Vinegar.** Soak a chicken bone in a glass of Heinz Vinegar for three days. It will bend like rubber.

Watch seedlings grow roots with . . .
- **Jell-O.** For a great science experiment for children, grow seeds in Jell-O and observe the root structures.

Write with invisible ink with . . .
- **ReaLemon.** Use a Q-Tips Cotton Swab as a pen to write in ReaLemon on a piece of white paper. Once it dries, hold the paper near a hot lightbulb. The writing will turn brown.

THE MOST POPULAR CRAYON COLORS
Red and black are the most popular crayon colors, mostly because children tend to use them for outlining.

Furniture
Clean high chairs, car seats, strollers, and plastic mattress protectors with . . .
- **Arm & Hammer Baking Soda.** Sprinkle Arm & Hammer Baking Soda on a damp sponge, wipe clean, and dry.

Polish chrome with . . .
- **Reynolds Wrap.** Use a piece of crumpled-up

Reynolds Wrap to polish the chrome on strollers, high chairs, and playpens.

Games

Store game pieces with . . .
- **Huggies Baby Wipes.** Store loose dice, cards, playing pieces, and small toys in an empty Huggies Baby Wipes box.

Draw on sidewalks with . . .
- **Crayola Chalk.** Create games, maps, and adventures.

Reinforce game and puzzle boxes with . . .
- **Scotch Packaging Tape.** Fortify the corners of boxes with Scotch Packaging Tape.

Gum

(See page 339)

Hair Dye

Dye kids' hair temporarily with . . .
- **Kool-Aid.** Mix a thick paste using Kool-Aid and water, then apply as you would hair dye, let sit five minutes, then rinse.

Kool-Aid Mustaches

Remove fruit drink mustaches from kids' faces with . . .
- **Colgate Toothpaste.** Rub on Colgate and rinse thoroughly.

Lunch Box Desserts

Make your own Jell-O dessert packs with . . .

- **Gerber Applesauce.** Fill clean, empty Gerber baby food jars with Jell-O and freeze. Pack the frozen Jell-O in your child's lunch box. By noon, the Jell-O will be defrosted and ready to eat.

Add an inexpensive dessert to lunch box meals with . . .

- **Gerber Applesauce.** Gerber Applesauce (and other Gerber desserts) makes an excellent and inexpensive single serving of dessert for adults or children.

CRAYONS: THE INTERNATIONAL LANGUAGE

Crayola Crayon boxes are printed in eleven languages: Danish, Dutch, English, Finnish, French, German, Italian, Norwegian, Portuguese, Spanish, and Swedish.

Playhouse

Create your own playhouse with . . .

- **Con-Tact Paper.** Cut doors and windows out of a large cardboard box and then decorate the house or fort with Con-Tact Paper.

Playpens

Repair the mesh screening on playpens with . . .

- **Oral-B Mint Waxed Floss.** Sew up the rip with Oral-B Mint Waxed Floss.

Secure the blanket in place in a playpen with . . .

- **Velcro.** Put Velcro on the four corners of the blanket and on the floor of the playpen to keep the blanket from sliding around.

Popsicles

Prevent a Popsicle from dripping with a . . .

● **Mr. Coffee Filter.** Poke one or two holes as needed in a Mr. Coffee Filter, insert the Popsicle, and let the filter catch the drips.

Portable Sponges

Carry a wet sponge or cloth for sticky fingers with . . .

● **Ziploc Storage Bags.** Travel with your own dampened wipe in a Ziploc Storage Bag.

School Supplies

(See School and Office, page 313)

Shampoo

Keep shampoo from getting into a baby's eyes with . . .

● **Vaseline.** Rub a line of Vaseline Petroleum Jelly above the baby's eyebrows so shampoo runs off to the side.

Shoes

Teach toddlers which shoe goes on which foot with . . .

● **Con-Tact Paper.** Trace the toddler's feet onto brightly colored Con-Tact Paper, cut out the footprints, and adhere them to a sturdy board. The child can then match the shoe with the correct footprint.

Sleep

Make children sleepy at bedtime and help prevent small children from wetting the bed with . . .

● **SueBee Honey.** A teaspoon of honey at bedtime will act as a sedative to a child's nervous system and will attract and hold fluid in a child's body during the hours of sleeping. When a child over one year old is given honey, the blood and tissue calcium begins to increase. The calcium unites with excess phosphorous to form a compound that makes bones, teeth, hair, and fingernails. The sedative effect on the nervous system of a child may be observed within an hour. Honey should not be fed to infants under one year of age. Honey is a safe and wholesome food for older children and adults.

Stilts

Make stilts with . . .

● **Maxwell House Coffee.** String rope through holes punched in the closed ends of two empty Maxwell House Coffee cans. Stand on the bottoms of the coffee cans and hold a rope loop in each hand for balance.

Stuffed Animals

Clean stuffed animals with . . .

● **Arm & Hammer Baking Soda.** Sprinkle Arm & Hammer Baking Soda on the stuffed animal, let sit for fifteen minutes, then brush off.

● **Kingsford's Corn Starch.** Rub Kingsford's Corn Starch onto the toy, let stand for five minutes, then brush off.

Toy Logs

Create toy logs for kids with . . .

- **Con-Tact Paper.** Cover empty Quaker Oats canisters with woodgrain Con-Tact Paper.

Toys

Make a carrier for small children's toys and crayons with . . .

- **Clorox.** Cut a hole in the side of an empty, clean Clorox Bleach jug opposite the handle.

Fix battery-operated toys or appliances with . . .

- **Reynolds Wrap.** If the batteries in a Walkman or a toy are loose as the result of a broken spring, wedge a small piece of Reynolds Wrap between the battery and the spring.

Prevent strings on pull toys from getting tangled with . . .

- **Glad Flexible Straws.** Run the string through one or more Glad Flexible Straws and knot it at the end.

Label children's toys with . . .

- **Cover Girl NailSlicks Classic Red.** Simply paint your child's name on the bottom of his or her favorite toys with Cover Girl NailSlicks Classic Red Nail Polish so they won't get lost.

Revitalize old toys with . . .

- **Con-Tact Paper.** Redecorate the toys with different Con-Tact Paper patterns.

Travel

Pack a child's suitcase with ease with . . .

●**Ziploc Storage Bags.** Organize your children's outfits in jumbo Ziploc Storage Bags. Put a matching top and bottom, and a pair of underwear and socks in each bag, so kids know exactly what they're going to wear each day of a vacation.

Writing

Teach kids how to write their name with . . .

●**Elmer's Glue-All.** Use crayon to write the child's name on a piece of paper, then trace over the letters using Elmer's Glue-All. When the glue dries, children can use their fingers to trace along the tactile letters of their names, making it easier to understand the shapes of the letters.

Accidents That Paid Off

Avon

During the 1880s, door-to-door book salesman David McConnell gave small bottles of perfume to New York housewives who listened to his sales pitch. The perfume was more popular than the books, so McConnell created the California Perfume Company in 1886, hiring women to sell door-to-door. Renamed Avon, after the Avon River in England, in 1950, the company became the world's largest cosmetic company.

Coca-Cola

Dr. John Styth Pemberton—inventor of Globe of Flower Cough Syrup, Indian Queen Hair Dye, Triplex Liver Pills, and Extract of Styllinger—was eager to duplicate Vin Mariani, a popular wine elixir made with coca. In his backyard at 107 Marietta Street in Atlanta, Georgia, Pemberton developed a thick syrup drink from sugar water, a kola nut extract, and coca. Pemberton brought his new syrup elixir to Jacob's Drug Store, where druggist Willis Venable added carbonated water—inadvertently creating the world's most popular soft drink.

Dixie Cups

In 1908, Hugh Moore started the American Water Supply Company of New England to market a vending machine that for one penny would dispense a cool drink of water in an individual, clean, disposable paper cup. When

Dr. Samuel Crumbine, a health official in Dodge City, Kansas, began crusading for a law to ban the public tin dipper, Moore soon realized that his sanitary cups had greater sales potential than his water. In 1909, Kansas passed the first state law abolishing the public dipper, and Professor Alvin Davison of Lafayette College published a study reporting the germs of communicable diseases found on public dipping tins. As state after state outlawed public drinking tins, sales of Moore's Health Kups skyrocketed—compelling him to change the name in 1919 to Dixie Cups.

Frisbee

In the 1870s, William Russell Frisbie opened a bakery called the Frisbie Pie Company in Bridgeport, Connecticut. His lightweight pie tins were embossed with the family name. In the mid-1940s, students at Yale University tossed the empty pie tins as a game. In the 1950s, Walter Frederick Morrison, a Los Angeles building inspector determined to capitalize on Hollywood's obsession with UFOs, designed a lightweight plastic disk, based on the Frisbie bakery's pie tins, but changed the name to Flyin' Saucer to avoid legal hassles. Morrison sold the rights to the Wham-O Manufacturing Co. of San Gabriel, California, and on January 13, 1957, Americans were introduced to the Frisbee. In 1958, the Frisbie Pie Company went out of business, but its pie tins live on, reincarnated as the Frisbee.

Ivory Soap

When Harley Procter decided to develop a creamy white soap to compete with imported castile soaps, he asked his cousin,

chemist James Gamble, to formulate the product. One day after the soap went into production, a factory worker (who remains anonymous) forgot to switch off the master mixing machine when he went to lunch and too much air was whipped into a batch of soap. Consumers, delighted by the floating soap, demanded more, and from then on, Procter and Gamble gave all Ivory Soap an extra-long whipping.

Kotex

In 1872, John Kimberly, Charles Clark, Havilah Babcock, and Frank Shattuck founded Kimberly, Clark & Company in Neenah, Wisconsin, to manufacture newsprint from rags. In 1889, the company built a pulp and paper plant on the Fox River, and in 1914, it developed cellucotton, a cotton substitute used by the U.S. Army as surgical cotton during World War I. Army nurses used cellucotton pads as disposable sanitary napkins, prompting the company to introduce Kotex, the first disposable feminine hygiene product, in 1920.

Lea & Perrins Worcestershire Sauce

In 1835, when Lord Marcus Sandys, governor of Bengal, retired to Ombersley, England, he longed for his favorite Indian sauce. He took the recipe to a drugstore on Broad Street in nearby Worcester where he commissioned the shopkeepers, John Lea and William Perrins, to mix up a batch. Lea and Perrins made a large batch, hoping to sell the excess to other customers. The pungent fishy concoction wound up in the cellar, where it sat undisturbed until Lea and Perrins rediscovered it two years later when housecleaning. Upon tasting the aged sauce, Lea and Perrins bottled "Worcester sauce"

as a local dip. When Lea and Perrins's salesmen convinced British passenger ships to put the sauce on their dining room tables, Worcestershire Sauce became an established steak sauce across Europe and the United States. To this day, the ingredients in Worcestershire Sauce are stirred together and allowed to sit for two years before being bottled.

Listerine

Impressed by Sir Joseph Lister's views on germs and his plea for "antiseptic surgery," Dr. Joseph Lawrence developed Listerine in his St. Louis laboratory as a safe and effective antiseptic for use in surgical procedures. In 1895, the local Lambert Pharmacal Company extended the sale and promotion of Listerine to the dental profession as an antibacterial mouthwash and gargle—forever ending Listerine's use in surgery.

Lubriderm

Texas Pharmacal developed Lubriderm Lotion in 1948 for dermatologists to use as a base for their own formulations of topical drugs to treat serious dermatological conditions. Lubriderm quickly gained a reputation as the dermatologist's choice as a compounding base, and demand for the moisturizer escalated.

Nestea

At the 1904 St. Louis World's Fair, a merchant having difficulty selling warm tea on a hot summer day poured the tepid brew over ice and invented iced tea. Ironically, iced tea did not become popular until 1948, when Nestlé scientists intro-

duced Nestea hot tea mix, which people used to make iced tea. Since Nestea hot tea mix did not dissolve completely in cold water, in 1956 Nestlé scientists developed Nestea iced tea mix.

Noxzema

In 1914, pharmacist Dr. George Bunting combined medication and vanishing cream in the prescription room of his Baltimore drugstore to create Dr. Bunting's Sunburn Remedy. A customer told Bunting, "Your cream knocked my eczema," inspiring Bunting to change the name of his sunburn remedy to Noxzema.

Scotchgard

In 1944, 3M bought the rights to a process for producing fluorochemical compounds. The company's researchers could not find any practical uses for the process or its reactive, fluorine-containing by-products—until a laboratory assistant accidentally spilled a sample of the substance on her tennis shoes. The assistant could not wash the stuff off with water or hydrocarbon solvents, and the stained spot on her tennis shoe also resisted soiling. Company chemists Patsy Sherman and Sam Smith realized that this substance might be used to make textiles resist water and oil stains and went to work to enhance the compound's ability to repel liquids, giving birth to Scotchgard.

Silly Putty

In the 1940s, when the United States War Production Board asked General Electric to synthesize a cheap substitute for

rubber, James Wright, a company engineer assigned to the project in New Haven, Connecticut, developed a pliant compound dubbed "nutty putty" with no real advantages over synthetic rubber. In 1949, Paul Hodgson, a former advertising copywriter running a New Haven toy store, happened to witness a demonstration of the "nutty putty" at a party. He bought twenty-one pounds of the putty for $147, hired a Yale student to separate it into half-ounce balls, and marketed the putty inside colored plastic eggs as Silly Putty. When it outsold every other item in his store, Hodgson mass-produced Silly Putty as "the toy with one moving part," selling up to three hundred eggs a day. The *New Yorker* featured a short piece on Silly Putty in "Talk of the Town," launching an overnight novelty.

S.O.S

In 1917, Edwin Cox, a struggling door-to-door aluminum cookware salesman in San Francisco, developed in his kitchen a steel wool scouring pad caked with dried soap as a free gift to housewives to get himself invited inside their homes to demonstrate his wares and boost sales. A few months later, demand for the soap-encrusted pads snowballed. Cox quit the aluminum cookware business and went to work for himself.

Tabasco Pepper Sauce

In 1862, when Union troops entered St. Louis, Edmund McIlhenny, a successful banker, fled with his wife, Mary Avery McIlhenny, to Avery Island, an island of solid salt approximately 140 miles west of New Orleans and the site of

America's first salt mine. In 1863, Union forces invaded the island, destroyed the salt mines, and the McIlhennys fled to Texas. After the Civil War, Edmund McIlhenny returned to Avery Island to find his wife's family mansion plundered but some capsicum hot peppers surviving. Determined to turn the peppers into income, McIlhenny made a pepper sauce by mixing crushed peppers and salt in crockery jars and letting the concoction age for thirty days. He then added "the best French wine vinegar" and let the mixture age for another thirty days. He strained the sauce, filled several small cologne bottles, and tried the sauce on friends. In 1868, McIlhenny sent 350 bottles of his pepper sauce under the trademark Tabasco to a carefully selected group of southern wholesalers, and a year later he sold several thousand bottles at a dollar each. The company is family run to this very day.

Vaseline

In 1859, Robert Augustus Chesebrough, a Brooklyn chemist whose kerosene business faced impending closure, traveled to Titusville, Pennsylvania, to enter the competing petroleum business. Intrigued by the jelly residue that gunked up drilling rods, Chesebrough learned from workers that the jelly quickened healing when rubbed on a wound or burn. Chesebrough brought jars of the whipped gunk back to Brooklyn, where he purified the petroleum lard into a clear, smooth gel he called "petroleum jelly" and started manufacturing Vaseline in 1887.

WD-40

The aerospace industry needed a product to eliminate mois-

ture from electrical circuitry and to prevent corrosion on airplanes and Atlas Missile nosecones. The newly developed WD-40 worked so well, engineers working at the Rocket Chemical Company began sneaking it out of the plant for home use on squeaky doors and stuck locks, inspiring the company to make WD-40 available to the public.

Wrigley's Gum

In 1891, William Wrigley Jr. moved to Chicago to sell soap and baking powder. At twenty-nine, he started his own business in Chicago—with a wife and child and $32 in cash. When he began offering customers free chewing gum made by Zeno Manufacturing, customers offered to buy the gum—accidentally starting Wrigley's career in the chewing gum business.

14

KITCHEN

Protect China

with Mr. Coffee Filters

Appliances

Clean white appliances with . . .

- **Clorox.** Mix three-quarters cup Clorox Bleach per gallon of water, apply with a sponge, let stand for ten minutes, then rinse and dry thoroughly.

Unblock small appliance vents with . . .

- **Oral-B Toothbrushes.** Gently clear lint and dust from vents with a clean, old Oral-B Toothbrush.

Shine kitchen appliances with . . .

- **Reynolds Cut-Rite Wax Paper.** Buff appliance exteriors with a sheet of Reynolds Cut-Rite Wax Paper.

Bottles

Remove dry glue from bottles with . . .

- **Alberto VO5 Hair Spray.** Spray Alberto VO5 Hair Spray on the dry glue, wipe off, and wash the bottle in soapy water. The propanes, butanes, and acetones in

Alberto VO5 Hair Spray dissolve glue.

Wash bottles with . . .

- **L'eggs Sheer Energy.** Wrap a section of L'eggs around the bristles of a bottle washer brush, fasten with a rubber band, and scrub.

Deodorize bottles with . . .

- **Gulden's Mustard.** Mix two teaspoons Gulden's Mustard with one quart water. Rinse well.

Butcher Block

Clean butcher blocks to prevent bacteria from breeding with . . .

- **Clorox.** Wash the cutting board with hot, sudsy water and rinse clean. Then apply a solution of three table-spoons Clorox Bleach per gallon of water. Keep wet for two minutes, then rinse clean.

Oil butcher blocks with . . .

- **Wesson Corn Oil.** Put Wesson Corn Oil on a Viva Paper Towel, rub it into the wood, then wipe clean.

Can Openers

Clean the blade of an electric (or manual) can opener with . . .

- **Oral-B Toothbrushes.** Unplug the can opener and use a clean, old Oral-B Toothbrush dipped in alcohol to clean the blade.

Candles

(See page 53)

Cast-Iron

Season new cast-iron cookware with . . .

- **Crisco All-Vegetable Shortening.** Rub the cookware with a thin coating of solid, unsalted Crisco All-Vegetable Shortening, then bake in an oven heated to 200°F for two hours. Repeat this procedure after the first few uses.

- **Pam No Stick Cooking Spray.** Wash in warm, soapy water after each use, wipe thoroughly dry, coat the inside with Pam No Stick Cooking Spray, then wipe clean with a sheet of Viva Paper Towels.

- **Wesson Corn Oil.** Rub a drop of Wesson Corn Oil on the inside of the pan to keep it seasoned. Place a Viva Paper Towel over and under the skillet when storing. To season a new cast-iron skillet, grease with unsalted Wesson Corn Oil and warm in an oven for two hours. Repeat after washing the skillet for several weeks.

Remove rust spots from a cast-iron skillet with . . .

- **Wesson Corn Oil.** Apply Wesson Corn Oil, let stand, then wipe thoroughly. Repeat if necessary.

Prevent cast-iron skillets from rusting with . . .

- **Mr. Coffee Filters.** Place a Mr. Coffee Filter in the skillet to absorb moisture and prevent rust.

- **Viva Paper Towels.** Place a sheet of Viva Paper Towels between your cast-iron pots and pans in the cupboard. Viva Paper Towels absorb moisture.

China

Shine china with . . .

- **20 Mule Team Borax.** Add one-half cup 20 Mule Team Borax to a sinkful of warm water, rinse fine china, then rinse again in clean water.

Remove coffee or tea stains from china with . . .

- **Arm & Hammer Baking Soda.** Dip a damp cloth in Arm & Hammer Baking Soda, gently rub the china, and rinse clean.
- **Clorox.** Soak clean china cups for five to ten minutes in a solution of one tablespoon Clorox Bleach per gallon of water.
- **Morton Salt.** Mix equal amounts of Morton Salt and white vinegar.

Protect china with . . .

- **Kleenex Tissue.** Separate your good dishes by putting a Kleenex Tissue between each dish.
- **Mr. Coffee Filters.** Separate your good dishes by putting a Mr. Coffee Filter between each dish.

Chrome

Shine chrome faucets and handles with . . .

- **Alberto VO5 Conditioning Hairdressing.** Put a little Alberto VO5 Conditioning Hairdressing on a soft, dry cloth and buff lightly.
- **Baby Oil.** Apply baby oil with a damp cloth, and polish with a clean, soft cloth.

Cleansers

Clean dirt, grime, and scuff marks from doors, stoves, laminated tabletops, linoleum floors, and tile with . . .

- **Arm & Hammer Baking Soda.** Sprinkle Arm & Hammer Baking Soda on a damp sponge, wipe clean, and dry.

Make your own household cleanser for walls and floors with . . .

- **20 Mule Team Borax.** Add one-half cup 20 Mule Team Borax, one-half teaspoon Dawn dishwashing liquid, and one teaspoon ammonia to two gallons warm water.

Clean dirt, grease, and grime from walls, glass, porcelain, wooden furniture, and the outsides of appliances with . . .

● **Cascade.** Dissolve one-quarter cup Cascade in one gallon of very hot water. Scrub, then wipe clean with a dry cloth. Cascade is spot-resistant and contains water-softening agents, so everything gets clean without rinsing.

Coffeemakers

Clean an electric coffeemaker with . . .

● **Kool-Aid.** Run Kool-Aid through an entire cycle, then rinse and dry thoroughly.

Clean lime deposits and calcium sludge from an automatic drip coffeemaker with . . .

● **Heinz Vinegar.** Once a month, fill the reservoir with Heinz White Vinegar and run through the brew cycle. Rinse thoroughly with two cycles of cold water.

Coffeepots

Clean a metal coffeepot with . . .

● **20 Mule Team Borax.** Fill the percolator with water and add one teaspoon 20 Mule Team Borax and one teaspoon detergent powder. Boil the water, let the mixture sit for a few minutes, then rinse clean.

Clean glass coffeepots with . . .

- **Arm & Hammer Baking Soda.** Wash in a solution of one-quarter cup Arm & Hammer Baking Soda and one quart warm water, then rinse clean.

Cookware

Clean badly stained Pyrex or Corningware dishes with . . .

- **Cascade.** Soak the glassware in a solution of two tablespoons Cascade to a pot of warm water.

Clean baked-on food from cookware with . . .

- **Alka-Seltzer.** Fill the pot or pan with water, drop in six Alka-Seltzer tablets, let soak for one hour, then scrub as usual.
- **Arm & Hammer Baking Soda.** Dampen area, sprinkle with Arm & Hammer Baking Soda, let soak overnight, then scrub with a sponge, rinse, and dry.
- **Bounce.** Put a sheet in the pan, fill with water, let sit overnight and sponge clean. The antistatic agents apparently weaken the bond between the food and the pan, and the fabric-softening agents soften the baked-on food.
- **Efferdent.** Fill the pot or pan with water, drop in two Efferdent tablets, let soak for one hour, then scrub as usual.
- **Heinz Vinegar.** Fill the pots and pans with Heinz White Vinegar and let stand for thirty minutes. Then rinse in hot, soapy water.
- **WD-40.** Spray WD-40 on a cookie pan and wipe clean. Then wash with soap and water.

Gently clean aluminum cookware with . . .

- **McCormick/Schilling Cream of Tartar.** Boil a solution two teaspoons of Cream of Tartar and one quart water in the pot for several minutes.

- **20 Mule Team Borax.** Sprinkle 20 Mule Team Borax on pots and pans, rub with a damp dishcloth, and rinse thoroughly.

Copper Pots
Remove tarnish from copper pots with . . .
- **Heinz Ketchup.** Rub with Heinz Ketchup.
- **Hunt's Tomato Paste.** Rub copper pots with Hunt's Tomato Paste.
- **Lea & Perrins Worcestershire Sauce.** With a soft cloth, rub Worcestershire Sauce on the tarnish.
- **Morton Salt** and **ReaLemon.** Make a paste from ReaLemon and Morton Salt, scrub gently, then rinse with water.

Countertops
Clean grease and dirt from Formica surfaces and oven range hoods with . . .
- **Coppertone.** Squeeze Coppertone onto a soft cloth and polish.

Clean kitchen counters with . . .
- **Canada Dry Club Soda.** Pour Canada Dry Club Soda directly on the counter, wipe with a soft cloth, then rinse with warm water and wipe dry.
- **Reynolds Cut-Rite Wax Paper.** Buff countertops with a sheet of Reynolds Cut-Rite Wax Paper.

Coupons
Organize store coupons with . . .
- **Ziploc Storage Bags.** Keep coupons in Ziploc Storage Bags for easy reference.

Crevices
(See page 59)

Cutting Boards
Clean and deodorize a cutting board with . . .

- **Arm & Hammer Baking Soda.** Sprinkle Arm & Hammer Baking Soda on a damp sponge, rub the cutting board, and rinse clean.
- **ReaLemon.** Wash the cutting board with ReaLemon lemon juice to get rid of the smell of garlic, onions, or fish.

Preserve a wooden cutting board with . . .

- **Crisco All-Vegetable Shortening.** Rub Crisco All-Vegetable Shortening over the cutting board, let sit overnight, then remove excess with paper towels.
- **Wesson Corn Oil.** Put Wesson Corn Oil on a Viva Paper Towel, rub it into the wood, then wipe clean.

Dishes
Wash dishes with . . .

- **Clairol Herbal Essences.** If you run out of dishwashing soap, wash your dishes in the kitchen sink with Clairol Herbal Essences. Perfect for camping since it's biodegradable.

Make a slight crack in a dish or plate disappear with . . .

- **Carnation Nonfat Dry Milk.** Mix one and one-third cup Carnation Nonfat Dry Milk with three and three-quarters cups water. Place the dish or plate in a pan, cover with the milk solution, then bring to a boil and simmer for forty-five minutes at low heat. In most cases the crack will vanish.

Dishwashers

Prevent dishwasher runners from sticking with . . .

- **Pam No Stick Cooking Spray.** Spray the runners with Pam No Stick Cooking Spray.

Reduce water spots on glasses and dishes with . . .

- **20 Mule Team Borax.** Add one tablespoon 20 Mule Team Borax to the dishwasher.

Clean your dishwasher with . . .

- **Kool-Aid.** Fill the detergent cup with Kool-Aid and run the machine through its normal cycle. The citric acid in Kool-Aid removes grunge and soap scum from the inside of a dishwasher.

- **Tang.** Put Tang in the detergent cup and run the machine through its normal cycle. The citric acid in Tang will clean soap scum from the inside of a dishwasher.

Deodorize a dishwasher with . . .

- **Arm & Hammer Baking Soda.** Sprinkle one-half cup Arm & Hammer Baking Soda on the bottom of the dishwasher between loads.

Make your own automatic dishwashing soap with . . .

- **20 Mule Team Borax.** Use equal parts 20 Mule Team Borax and washing soda.

Dishwashing Liquid

Boost the strength of dishwashing liquid with . . .

- **Arm & Hammer Baking Soda.** Add two full tablespoons Arm & Hammer Baking Soda to the usual amount of detergent you use.

Drainboards
Prevent stains on kitchen drainboards with . . .
- **Endust.** Coat rubber drainboard trays with a light coat of Endust.

Drains
Deodorize sink drains with . . .
- **Arm & Hammer Baking Soda.** Instead of throwing out that old box of Arm & Hammer Baking Soda that's been sitting in the refrigerator or freezer, gradually pour it down the drain and flush with water.

Keep drains open with . . .
- **Heinz Vinegar.** Pour one-half box of old baking soda down the drain, followed by one cup Heinz White Vinegar. When the bubbling stops, run the hot water.

Unclog a drain with . . .
- **Alka-Seltzer.** Clear the sink drain by dropping three Alka-Seltzer tablets down the drain, followed by a cup of Heinz White Vinegar. Wait a few minutes, then run the hot water.
- **Efferdent.** Drop several Efferdent tablets into the sink and let it sit overnight.

Food Graters
Clean a food grater with . . .
- **Oral-B Toothbrushes.** Scrub the grater with a clean, old Oral-B Toothbrush dipped in dishwashing liquid.

Make cleaning a grater less grating with . . .
- **Pam No Stick Cooking Spray.** Before using the

So Good It Sells without a Slogan

"57 Varieties"

In 1896, while riding an elevated train in New York City, company founder H. J. Heinz spotted an advertisement for a shoe store announcing "21 Styles" of shoes. Inspired by the concept, Heinz immediately decided to use it to advertise his pickles and condiments. Although Heinz made more than sixty different products at the time, he settled on the slogan "57 Varieties" because he liked the way it looked in print. Today, Heinz has over three thousand varieties, but it still uses the "57 Varieties" slogan.

"Good to the Last Drop"

Legend has it that Theodore Roosevelt tasted Maxwell House Coffee while a guest at the Hermitage, Andrew Jackson's old Nashville home. When asked if he wanted another cup, Roosevelt purportedly responded, "Will I have another? Delighted! It's good to the last drop!" thus giving birth to the catchy slogan and the trademark depicting a tilted coffee cup with one last drop.

Maxwell House Coffee's slogan, "Good to the Last Drop," ignited a controversy over the proper use of the word *to*. Pundits asked, "What's wrong with the last drop?" A renowned English professor at Columbia University finally decreed that the word *to* is good usage

and includes the last drop. The word *until* would pre-clude the last drop. The slogan was first used by Coca-Cola in 1908.

"99-44/100% Pure" and "It Floats"

A chemist's analysis of Ivory Soap indicated that 56/100 of the ingredients did not fall into the category of pure soap. Company founder Harley Procter subtracted from 100, and wrote the slogan "99-44/100% Pure," which first appeared in Ivory's advertising in 1882. "It Floats" was added to Ivory's slogan in 1891.

"When It Rains It Pours"

Joy Morton's son, Sterling Morton II, then president of the company, suggested the slogan "When It Rains It Pours" to convey the message that Morton Salt would run even in damp weather.

grater, spray it with Pam No Stick Cooking Spray to make cleanup easier.

Freezers
Make defrosting the freezer easier with . . .
- **Pam No Stick Cooking Spray.** After defrosting the freezer, spray it with Pam No Stick Cooking Spray.

Deodorize the freezer with . . .
- **Maxwell House Coffee.** Place a bowl filled with Maxwell House Coffee grounds on the back shelf.

Funnels
Improvise a funnel with . . .
- **Clorox.** Cut an empty, clean Clorox Bleach bottle in half, remove the cap, and keep it under your sink.
- **Dixie Cups.** Punch a hole in the bottom of a Dixie Cup near the edge.
- **Reynolds Wrap.** Double over a piece of Reynolds Wrap and roll into the shape of a cone.

Garbage
Deodorize kitchen garbage with . . .
- **Arm & Hammer Baking Soda.** Sprinkle a handful of Arm & Hammer Baking Soda into the garbage pail each time you add garbage.

Garbage Disposers

Deodorize garbage disposers with . . .

- **Arm & Hammer Baking Soda.** Instead of throwing out that old box of Arm & Hammer Baking Soda that's been sitting in the refrigerator or freezer, gradually pour it down the drain and flush with water. Or better yet, pour two tablespoons Arm & Hammer Baking Soda down the garbage disposer every week.
- **Clorox.** Pour Clorox Bleach down your sink.
- **Heinz Vinegar.** Mix one cup of Heinz Vinegar in enough water to fill an ice cube tray, freeze the mixture, grind the cubes through the disposal, and flush with cold water.
- **20 Mule Team Borax.** Sprinkle two to three tablespoons 20 Mule Team Borax into the drain, let it stand for fifteen minutes, then flush with water with the disposer on. Borax helps deodorize garbage disposers by neutralizing acidic odors.

Glassware

Prevent soapy film on glassware with . . .

- **Heinz Vinegar.** Place a cup of Heinz White Vinegar on the bottom rack of your dishwasher, run for five minutes, then run though the full cycle. A cup of white vinegar run through the entire cycle once a month will also reduce soap scum on the inner workings.

Pry apart two bowls or glasses with . . .

- **Baby Oil.** Dribble baby oil between the stuck glassware, allow it to seep in, and gently pull the glasses apart.

- **Coppertone.** Dribble a few drops of Coppertone down the sides, then slip the bowls or glasses apart.

Remove scratches on glassware with . . .
- **Colgate Toothpaste.** Polish with a dollop of Colgate.

Hands
Remove fruit or berry stains from your hands with . . .
- **ReaLemon.** Rinse hands with ReaLemon juice.

Clean garlic, onion, or fish odors from your hands with . . .
- **Campbell's Tomato Juice.** Wash your hands with Campbell's Tomato Juice.

Lacquered Metal
Polish lacquered metal with . . .
- **Star Olive Oil.** Use a few drops of Star Olive Oil on a soft cloth.

Lunch Boxes
Deodorize a stale lunch box with . . .
- **Heinz Vinegar.** Soak a paper napkin in Heinz Vinegar and leave it inside the closed lunch box overnight.
- **Wonder Bread.** Soak a piece of Wonder Bread in Heinz Vinegar and leave it inside the closed lunch box overnight.

Mealworms
(See page 151)

Measuring Cups
Repaint faded gradation marks on measuring cups with . . .
- **Cover Girl NailSlicks Classic Red.** Carefully repaint the gradation marks with Cover Girl NailSlicks Classic Red Nail Polish.

Microwave Ovens

Clean a microwave oven with . . .

- **Arm & Hammer Baking Soda.** Sprinkle Arm & Hammer Baking Soda on a damp sponge, scrub, and rinse.
- **ReaLemon.** Add four tablespoons ReaLemon to one cup water in a microwave-safe, four-cup bowl. Boil for five minutes in the microwave, allowing the steam to condense on the inside walls of the oven. Then wipe clean.

Prevent spatters in the microwave with . . .

- **Reynolds Cut-Rite Wax Paper.** Cover spaghetti and meatballs, chili, or other saucy foods with Reynolds Cut-Rite Wax Paper.

Odors

Deodorize food containers with . . .

- **Arm & Hammer Baking Soda.** Mix one-quarter cup Arm & Hammer Baking Soda with one quart water, swish food containers in the solution, soak overnight, then rinse clean.

Eliminate cooking odors in the kitchen with . . .

- **Heinz Vinegar.** Boil one tablespoon Heinz White Vinegar with one cup water.

Eliminate odors from used jars with . . .

- **Heinz Vinegar.** Rinse peanut butter and mayonnaise jars with Heinz White Vinegar.

Neutralize sour spilled milk odors with . . .

- **20 Mule Team Borax.** Dampen the spot, rub in 20 Mule Team Borax, let dry, then vacuum or brush clean.

Ovens

Catch messy oven drips with . . .

● **Reynolds Wrap.** Tear off a sheet of Reynolds Wrap a few inches larger than baking pan. Place foil on the oven rack below the food being baked. (To prevent damage to the oven, do not use foil to line the bottom of the oven.)

Make cleaning the broiler pan easier with . . .

● **Pam No Stick Cooking Spray.** Spray the pan with Pam No Stick Cooking Spray before cooking.

Clean an oven with . . .

● **Cascade.** Sprinkle the bottom of the cold oven with Cascade and cover with wet sheets of Viva Paper Towels. Let stand for a few hours.

Prevent stains on the wallpaper behind your oven range with . . .

● **Con-Tact Paper.** Clean the wallpaper thoroughly, let dry, then paper over it with clear, washable Con-Tact Paper.

Popcorn Popper

Clean cooked-on oil from a popcorn popper or baked-on food from a pot or pan with . . .

● **Cascade.** Mix a heaping tablespoon of Cascade with hot water, put it in the popper, and let soak overnight.

Popsicles

Prevent a Popsicle from dripping with a . . .

● **Mr. Coffee Filter.** Poke one or two holes as needed in a Mr. Coffee Filter, insert the Popsicle, and let the filter catch the drips.

Price Tags

(See page 63)

Recycling

Collect aluminum cans for recycling with . . .

- **Glad Trash Bags.** Hang a Glad Trash Bag on the inside of a kitchen cabinet, closet, or pantry door.

Refrigerator

Clean and deodorize a refrigerator with . . .

- **Arm & Hammer Baking Soda.** Sprinkle Arm & Hammer Baking Soda on a damp sponge, scrub, and rinse clean.
- **20 Mule Team Borax.** Mix one tablespoon 20 Mule Team Borax in one quart warm water. Wash spilled food with a sponge and soft cloth. Rinse with cold water.

Clean the dust from under a refrigerator with . . .

- **L'eggs Sheer Energy.** Place one stocking leg over the end of a broomstick and secure with a rubber band. Slide the broomstick under the refrigerator and move it back and forth.

Deodorize a refrigerator with . . .

- **McCormick/Schilling Vanilla Extract.** Dampen a cotton ball with McCormick/Schilling Vanilla Extract (or lemon or peppermint extract) and place it on a dish in your refrigerator.
- **Kingsford Charcoal Briquets.** A cup of charcoal briquets in the back of the refrigerator keeps it smelling fresh and clean, according to household hints columnist Mary Ellen.
- **Maxwell House Coffee.** Place a bowl filled with Maxwell House Coffee on the back shelf.
- **Tidy Cat.** Pour unused Tidy Cat into a flat box, place it on the middle shelf, and shut the door for five days.

Defrost a jammed automatic ice maker with a . . .

- **Conair Pro Style 1600.** Hold a Conair Pro Style 1600 eight inches from the frozen mass of ice cubes until they melt apart.

Stop refrigerator racks from sticking with . . .

- **Alberto VO5 Conditioning Hairdressing.** Coat the edges of the racks with a thin layer of Alberto VO5 Conditioning Hairdressing so the racks glide easily.
- **Vaseline.** Coat the edges of the racks with Vaseline Petroleum Jelly.

Rubber Gloves

Help rubber gloves slip on easily with . . .

- **Kingsford's Corn Starch.** Sprinkle Kingsford's Corn Starch inside the gloves.
- **Lubriderm.** Apply Lubriderm before putting on rubber gloves. The heat from washing dishes will also help the moisturizing hand cream melt in.

Silverware

Polish silverware with . . .

- **Carnation Nonfat Dry Milk.** Mix five ounces Carnation Nonfat Dry Milk, twelve ounces water, and one tablespoon Heinz White Vinegar or ReaLemon. Let sil-

WARNING: DO NOT USE FOR INDOOR HEATING OR COOKING UNLESS VENTILATION IS PROVIDED FOR EXHAUSTING FUMES TO OUTSIDE. TOXIC FUMES MAY ACCUMULATE AND CAUSE DEATH.

SATISFACTION GUARANTEED

KINGSFORD

ORIGINAL Charcoal Briquets

AMERICA'S FASTEST LIGHTING

5 LBS NET WT

ver stand overnight in the mixture, then rinse clean and dry thoroughly.

● **Colgate Toothpaste.** Colgate will shine up silver. Rinse thoroughly.

● **Kingsford's Corn Starch.** Make a paste with Kingsford's Corn Starch and water. Apply with a damp cloth, let dry, then rub off with cheesecloth.

Prevent silverware from tarnishing with . . .

● **Alberto VO5 Conditioning Hairdressing.** Apply a thin coat of Alberto VO5 Conditioning Hairdressing with a soft cloth to clean, polished, dry silver candlesticks, picture frames, silver sets, and other decorative items. Wipe off excess, leaving behind a very thin, virtually invisible protective coating. VO5's organic protectants actually prevent tarnishing.

● **Crayola Chalk.** Place a piece of Crayola Chalk in your silver chest to absorb moisture.

Remove tarnish from silver with . . .

● **Arm & Hammer Baking Soda.** Mix a thick paste of Arm & Hammer Baking Soda with water, apply to the silver with a damp sponge, rub, rinse, and buff dry.

● **Reynolds Wrap.** Line a metal cake pan with Reynolds Wrap and fill with enough water to cover the silverware. Add two tablespoons baking soda per quart of water. Heat the water above 150° F. Place the tarnished silverware in the pan so it touches the aluminum foil. Do not let the water boil. The hydrogen produced by heating baking soda combines with the sulfur in the tarnish, removing the stains.

Sinks
(Also see page 25)
Dissolve soap suds in the sink with . . .
- **Morton Salt.** Sprinkle Morton Salt on soap bubbles to make them pop.

Shine a stainless steel sink with . . .
- **Alberto VO5 Conditioning Hairdressing.** Shine the sink with a dab of Alberto VO5 Conditioning Hairdressing on a soft cloth.

- **Baby Oil.** Polish with a drop of baby oil, dry with a paper towel, and polish with a few more drops.
- **Wesson Corn Oil.** Wipe the sink with a few drops of Wesson Corn Oil on a soft cloth.

Clean a stainless steel sink with . . .
- **Arm & Hammer Baking Soda.** Sprinkle Arm & Hammer Baking Soda on a damp sponge, scrub the sink, and rinse clean.
- **Morton Salt** and **ReaLemon.** Make a paste from ReaLemon and Morton Salt, scrub gently, then rinse with water.

Sink Mats
Clean a rubber sink mat with . . .
- **Clorox.** Fill the sink with water, add one-quarter cup Clorox Bleach, and soak the sink mat five to ten minutes.

Spills

Absorb spilled cooking grease or a broken egg with . . .

- **Morton Salt.** Pour Morton Salt immediately on the spill, let sit for twenty minutes, then wipe it up.

Steel Wool

Prevent steel wool from rusting with . . .

- **Reynolds Wrap.** Wrap the pad in Reynolds Wrap and store it in the freezer.

Stoves

Make cleaning grease splatters on the wall behind the stove easier with . . .

- **Endust.** Spray the clean, painted wall behind your stove with a generous coat of Endust and buff well. Future grease spatters can be wiped away easily with a dry sheet of Viva Paper Towels.

Teapots

Clean teapots with . . .

- **Arm & Hammer Baking Soda.** Wash in a solution of one-quarter cup Arm & Hammer Baking Soda and one quart warm water, then rinse clean.

Thermos Bottles

Clean a Thermos bottle with . . .

- **Alka-Seltzer.** Fill the bottle with water, drop in four Alka-Seltzer tablets, and let soak for an hour—or longer if necessary.
- **Cascade.** Fill the bottle with two tablespoons Cas-

cade and hot water. Let sit for thirty minutes, then swish clean with a bottle brush and rinse thoroughly.

- **Efferdent.** Fill the bottle with water, drop in three Efferdent tablets, and let it soak for an hour.

Clean coffee stains from a Thermos bottle with . . .

- **Uncle Ben's Converted Brand Rice.** Pour in a tablespoon of uncooked rice and a cup of warm water. Shake vigorously, then rinse.

Deodorize Thermos bottles with . . .

- **Clorox.** Wash with diluted Clorox Bleach, then rinse.

Vegetables

Keep vegetables fresher longer with . . .

- **Viva Paper Towels.** Line the bottom of the vegetable bin in your refrigerator with Viva Paper Towels to absorb the excess moisture.

Wine or Champagne

Cork a wine or champagne bottle with . . .

- **Scotch Packaging Tape.** Wipe the lip of the bottle dry and seal tightly with a small piece of Scotch Packaging Tape.

Filter broken cork from wine with . . .

- **Mr. Coffee Filters.** If you break the cork when opening a wine bottle, filter the wine through a Mr. Coffee Filter.

Wooden Salad Bowls

Revitalize wooden salad bowls with . . .

- **Crisco All-Vegetable Shortening.** Rub with Crisco All-Vegetable Shortening inside and out, let sit overnight, then remove excess with paper towels.

● **Reynolds Cut-Rite Wax Paper.** Wash and dry the wooden salad bowl thoroughly, then rub the entire bowl with a sheet of Reynolds Cut-Rite Wax Paper.

Wooden Spoons

Oil wooden spoons with . . .

● **Crisco All-Vegetable Shortening.** Rub Crisco All-Vegetable Shortening over the wooden spoon, let sit overnight, then remove excess with paper towels.

● **Wesson Corn Oil.** Put Wesson Corn Oil on a Viva Paper Towels, rub it into the wood, then wipe clean.

Reduce Static Cling

with Wilson Tennis Balls

Baby Clothes

Make baby clothes smell even fresher with . . .

● **Arm & Hammer Baking Soda.** Add one-half cup Arm & Hammer Baking Soda to baby's laundry.

Wash baby clothes with . . .

● **20 Mule Team Borax.** Wash linens, bibs, slips, and cotton crib liners in hot water, adding one-half cup 20 Mule Team Borax and detergent. Borax helps get rid of odors and reduce staining.

Remove stains from baby clothes with . . .

● **Clorox.** Mix one-quarter cup Clorox Bleach to one gallon of water in a plastic bucket. Add the clothes and soak for five minutes. Rinse well, then run the clothes through a regular cycle in the washing machine.

Bleach Booster

Boost bleach with . . .

- **Arm & Hammer Baking Soda.** Use one-half cup Arm & Hammer Baking Soda with your normal liquid bleach to boost the bleaching action and freshen the wash.

Bleach Spots

Hide small bleach spots on clothing with . . .

- **Crayola Crayons.** Color the spot with a Crayola Crayon that matches the color of the fabric, then cover with wax paper, and iron on low setting.
- **McCormick/Schilling Food Coloring.** Mix food coloring with water to make the proper shade and apply to the spot.

Bloodstains

Clean bloodstains with . . .

- **Kingsford's Corn Starch.** Immediately cover the spot with a paste of Kingsford's Corn Starch and cold water. Rub gently, place the object in the sun until dry to draw the blood into the corn starch, then brush off. Repeat if necessary.
- **McCormick/Schilling Meat Tenderizer.** Cover the stain with McCormick/Schilling Meat Tenderizer and add cool water. Wait fifteen to thirty minutes and sponge off with cool water.

Brighter Brights

Prevent bright-colored clothes from fading with . . .

- **Heinz Vinegar.** Before putting the article in the

washing machine, soak it in Heinz White Vinegar for ten minutes.

● **Morton Salt.** Add one cup coarse Morton Salt to your detergent in the washing machine.

Stop colors from running with . . .

● **McCormick/Schilling Black Pepper.** Add a teaspoon of McCormick/Schilling Black Pepper to the first suds when you are washing cottons.

Chocolate Stains

Clean chocolate from clothing with . . .

● **20 Mule Team Borax.** Sponge the spot with a solution of one tablespoon 20 Mule Team Borax and one cup warm water. Flush with water. If that doesn't work, make a paste with borax and water, work into the stain, let set for one hour, flush well with warm water, and launder as usual.

Clothespins

Make a clothespin holder with . . .

● **Clorox.** Cut a hole in the side of an empty, clean Clorox Bleach jug opposite the handle, and punch small holes in the bottom for drainage. Hang your new clothespin holder on the clothesline.

Collars

Protect shirt and collars with . . .

● **Kleenex Tissue.** Fold a Kleenex Tissue into a one-inch wide strip and place under the shirt or dress collar while on wire hangers.

Delicate Hand Washables

Wash delicate hand washables with . . .

● **20 Mule Team Borax.** Dissolve one-quarter cup 20 Mule Team Borax and two tablespoons detergent in a basin of warm water. Soak hand washables for ten minutes, rinse in clear, cool water, blot with a towel, and lay flat (woolens) or hang to dry (away from sunlight and direct heat).

Detergent Booster
Boost laundry detergent with . . .

● **Arm & Hammer Baking Soda.** Add one-half cup Arm & Hammer Baking Soda with the usual amount of detergent in your regular wash cycle.

● **20 Mule Team Borax.** Add one-half cup 20 Mule Team Borax to each washload along with the recommended amount of detergent. For large-capacity and front-loading machines, add three-quarters cup. Borax acts as a water conditioner, boosting the cleaning power of detergent by controlling alkalinity, deodorizing the clothes, and aiding the removal of stains and soil.

Diapers
Deodorize cloth diapers with . . .

● **Arm & Hammer Baking Soda.** Mix one-half cup Arm & Hammer Baking Soda in two quarts water, and soak diapers in the solution.

Wash diapers with . . .

● **20 Mule Team Borax.** Flush out dirty diapers and soak as soon as possible in a diaper pail filled with warm water and one-half cup 20 Mule Team Borax. Presoak for at least thirty minutes before washing in warm water, adding one-half cup borax with the recommended amount of detergent. Borax helps get rid of odors, reduce staining, and make diapers more absorbent.

Double-Knits
Clean grease stains from double-knit fabrics with . . .
- **Canada Dry Club Soda.** Pour on Canada Dry Club Soda and scrub gently.

Down Jackets
Fluff your down jacket in the dryer with . . .
- **Wilson Tennis Balls.** Throw in a handful of Wilson Tennis Balls to fluff the down while the jacket is tumbling in the dryer.

Dye
Dye fabric brown inexpensively with . . .
- **Lipton Tea Bags.** If Clorox Bleach won't whiten a graying white garment, soak the item in hot, strong-brewed Lipton Tea until it is a shade darker than you desire. Then rinse in cold water and let dry.
- **Maxwell House Coffee.** Soak the fabric in a bucket of strong black Maxwell House Coffee. This technique is also a good way to cover up an unremovable coffee stain on a white tablecloth.

Food Stains

Remove food stains from clothes with . . .

- **Canada Dry Club Soda.** Immediately blot up the spills on any washable fabric, sponge with Canada Dry Club Soda, then wash the item in the washing machine through a regular cycle.

- **Palmolive** and **Heinz Vinegar.** Mix two teaspoons Palmolive, two teaspoons Heinz Vinegar, and two quarts warm water. Wash lightly, and blot up the moisture.

Grease Stains

Remove grease from clothes with . . .

- **Coca-Cola.** Empty a can of Coke into a load of greasy work clothes, add detergent, and run through a regular wash cycle. The Coca-Cola will help loosen grease stains, according to household-hints columnist Mary Ellen.

- **Crayola Chalk.** Rub Crayola Chalk on a grease spot on clothing or table linens, let the chalk absorb the oil, then brush off. Launder as usual.

- **Kingsford's Corn Starch.** Apply Kingsford's Corn Starch to the spot, wait twelve hours, brush off, then launder as usual.

Remove grease stains from linen with . . .

- **WD-40.** Spray WD-40 directly to the stain, rub it in, let it soak for a few minutes, then run through a regular wash cycle.

Ink Spots

Remove ink spots from clothing with . . .

- **Alberto VO5 Hair Spray.** Spray Alberto VO5 Hair Spray on the stain, blot until the stain comes up, and wash.

- **Colgate Toothpaste.** Squeeze Colgate on the spot, scrub, and rinse thoroughly.
- **ReaLemon.** While ink is wet, apply ReaLemon liberally to the spot, then wash the garment in normal cycle with regular detergent in cold water.

Ironing

Speed up your ironing with . . .

- **Reynolds Wrap.** Place a piece of aluminum foil under the ironing board cover to reflect the heat from the iron.

Clean mineral deposits from a steam iron with . . .

- **Heinz Vinegar.** Fill the iron's water reservoir with Heinz White Vinegar. Turn the iron to a steam setting and steam-iron a soft utility rag to clean the steam ports. Repeat the process with water, then thoroughly rinse out the inside of your iron.

Clean starch off an iron with . . .

- **Reynolds Wrap.** Run the iron over a piece of Reynolds Wrap.

Jeans

(See page 78)

Laundromats

Disinfect a washing machine at a Laundromat with . . .

- **Listerine.** To avoid getting germs from another family, wipe off the surface of the machine with Listerine and add one-half cup Listerine to the wash cycle to disinfect the inside of the machine.

Laundry Bags

Travel with a laundry bag with . . .

- **Glad Trash Bags.** Pack a Glad Trash Bag in your suitcase.

BRAND X

Ajax   Kleenex   Pyrex
Balmex   Kotex   Rolex
Borax   Lenox   Tampax
Clorox   Lux   Tilex
Cutex   Playtex   Timex
Desenex   Purex   Windex

Conspiracy or mere coincidence?

Lint

Prevent lint from clinging to clothes with . . .

- **Heinz Vinegar.** Add one cup Heinz Vinegar to each wash load.
- **L'eggs Sheer Energy.** Throw a pair of L'eggs into the dryer with your wet clothes.

Lipstick Stains

Remove lipstick stains from linen napkins with . . .

- **Crisco All-Vegetable Shortening.** Rub in a dab of Crisco All-Vegetable Shortening, then rinse the stained area with Canada Dry Club Soda.
- **Vaseline.** Apply Vaseline Petroleum Jelly before washing.

Odors

Keep clothes and linens smelling fresh with . . .

- **Ivory Soap.** Place an unwrapped bar of Ivory Soap in drawers, linen closets, and storage trunks.

Minimize the smell of dirty laundry with . . .

- **Arm & Hammer Baking Soda.** Sprinkle some Arm & Hammer Baking Soda into your hamper or laundry bag.

- **Bounce.** Place an individual sheet of Bounce at the bottom of a laundry bag or hamper.

Perspiration Stains

Remove perspiration stains from sheets, towels, and clothes with . . .

- **Heinz Vinegar.** Apply one part Heinz White Vinegar to four parts water, then rinse.

Ring-around-the-collar

Clean ring-around-the-collar with . . .

- **Clairol Herbal Essences.** Since the dirt rings in collars are oil stains, Clairol Herbal Essences will remove them when rubbed into the fabric.
- **Crayola Chalk.** Mark the stain heavily with white Crayola Chalk. The chalk will absorb the sebum oil that holds in the dirt.
- **McCormick/Schilling Cream of Tartar.** Wet the collar with warm or hot water, rub in Cream of Tartar, then launder as usual.

Rust Stains

Remove rust stains from washable fabrics with . . .

- **McCormick/Schilling Alum.** Mix one part McCormick/Schilling Alum, one part Cream of Tartar, and enough water to make a paste. Work into the fabric, let stand for five minutes, then flush with warm water.
- **McCormick/Schilling Cream of Tartar.** Make a paste of Cream of Tartar and hot water, rub into the stain, let sit, then launder as usual.
- **ReaLemon.** Use one cup ReaLemon in the washer.

Scorch Marks

Remove light scorch marks from fabrics with . . .

- **Heinz Vinegar.** Rub lightly with Heinz White Vinegar, then wipe with a clean cloth.

Spray Starch

Make spray starch for clothing with . . .

- **Kingsford's Corn Starch.** Mix one tablespoon Kingsford's Corn Starch and one pint cold water in a spray bottle. Use as you would any spray starch. Shake well before each use.

Stains

Prewash stains on clothes with . . .

- **Cascade.** Wet the fabric and sprinkle Cascade on the stain. Scrub gently with an old toothbrush, rinse, and run through the regular wash cycle.
- **Murphy's Oil Soap.** Wet the stain and apply Murphy's Oil Soap full strength just prior to washing.

Static Cling

Reduce static cling with . . .

- **Wilson Tennis Balls.** Throw in a handful of Wilson Tennis Balls while the clothes are tumbling in the dryer.

Suede

Cover spots on black suede with . . .

- **Maxwell House Coffee.** Sponge on a little black Maxwell House Coffee.

And the Rest Is History

- King Louis XI of France (1423-1483) carried his own personal pot of mustard, made for him by a Dijon mustard maker, wherever he went.
- In 1900, New York City's first electric sign—six stories high and lit with 1,200 lights—advertised Heinz's 57 Varieties with the outline of the Heinz pickle at the top.
- Derry Church, Pennsylvania, the home of Hershey's Foods, was renamed Hershey in 1906.
- Explorer Robert Peary carried Quaker Oats to the North Pole, and explorer Admiral Richard Byrd carried Quaker Oats to the South Pole.
- Explorer Robert Peary brought Vaseline Petroleum Jelly to the North Pole to protect his skin from chapping and his mechanical equipment from rusting.
- Sales of Vaseline Petroleum Jelly soared in Russia in 1916, when peasants discovered that adding the petroleum jelly to the oil they burned in their holy lamps eliminated the choking smoke fumes.
- Sales of Vaseline Petroleum Jelly soared in China with Sun Yat-sen's liberation of the Chinese people in 1917. Coolies, ordered to clip off their pigtails (a mark of

subrogation), discovered that Vaseline eased the discomfort caused by the bristle of the severed pigtail.

● In a famous photograph taken on September 30, 1938 of Neville Chamberlain having dinner with Adolf Hitler, Benito Mussolini, and Edouard Daladier, a bottle of Lea & Perrins Worcestershire Sauce sits on the table.

● In the 1940s, Eleanor Roosevelt was voted the most well-known woman in America, followed by Betty Crocker.

● During World War II, 3M stopped selling Scotch Tape to civilians because the military wanted it all. At least one American munitions factory used Scotch Transparent Tape as a conveyor belt to move bullets.

● The universally popular Hershey bar was used overseas during World War II as currency.

● During World War II, gum, considered an emergency ration, was also given to soldiers to relieve tension and dry throats on long marches. GIs used chewed gum to patch jeep tires, gas tanks, life rafts, and parts of airplanes. Wrigley advertisements recommended five sticks of gum per day for every war worker, insisting, "Factory tests show how chewing gum helps men feel better, work better." Since World War II, American soldiers have been issued gum with their K rations and survival kits.

● In 1961, Silly Putty attracted hundreds of Russians to the United States Plastics Expo in Moscow.

● Kraft celebrated the fiftieth anniversary of Miracle Whip in 1983 at the Waldorf-Astoria in New York City with a five-foot-high cake in the shape of a Miracle Whip Salad Dressing jar—complete with the famous red, white, and blue label.

● During Operation Bring Hope in Somalia, U.S. troops bartered for Huggies because the disposable diapers, when moistened, provide a refreshing rubdown, almost as good as a bath.

● In 1990, during Operation Desert Storm, Hershey Foods sent 144,000 "heat-resistant" milk chocolate Desert Bars—capable of withstanding temperatures up to 100°F—to American troops in Saudi Arabia.

● In the 1950s, Sandoz—now the parent company of Gerber—developed psychoactive drugs, including LSD.

● According to *The 1993 Guinness Book of Records*, the world record for the largest single amount of Jell-O is held by Paul Squire and Geoff Ross, who made 7,700 gallons of watermelon-flavored pink Jell-O in a tank supplied by Pool Fab on February 5, 1981, at Roma Street Forum in Brisbane, Australia.

● Procter & Gamble introduced Pringles Potato Crisps at the same time General Foods introduced Pringles Pretzel Snacks. Procter & Gamble ended up buying the rights to the Pringles name from General Foods for an undisclosed sum.

● Queen Elizabeth I loved vanilla so much that she eventually refused all foods prepared without it.

● The Pilgrims landed at Plymouth Rock in December 1620 because, in the words of a diarist aboard the *Mayflower*, "We could not now take time for further search or consideration, our victuals being much spent, especially our beere."

● During the Depression, banks first used Scotch Tape to mend torn currency.

● Baking soda was used to clean the Statue of Liberty for the 1976 bicentennial celebration.

Tar Stains

Remove tar from clothing with . . .

- **Crisco All-Vegetable Shortening.** Scrape off as much tar as possible, place a small lump of Crisco All-Vegetable Shortening over the spot, wait three hours, then wash.

Washing Machine

Dissolve excess soap suds in your washing machine with . . .

- **Downy Fabric Softener.** Add a capful of Downy Fabric Softener to the washload.

Renew the worn dial on a washer or other appliance with . . .

- **Crayola Crayons.** Rub the knob with a red or black Crayola Crayon until the indentations of the letters and numbers are filled with colored wax. Then wipe off the excess crayon.

Clean the hoses and unclog soap scum from a washing machine with . . .

- **Heinz Vinegar.** Once a month, pour one cup of Heinz White Vinegar into the washing machine and run the machine through a normal cycle, without clothes.

Whiter Whites

Whiten white polyester with . . .

- **Cascade.** Mix one cup Cascade and one gallon warm water in a plastic bucket. Soak the clothes in this mixture overnight, then run them through the washing machine. Cascade removes the gray due to detergent residue buildup from white polyester. Be sure to test an inconspicuous area of the fabric first.

Whiten socks and dirty clothes with . . .

- **Arm & Hammer Baking Soda.** Add one-half cup

Arm & Hammer Baking Soda to your regular liquid laundry detergent.

Get your whites whiter than white with . . .

- **Cascade, Clorox,** and **Heinz Vinegar.** Mix one-half cup Cascade, one-half cup Clorox Bleach, and one gallon hot water in a plastic bucket. Soak clothing in this mixture overnight, dump the solution and clothes into the washing machine, and wash as usual. Add one-half cup Heinz White Vinegar to the rinse water. Be sure to test an inconspicuous area of the fabric first.

Wool

Clean wool with . . .

- **Dr. Bronner's Peppermint Soap.** Add one-quarter teaspoon of Dr. Bronner's Peppermint Soap to a sink full of water and wash the garment.

Deodorize a wool sweater with . . .

- **Heinz Vinegar.** Wash the sweater, then rinse in equal parts Heinz Vinegar and water to remove odor.

Deodorize Your Feet

with Lipton Tea Bags

Arthritis

Relieve arthritis with . . .

- **Gulden's Mustard.** Rub Gulden's Mustard into your hands.
- **Heinz Vinegar.** Before each meal, drink a glass of water containing two teaspoons Heinz Apple Cider Vinegar. Give this folk remedy at least three weeks to start working.

Athlete's Foot

Cure athlete's foot with . . .

- **Dr. Bronner's Peppermint Soap.** Soap up your feet with Dr. Bronner's Peppermint Soap, dry your feet, then apply a dash of soap as a lotion to your dry feet.
- **Kingsford's Corn Starch.** Sprinkle Kingsford's Corn Starch on your feet and in your shoes to absorb moisture and reduce friction.

Backache

Keep backache away with . . .

● **Bayer Aspirin.** Bayer Aspirin is an antiinflammatory, and taking one aspirin a day can help eliminate inflammation around the site of the pain.

Bandages

Remove adhesive bandages painlessly with . . .

● **Alberto VO5 Conditioning Hairdressing.** Rub a little Alberto VO5 Conditioning Hairdressing into the bandage wings, wait a few minutes, then peel off.

● **Baby Oil.** Rub baby oil around the bandage before pulling it off.

● **Conair Pro Style 1600.** Blowing hot air at the bandage with a Conair Pro Style 1600 will soften the adhesive so you can ease off the bandage.

Bee Stings

Relieve a bee sting with . . .

● **McCormick/Schilling Meat Tenderizer.** Make sure the stinger is removed, then make a paste with meat tenderizer and water, and apply to the skin. The enzymes in meat tenderizer break down the proteins in bee venom.

Bleeding

Control heavy bleeding with . . .

● **Pampers.** Use a pair of Pampers as a compress.

- **Tampax Tampons.** A tampon can be used as a compress for wounds or lacerations.

Stop bleeding and disinfect minor wounds with . . .
- **McCormick/Schilling Alum.** Help clot a minor cut by dabbing on McCormick/Schilling Alum. Alum is both an antiseptic and a pain reliever that can prevent the infection from getting worse.

- **ReaLemon.** Pour ReaLemon on a cut or apply with a cotton ball.

Broken Bones
Provide first aid in an emergency with . . .
- **Scotch Packaging Tape.** Make emergency splints with two-by-fours and Scotch Packaging Tape.

Burned Tongue
Soothe a burned tongue with . . .
- **Domino Sugar.** Sprinkle a dash of Domino Sugar on your tongue if it has been burned by hot soup, tea, or coffee.

Burns
Treat minor burns with . . .
- **Betty Crocker Potato Buds.** Mix Betty Crocker Potato Buds with

enough water to make a thick paste, and apply to the burn.

● **Lipton Tea Bags.** Apply wet Lipton Flo-Thru Tea Bags directly to the burn, or secure in place with gauze.

● **Miracle Whip.** Rub Miracle Whip into the burn. Let it set, then wipe off.

● **SueBee Honey.** Apply SueBee Honey to the injury. Honey is hygroscopic and absorbs water, creating an environment in which disease-producing microorganisms, deprived of their moisture, cannot live.

Speed up the healing of a burn with . . .

● **Preparation H.** Apply Preparation H to the burn and cover with a fresh sterile bandage every day.

Bursitis

Relieve bursitis with . . .

● **Star Olive Oil.** Heat Star Olive Oil and massage into the shoulder or upper arm daily.

Calluses

Soften calluses on feet with . . .

● **Bayer Aspirin.** Crush six Bayer Aspirin tablets into a powder using a mortar and pestle. Add one-half teaspoon ReaLemon and one-half teaspoon water, and mix into a paste. Apply to feet, then place a plastic bag over each foot and wrap in a warm towel for ten minutes, allowing the paste to penetrate the skin. Then unwrap each foot and scrub with a pumice stone. If you are allergic or sensitive to aspirin, do not use aspirin on your skin to avoid the remote possibility of a reaction.

Canker Sores

Soothe canker sores with . . .

- **Dannon Yogurt.** Eat two servings of Dannon Yogurt a day until the sores clear.
- **Lipton Tea.** Apply a wet Lipton Tea Bag to the canker sore. Tannin is an astringent that relieves pain.
- **McCormick/Schilling Alum.** McCormick/Schilling Alum is both an antiseptic and a pain reliever that can prevent the infection from getting worse.
- **Phillips' Milk of Magnesia.** Swish Phillips' Milk of Magnesia around your mouth to coat the canker sore. Milk of Magnesia counteracts the acid environment in which the bacteria thrive.

Chapped Lips
Heal chapped lips with . . .

- **Alberto VO5 Conditioning Hairdressing.** Rub in a small amount of Alberto VO5 Conditioning Hairdressing.
- **Balmex.** Apply Balmex to your lips.
- **Vaseline.** Apply a little Vaseline Petroleum Jelly to your lips before going outdoors and again before going to bed.

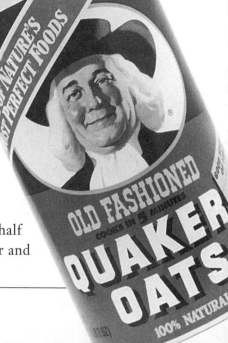

Chicken Pox
Relieve itching from chicken pox with . . .

- **Quaker Oats.** Pour one-half cup Quaker Oats in a blender and blend into a powder on medium-high speed, then sift. Put two tablespoons into a warm bath and soak in the oatmeal for thirty minutes.

Colds
Relieve a cold with . . .

- **Gold's Horse Radish.** Gold's Horse Radish is a natural cure for a congested nose.
- **Gulden's Mustard.** Rub Gulden's Mustard on your chest.
- **Heinz Vinegar.** Mix one-quarter cup Heinz Apple Cider Vinegar with one-quarter cup honey. Take one tablespoon six to eight times daily.
- **McCormick/Schilling Garlic Powder.** Spice a bowl of chicken soup with McCormick/Schilling Garlic Powder. Garlic is a natural antibiotic and antiseptic.
- **Tabasco Pepper Sauce.** Mix ten to twenty drops Tabasco Pepper Sauce in a glass of tomato juice.

Drink several of these decongestant tonics daily to help relieve congestion in the nose, sinuses, and lungs. Or gargle with ten to twenty drops Tabasco Pepper Sauce mixed in a glass of water to clear out the respiratory tract.

Cold Sores
Help heal, relieve, and soften cold sores with . . .

- **Balmex.** Apply Balmex the moment you feel a cold sore forming.

Constipation

Relieve constipation with . . .

- **ReaLemon.** Before breakfast, drink four tablespoons ReaLemon in one cup warm water. Sweeten with honey to taste.
- **Star Olive Oil.** Take one to three tablespoons Star Olive Oil as a mild laxative.

Corns

Remove corns with . . .

- **Heinz Vinegar** and **Wonder Bread.** Make a poultice of one crumbled piece of Wonder Bread soaked in one-quarter cup Heinz Vinegar. Let poultice sit for one-half hour, then apply to the corn and tape in place overnight. If corn does not peel off by morning, reapply the poultice for several consecutive nights.
- **Nestea.** Soak the corn in warm Nestea for one-half hour each day for a week or two until the tannic acid in the tea dissolves the corn.

Relieve corns with . . .

- **Epsom Salt.** Soak your feet in a solution of Epsom Salt and warm water.

Coughs

Relieve a cough with . . .

- **Heinz Vinegar.** Mix one-half cup Heinz Apple Cider Vinegar, one-half cup water, one teaspoon cayenne pepper, and four teaspoons honey. Take one tablespoon when cough acts up. Take another tablespoon at bedtime.

● **ReaLemon, Star Olive Oil,** and **SueBee Honey.** Mix four tablespoons ReaLemon, one-half cup Star Olive Oil, and one cup SueBee Honey. Heat five minutes, then stir vigorously for two minutes. Take one teaspoon every two hours.

● **SueBee Honey** and **ReaLemon.** Dissolve one tablespoon SueBee Honey and one tablespoon ReaLemon in a small glass of warm water and sip it. For a stronger solution, combine equal parts SueBee Honey and ReaLemon, and take one teaspoon at bedtime. Both mixtures may help loosen phlegm.

Dandruff

Get rid of dandruff with . . .

● **Listerine.** Wash your hair with Listerine.

● **ReaLemon.** Apply one tablespoon ReaLemon to your hair. Shampoo, then rinse with water. Rinse again with a mixture of two tablespoons ReaLemon and two cups water. Repeat every other day until dandruff disappears.

Remove dandruff with . . .

● **Morton Salt.** Shake one tablespoon Morton Salt into dry hair. Massage gently and shampoo.

Diarrhea

Prevent diarrhea while taking antibiotics with . . .

● **Dannon Yogurt.** Eat Dannon Yogurt with active cultures while taking antibiotics. Antibiotics may kill healthful bacteria in addition to disease-bearing ones, but the *Lactobacillus acidophilus* in yogurt produce bacteriocins that restore natural intestinal cultures.

Help relieve diarrhea with . . .

- **Lipton Tea Bags.** Drink plenty of Lipton Tea and eat toast. The tannin in tea is reported to be helpful in cases of diarrhea, while its liquid replaces fluids lost by the body.

- **Uncle Ben's Converted Brand Rice.** Eating plain Uncle Ben's Converted Brand Rice will help cure diarrhea, according to *Prevention* magazine.

Digestion

Aid digestion with . . .

- **Gulden's Mustard.** Mustard's properties for aiding digestion have never been disputed.

Earaches

Alleviate an earache caused by a cold, sinus infection, or allergy with . . .

- **Wrigley's Spearmint Gum.** The muscular action of chewing Wrigley's Spearmint Gum will open the eustachian tubes (which lead from the back of the throat to the middle ear).

Soothe an earache with . . .

DR. KRAZY GLUE

Surgeons treat arterial venous fistulas (entangled clusters of arteries) by injecting liquid acrylic agents into the abnormal blood vessels to seal off the excessive flow of blood. The material used, N-butyl cyanoacrylate, is similar to the ingredients in Krazy Glue. Physicians in Canada use an adhesive similar to Krazy Glue instead of stitches, lowering the possibility of bacterial infection and minimizing scarring.

- **Star Olive Oil.** Warm and insert a few drops of Star Olive Oil into the affected ear, plug with cotton, and apply a hot water bottle.

Relieve an earache caused by the change in pressure in an airplane with . . .

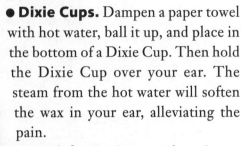

- **Dixie Cups.** Dampen a paper towel with hot water, ball it up, and place in the bottom of a Dixie Cup. Then hold the Dixie Cup over your ear. The steam from the hot water will soften the wax in your ear, alleviating the pain.
- **Wrigley's Spearmint Gum.** Open the eustachian tubes in your ears by chewing Wrigley's Spearmint Gum on an airplane flight.

Episiotomies

After an episiotomy, instead of toilet paper, use . . .

- **Huggies Baby Wipes.** Huggies Baby Wipes are gentle enough for a baby and perfect after an operation on the more sensitive areas of your body.

Erysipelas

Help heal erysipelas with . . .

- **SueBee Honey.** Generously cover the affected area with honey, then cover with cotton for twenty-four hours. Repeat if necessary.

Eyes

Soothe tired eyes with . . .

- **Lipton Tea Bags.** Place Lipton Flo-Thru Tea Bags soaked in cool water or lukewarm water over your closed eyes for at least fifteen minutes.

Improvise an eyedropper with . . .

- **Glad Flexible Straws.** Insert a Glad Flexible Straw into the liquid, cover the open end of the straw with your finger, and lift. The liquid will stay in the straw until you release your finger.

YOGURT: MILK WITH CULTURE

In 1992, researchers from the University of Southern California School of Medicine in Los Angeles reported that people who ate yogurt, even as little as three to four times a month, showed lower relative risk of developing colon cancer.

Feet

Deodorize your feet with . . .

- **Lipton Tea Bags.** Boil three or four Lipton Flo-Thru Tea Bags in one quart of water for ten minutes. Add enough cold water to make a comfortable soak. Soak your feet for twenty to thirty minutes, then dry and apply foot powder. Do this twice a day until odor is under control. Then continue twice a week to keep odor under control. Tannin, which can be found in tea, is a drying agent.

Frostbite

Soothe frostbite with . . .

- **Star Olive Oil.** Warm some Star Olive Oil and gently dab on frostbitten skin.

Hangovers

Relieve a hangover with . . .

- **Maxwell House Coffee.** Drink a couple of cups of Maxwell House Coffee. Coffee acts as a vasoconstrictor, reducing the swelling of blood vessels that causes headache.
- **SueBee Honey.** Honey is a concentrated source of fructose. Eating SueBee Honey on crackers helps your body flush out whatever alcohol remains in the body.

Heart Attack

Prevent heart attack with . . .

- **Bayer Aspirin.** Take one Bayer Aspirin a day. Aspirin seems to prevent blood from clotting too easily, not getting through a narrowed artery, and triggering a heart attack. However, all heart patients should get their doctor's approval before taking any medication, including aspirin, on a daily basis.

Hemorrhoids

Soothe hemorrhoids with . . .

- **Huggies Baby Wipes.** Use Huggies Baby Wipes as toilet paper to avoid aggravating sensitive hemorrhoids.
- **Kingsford's Corn Starch.** Ben Charles Harris, author of *Kitchen Medicines*, suggests mixing one tablespoon Kingsford's Corn Starch in enough water to make a paste, gradually adding more water to measure a pint, boiling the mixture for a few minutes, allowing it to cool, and then using it in an enema.

Hiccups

Cure the hiccups with . . .

- **Heinz Vinegar.** Mix one teaspoon Heinz Apple Cider Vinegar in one cup warm water, and drink.

Hives

Relieve hives with . . .

- **Phillips' Milk of Magnesia.** Dab Phillips' Milk of Magnesia on your hives. The alkalinity helps relieve the itch.

Humidifiers

Eliminate odors in your humidifier with . . .

- **ReaLemon.** Pour three or four teaspoons of ReaLemon into the water.
- **20 Mule Team Borax.** Dissolve one tablespoon 20 Mule Team Borax per gallon of water before adding to the unit. Use this treatment once or twice a year.

Ice Pack

Make an ice pack with . . .

- **Playtex Living Gloves.** Fill a Playtex Living Glove with ice, then tie the cuff securely to prevent leaks.

Immunity Booster

Enhance your immune system with . . .

- **Dannon Yogurt.** According to the *International Journal of Immunotherapy*, yogurt with active cultures enhances the body's immune system by increasing the production of gamma interferons, which play a key role in fighting certain allergies and viral infections. Other studies indicate that yogurt can help prevent gastrointestinal infections (lactic acid helps inhibit the growth of food-borne pathogens, and yogurt cultures produce bacteriocins that restore natural intestinal cultures).

Indigestion
Relieve an upset stomach with . . .
- **Canada Dry Club Soda.** Drink Canada Dry Club Soda to soothe indigestion.
- **Heinz Vinegar.** Drink one teaspoon Heinz Apple Cider Vinegar in one-half cup water to quiet an upset stomach.

Flavor Alka-Seltzer with . . .
- **Domino Sugar** and **McCormick/ Schilling Pure Vanilla Extract.** Add a few drops of McCormick/Schilling Pure Vanilla Extract and one teaspoon Domino Sugar to a glass of Alka-Seltzer to improve the taste.

Insect Bites
Soothe insect bites with . . .
- **Alka-Seltzer.** Dissolve two Alka-Seltzer tablets in a glass of water, dip a cloth into the solution, and place it on the bite for twenty minutes.
- **Arm & Hammer Baking Soda.** Make a paste of Arm & Hammer Baking Soda and water, and apply to the affected area.
- **Bayer Aspirin.** Wet the skin and rub a Bayer Aspirin tablet over the bite to help control inflammation.
- **Betty Crocker Potato Buds.** Mix Betty Crocker Potato Buds with enough water to make a thick paste, and apply to the bite.

- **Carnation Nonfat Dry Milk.** Mix ten ounces Carnation Nonfat Dry Milk and twenty-

five ounces water in a quart container. Fill the container by adding ice cubes and two tablespoons of salt. Apply to infected area with a cloth for twenty minutes, three or four times daily.

- **Coppertone.** Applying Coppertone to the affected areas alleviates itching.
- **Epsom Salt.** Dissolve one tablespoon Epsom Salt in one quart hot water. Chill, then dip a clean, soft cloth into the solution and place on the bite for twenty minutes.
- **Heinz Vinegar.** Use a cotton ball to dab mosquito and other bug bites with Heinz Vinegar straight from the bottle.
- **Ivory Soap.** Apply wet Ivory to the bite. When the soap dries, the skin will feel anesthetized.
- **McCormick/Schilling Meat Tenderizer.** Make a paste of McCormick/Schilling Meat Tenderizer and water, and apply to the sting. The enzymes in meat tenderizer break down the proteins in insect venom.

Jellyfish Stings

Relieve a jellyfish sting with . . .

- **McCormick/Schilling Meat Tenderizer.** Dissolve McCormick/Schilling Meat

Tenderizer in salt water and pat it on the affected area. An enzyme in meat tenderizer deactivates venom protein.

- **Star Olive Oil.** Apply Star Olive Oil for immediate relief.

Laryngitis

Soothe laryngitis with . . .

- **Lipton Tea Bags.** Drink brewed Lipton Tea with ReaLemon or SueBee Honey.

Medicines

Locate the arrows or markings on childproof caps with . . .

- **Cover Girl NailSlicks Classic Red.** Paint the arrows or markings on childproof medicine bottles with Cover Girl NailSlicks Classic Red Nail Polish so you can line them up easier.

Label poisons and medicines with . . .

- **Cover Girl NailSlicks Classic Red.** Paint an *X* with Cover Girl NailSlicks Classic Red Nail Polish on containers of poison and medicine bottles, and teach your children to never touch any bottle or box labeled with a red *X*.

Muscles

Soothe sore muscles with . . .

- **Gulden's Mustard.** Apply a poultice of Gulden's Mustard.

Nicotine Withdrawal

Get short-term relief from nicotine withdrawal symptoms with . . .

- **Alka-Seltzer.** As long as you're not on a low-sodium diet or have peptic ulcers, drink two Alka-Seltzer tablets dissolved in a glass of water at every meal.

Poison Ivy

Soothe poison ivy with . . .

- **Arm & Hammer Baking Soda.** Make a paste of Arm & Hammer Baking Soda and water, and apply to the affected area.
- **Balmex.** Apply Balmex to the affected area until the oozing dries and stops.

- **Carnation Nonfat Dry Milk.** Mix ten ounces Carnation Nonfat Dry Milk and twenty-five ounces water in a quart container. Fill the container by adding ice cubes and two tablespoons of salt. Apply to infected area with a cloth for twenty minutes, three or four times daily.
- **ReaLemon.** Applying ReaLemon over the affected areas should soothe itching and alleviate the rash.

Portuguese Man-of-War Stings

Relieve a Portuguese man-of-war sting with . . .

- **Star Olive Oil.** Apply Star Olive Oil for immediate relief, then seek medical attention.

Prickly Heat
Soothe prickly heat with . . .
- **Arm & Hammer Baking Soda.** Dissolve one-half cup Arm & Hammer Baking Soda in a tepid bath. Soak in the bath for fifteen minutes.

Sinusitis
Help relieve sinusitis with . . .
- **McCormick/Schilling Garlic Powder.** Spice your foods with McCormick/Schilling Garlic Powder. Garlic contains a chemical that makes mucus less sticky, clearing the sinuses.

Skin Irritations
Soothe skin irritations with . . .
- **Kingsford's Corn Starch.** Apply a paste made of equal parts Kingsford's Corn Starch, zinc oxide, and castor oil.

Splinters
Remove a splinter with . . .
- **Elmer's Glue-All.** Coat the splinter with a drop of Elmer's Glue-All, wait for it to dry, then peel off the dried glue. The splinter should be stuck to it.
- **Scotch Packaging Tape.** Place Scotch Packaging Tape over the splinter and gently peel off.
- **Wesson Corn Oil.** Soak the wounded area in Wesson Corn Oil for a few minutes to soften the skin before trying to remove the splinter.

Sunburn

Soothe sunburn pain with . . .

- **Arm & Hammer Baking Soda.** Dissolve one-half cup Arm & Hammer Baking Soda in a tepid bath. Soak for fifteen minutes.
- **Carnation Nonfat Dry Milk.** Mix ten ounces Carnation Nonfat Dry Milk and twenty-five ounces water in a quart container. Fill the container by adding ice cubes and two tablespoons of salt. Apply to infected area with a cloth for twenty minutes, three or four times daily.
- **Dannon Yogurt.** Spread Dannon Yogurt on the sunburn, let sit for twenty minutes, then rinse clean with lukewarm water.
- **Heinz Vinegar.** Apply undiluted Heinz Vinegar to the burn.
- **Kingsford's Corn Starch.** Add enough water to Kingsford's Corn Starch to make a paste, and apply directly to the burn.
- **Lipton Tea Bags.** Pat your sunburn with wet Lipton Flo-Thru Tea Bags.
- **Lubriderm.** After soaking or using compresses, smooth on some bath oil. Then moisturize with Lubriderm.
- **Miracle Whip.** Use Miracle Whip as a skin cream.
- **Nestea.** Empty a jar of Nestea into a warm bath. Soak in the tea. The tannic acid will relieve the sunburn pain.

Teeth

Stop gums from bleeding after having a tooth pulled with . . .

- **Lipton Tea Bags.** With your finger, press a cool, moist Lipton Flo-Thru Tea Bag against the cavity.

Throat

Soothe a sore throat with . . .

- **Aunt Jemima Original Syrup.** Take two teaspoons Aunt Jemima Original Syrup to coat and soothe the throat.
- **Bosco.** Take two teaspoons Bosco chocolate syrup to coat and soothe a sore throat.
- **Gold's Horse Radish.** Mix one tablespoon Gold's Horse Radish, one teaspoon SueBue Honey, and one teaspoon ground cloves in a glass of warm water, and stir. Sip slowly, continually stirring to prevent the horseradish from settling.
- **Gulden's Mustard.** Mix two tablespoons Gulden's Mustard, juice of half a lemon, one tablespoon salt, one tablespoon honey, and one and a half cups boiling water. Cover and let cool for fifteen minutes, then gargle.
- **Heinz Vinegar.** Add two teaspoons of Heinz Vinegar to the water in your humidifier.
- **Lipton Tea Bags.** Drink brewed Lipton Tea with ReaLemon or SueBee Honey.
- **McCormick/Schilling Garlic Powder.** Spice your foods with McCormick/Schilling Garlic Powder. Garlic is a natural antibiotic and antiseptic.

- **SueBee Honey.** Take one teaspoon of SueBee Honey at bedtime, letting it trickle down your throat.

Relieve a scalded throat with . . .
- **Star Olive Oil.** Take two teaspoons Star Olive Oil to soothe and coat the throat.

Toothache

Relieve a toothache with . . .
- **Tabasco Pepper Sauce.** Apply a dab of Tabasco Pepper Sauce to the gum.

Walkers

Make a walker glide more easily with . . .
- **Wilson Tennis Balls.** Cut a hole in two Wilson Tennis Balls and fit them on the back feet of the walker.

Warts

Dissolve warts with . . .
- **Heinz Vinegar.** Mix one part Heinz Apple Cider Vinegar to one part glycerin into a lotion and apply daily to warts until they dissolve.

Wasp Stings

Relieve a wasp sting with . . .
- **McCormick/Schilling Meat Tenderizer.** Make sure the stinger is removed, then make a paste with meat tenderizer and water, and apply to the skin. The enzymes in meat tenderizer break down the proteins in bee venom.

Windburn

Soothe windburn pain with . . .

- **Arm & Hammer Baking Soda.** Dissolve one-half cup baking soda in a tepid bath. Soak in the bath for fifteen minutes.
- **Miracle Whip.** Use Miracle Whip as a skin cream.
- **Vaseline.** Apply a thin coat of Vaseline Petroleum Jelly.

Wounds

Lessen the pain of minor skin fissures and paper cuts with . . .
- **Krazy Glue.** Apply Krazy Glue to the thin cracks in the skin to relieve the pain. The Krazy Glue deprives the nerve endings of air.

Disinfect wounds with . . .
- **Listerine.** Listerine works as an astringent when poured on a laceration or abrasion.

Clean scrapes and bruises with . . .
- **Huggies Baby Wipes.** Huggies Baby Wipes are great for cleaning a minor abrasion.

Dress wounds with . . .
- **SueBee Honey.** Apply SueBee Honey to the injury. Honey is hygroscopic and absorbs water, creating an environment in which disease-producing microorganisms, deprived of their moisture, cannot live.

Relieve a bruise with . . .
- **Gulden's Mustard.** Combine three parts Gulden's Mustard, one part honey, and one part finely chopped onion, apply to affected area, and cover with a bandage or handkerchief.

Provide first aid in an emergency with . . .

- **Scotch Packaging Tape.** Bandage wounds with torn bedsheets and Scotch Packaging Tape.

Yeast infections

Prevent yeast infections with . . .

- **Heinz Vinegar.** Douche with one tablespoon Heinz White Vinegar to one quart warm water to adjust the pH balance in the vagina.

Reduce the occurrence of yeast infections with . . .

- **Dannon Yogurt.** The March 1992 issue of the *Annals of Internal Medicine* reports that daily consumption of yogurt containing *Lactobacillus acidophilus cultures* results in a threefold decrease in the incidence of candidal vaginitis (yeast infections).

Cure yeast infections with . . .

- **Dannon Yogurt.** Insert yogurt into the vagina. According to *The New Our Bodies, Ourselves,* some women claim that yogurt in the vagina is a remedy for *Candida albicans.*

Hide Your Valuables

in Wilson Tennis Balls

<u>Candles</u>
Store candles with . . .

> ● **Reynolds Cut-Rite Wax Paper.** Roll candles in a sheet of Cut-Rite Wax Paper before placing them in a drawer or storage box to protect them from getting scuffed.

<u>Drapes</u>
Tag the pull cord that opens the drapes with . . .

> ● **Scotch Packaging Tape.** Wrap a half-inch piece of Scotch Packaging Tape at eye level around the correct cord.

<u>Games</u>
Store game pieces with . . .

> ● **Ziploc Storage Bags.** Never lose dice, cards, playing pieces, or small toys again.

Store jigsaw puzzles with . . .

- **Ziploc Storage Bags.** Keep all the pieces in a Ziploc Storage Bag so you never lose that one pivotal piece of the puzzle again.

Important Papers

Protect important papers with . . .

- **Ziploc Storage Bags.** Store tax forms, important records, canceled checks, receipts, warranties, and instructions in a Ziploc Storage Bag.

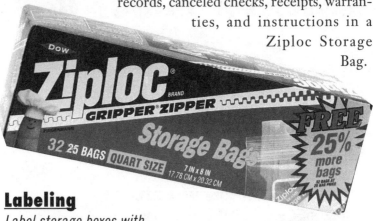

Labeling

Label storage boxes with . . .

- **Avery Laser Labels.** Label the contents of any box you put into storage or in the attic or garage with an Avery Laser Label so you can easily identify the contents.

Label your compact discs with . . .

- **Avery Laser Labels.** Print your name, address, and phone number on Avery Laser Labels and adhere them to CDs.

Luggage

Identify your luggage easily with . . .

- **Con-Tact Paper.** Mark your suitcases with an easily

Double Your Pleasure, Double Your Fun

- In 1915, William Wrigley Jr. sent four free sticks of gum to every person listed in a U.S. phone book.
- William Wrigley was the first distributor to place gum next to restaurant cash registers.
- Before World War II, the basic ingredient of all chewing gum was chicle, the sap of the sapodilla tree, indigenous to Central and South America. When chicle became difficult to obtain during World War II, the gum industry developed synthetic gum bases such as polyvinyl acetate, supplied almost entirely by the Hercule Powder Company, an explosives manufacturer.
- Psychiatrists have called gum chewing oral masturbation.

identifiable mark made from brightly patterned Con-Tact Paper so you can quickly spot your luggage in airports.

Maps

Protect road maps with . . .

- **Con-Tact Paper.** Cover those important maps with clean Con-Tact Paper. Trace your route with a dry erasable marker which you can wipe off after the trip.

The Toothbrush Throughout History

3000 B.C.	Egyptians invent the "chew stick," a twig with a frayed end of soft fibers that is rubbed against the teeth to clean them.
1498	The Chinese develop the first bristled toothbrush, made from bristles plucked from the backs of hogs' necks and fastened to bamboo or bone handles. Traders from the Orient introduce Europeans to the practice of brushing their teeth, and the few Europeans who adopt the practice opt for horsehair toothbrushes, though most prefer the Roman toothpick.
1937	The United States imports 1.5 million pounds of hog bristles for toothbrushes.
1938	After Du Pont chemists discover nylon in the 1930s, the company markets the first nylon-bristle toothbrush in 1938.
1940s	Periodontist Robert Hutson invents Oral-B Toothbrushes, the first multitufted, soft-nylon-bristle toothbrushes.
1961	The Squibb Company introduces the electric toothbrush.
1962	General Electric introduces the cordless electric toothbush.

Mothballs

Secure mothballs with . . .

- **L'eggs Sheer Energy.** Use a L'eggs stocking to hold mothballs in the closet.

Passports

Keep passports waterproof with . . .

- **Ziploc Storage Bags.** Store your passport in a Ziploc Storage Bag.

Remote Control

Prevent your remote controls from disappearing with . . .

- **Velcro.** Adhere hook-sided strips of Velcro to the back of the remote control and fluffy strips on the top of your television set or a nearby wall. The hook-sided strips will also adhere to fabric upholstery on a couch or chair.

Rubber Bands

Make rubber bands with . . .

- **Playtex Living Gloves.** When your Playtex Living Gloves wear out, slice up the cuff to make rubber bands.

Seasonal Items

Pack seasonal items away with . . .

- **Ziploc Storage Bags.** Store leftover holiday greet-

ing cards, valentines, and halloween decorations in Ziploc
Storage Bags.

Suitcases
Label suitcases with . . .
- **Scotch Packaging Tape.** Write your name and address on two index cards, and use Scotch Packaging Tape
to tape one card inside the suitcase and another on the
outside.

Prevent musty suitcases with . . .
- **Bounce.** Place an individual sheet of Bounce inside
empty luggage before storing.

Thermostats
Readjust your thermostat quickly with . . .
- **Cover Girl NailSlicks Classic Red.** Paint a dot of
Cover Girl NailSlicks Classic Red Nail Polish to mark
the temperature at which you usually set your thermo-
stat.

Toiletries
Pack toiletries when you travel with . . .
- **Ziploc Storage Bags.** Keep all your toiletry items
together in a Ziploc Storage Bag and prevent any unex-
pected leaks or spills.

Valuables
Store valuables with . . .
- **Tampax Tampons.** Remove a tampon from its card-
board applicator, roll up your money, insert it into the
empty applicator, and place it back in the box.
- **Wilson Tennis Balls.** Make a two-inch slit along one

seam of a Wilson Tennis Ball, then place valuables inside. If you hide the doctored tennis ball among your other sports equipment, remember not to use it.

Winter Clothes

Store your winter clothes with . . .

- **Glad Trash Bags.** Fill a Glad Trash Bag with your sweaters, add a few mothballs, and seal with a twist tie.

Make a Solar-Powered Camping Shower

with a Glad Trash Bag

Antenna

Improvise a radio or television antenna with a . . .

- **Slinky.** During the Vietnam War, communications soldiers would toss a Slinky over a high tree branch as a makeshift radio antenna.

Barbecues

Clean barbecue grills with . . .

- **Arm & Hammer Baking Soda.** Make a paste by mixing equal parts Arm & Hammer Baking Soda and water, apply with a wire brush, wipe clean, and dry with a cloth.
- **Reynolds Wrap.** After barbecuing, place a sheet of Reynolds Wrap on the hot grill. The next time you use

the barbecue, peel off the foil, crinkle it into a ball, and rub the grill clean, easily removing all the burned food.

- **WD-40.** Remove the grill from the barbecue, spray with WD-40, wait, and wipe clean. Then wash with soap and water.

Start a charcoal fire with . . .

- **Conair Pro Style 1600.** Use a Conair Pro Style 1600 to fan the charcoal briquets in a barbecue grill.

- **Maxwell House Coffee.** Remove the top and bottom of an empty Maxwell House Coffee can and punch a few holes in the sides of the can. Stand the can in your barbecue grill, fill it with charcoal briquets, add lighter fluid, and light. When the coals glow, remove the hot can with tongs and set in a safe place.

Make cleaning a barbecue grill easy with . . .

- **Wesson Corn Oil.** Before cooking, coat the grill with Wesson Corn Oil. Clean when the grill is cool to the touch.

Remove dirt and grime from barbecue grills with . . .

- **WD-40.** Remove the grill from the barbecue, spray with WD-40, wait, and wipe clean. Then wash with soap and water.

Identify rare, medium, and well-done steaks on your barbecue grill with . . .

- **Forster Toothpicks.** Use colored Forster Toothpicks to mark steaks on the barbecue.

Cover your barbecue with . . .

- **Glad Trash Bags.** Protect your outdoor grill by covering it with a Glad Trash Bag when it's cool.

Prevent grease fires in barbecue grills with . . .

- **Tidy Cat.** Cover bottom of grill with a three-quarter-inch layer of unused Tidy Cat to reduce fires.

Secure the lid on a barbecue grill for transportation purposes with . . .

- **Scotch Packaging Tape.** Simply use Scotch Packaging Tape.

Beach

Clean sand off wet skin with . . .

- **Kingsford's Corn Starch.** Sprinkle Kingsford's Corn Starch on skin to remove moisture, and the sand virtually falls off by itself.

Remove tar with . . .

- **Colgate Toothpaste.** Squeeze on Colgate and rub.
- **Miracle Whip.** Spread a teaspoon of Miracle Whip on tar, rub, and wipe off.

Birds

Make a bird feeder with . . .

- **Clorox.** Cut a hole in the side of an empty, clean Clorox Bleach jug opposite the handle.
- **Hartz Parakeet Seed.** Punch a hole in the top of an empty cardboard tube (from a used roll of toilet paper or paper towels). Roll the cardboard tube in honey, then roll the honey-coated tube in the Hartz Parakeet Seed. Hang the birdseed-coated tube outdoors.

Make a birdbath with a . . .

- **Frisbee.** Punch three equidistant holes along the circumference of the Frisbee, insert wire, and hang the Frisbee upside down from a tree or post. Fill with water, or let the rain do it naturally.

Deck Chairs

Prevent a deck chair from slipping through the cracks of a deck with . . .

● **Wilson Tennis Balls.** Slit four Wilson Tennis Balls and fit them on the feet of the deck chair.

Ground Cloth

Make a ground cloth for camping trips with . . .

● **Glad Trash Bags.** Place your sleeping bag on top of several Glad Trash Bags to keep out moisture.

Hoses

Repair a punctured garden hose with . . .

● **Forster Toothpicks.** Insert a Forster Toothpick into the hole, snap it off flush with the hose's outer skin, then wrap Scotch Mailing Tape around the spot. The wooden toothpick will absorb water, swelling to seal the hole.

● **Wrigley's Spearmint Gum.** Patch the holes with chewed Wrigley's Spearmint Gum.

Lighting

Prevent outdoor lightbulbs from sticking in fixtures when you go to change them with . . .

● **Vaseline.** Rub a thin coat of Vaseline Petroleum Jelly on the threads before inserting the bulbs to make removal easy.

Mosquitoes

(See page 152)

Packing

Store camping items with . . .

- **Ziploc Storage Bags.** Carry utensils, food, clothes, maps, medications, and first aid supplies in Ziploc Storage Bags.

Picnics

Prevent picnic tablecloths from blowing away with . . .

- **Scotch Packaging Tape.** Tape the corners to the table with Scotch Packaging Tape.
- **Velcro.** Adhere strips of Velcro on the four corners of the tablecloth and the table to keep the cloth from blowing off the table.

Deodorize a cooler with . . .

- **Clorox.** Wash with diluted Clorox Bleach, then rinse.
- **McCormick/Schilling Pure Vanilla Extract.** Wash out the cooler with a strong solution of Clorox Bleach and hot water, then saturate a cloth with McCormick/Schilling Pure Vanilla Extract and wipe down the insides.

Remove wrinkles from plastic tablecloths with a . . .

- **Conair Pro Style 1600.** Blow with a Conair Pro Style 1600 set on hot until the plastic softens.

Hold a paper plate with a . . .

- **Frisbee.** Fit a paper plate inside an upside-down Frisbee during a picnic.

Pools

Maintain the proper alkalinity in a swimming pool with . . .

- **Arm & Hammer Baking Soda.** Add 1.5 pounds of Arm & Hammer Baking Soda for every 10,000 gallons of water in the pool to raise total alkalinity by 10 ppm (parts per million parts of pool water), keeping the total alkalinity of the pool within the range of 80 to 150 ppm of alkalinity. Maintaining a proper level of total alkalinity minimizes changes in pH when acidic or basic pool chemicals or contaminants enter the water, reducing chloramine formation and the corrosivity of water, consequently reducing eye irritation and unpleasant odors while improving bactericidal effectiveness.

THE BEAR NECESSITIES

When wilderness camping, anything that smells like food, including toothpaste, can attract bears. Food, soap, and toothpaste should be stored in a waterproof sack hung from a twenty-foot-high rope strung between two trees.

Pots and Pans

Clean pots and pans when camping with . . .

- **Reynolds Wrap.** A crumpled-up piece of Reynolds Wrap makes an excellent pot scrubber.

Prevent campfire soot from sticking to the bottoms of pots and pans with . . .

- **Ivory Soap.** Thinly coat the bottoms of pots and pans with Ivory Soap before putting them over an open fire.

Propane Lanterns

Prolong and brighten propane lanterns with . . .

- **Heinz Vinegar.** Soak new wicks for several hours in

Heinz White Vinegar and let them dry before inserting. Propane lanterns will burn longer and brighter on the same amount of fuel.

Raincoats
Improvise a raincoat with . . .
- **Glad Trash Bags.** Cut slits in a Glad Trash Bag for head and arms.

Repairs
Fix leaks in inflatable inner tubes, air mattresses, or air pillows with . . .
- **Krazy Glue.** Apply Krazy Glue to seal holes or leaky valve stems.

Repair a tent or backpack with . . .
- **Oral-B Mint Waxed Floss.** When hiking or camping, Oral-B Mint Waxed Floss makes a durable, strong thread for tough repairs.

Sliding Boards
Resurface a metal sliding board with . . .
- **Reynolds Cut-Rite Wax Paper.** Rub a sheet of Reynolds Cut-Rite Wax Paper on the metal slide.
- **Turtle Wax.** Cover with two coats of Turtle Wax, polishing between applications.

Snow
Prevent snow from sticking to a shovel with . . .
- **Crisco All-Vegetable Shortening.** Lubricate the

shovel with Crisco All-Vegetable Shortening before you start shoveling.

- **Pam No Stick Cooking Spray.** Spray Pam No Stick Cooking Spray on the snow shovel.
- **Turtle Wax.** Cover the shovel with two thick coats of Turtle Wax.
- **Wesson Corn Oil.** Coat the shovel with Wesson Corn Oil.

Paint snow with . . .

- **McCormick/Schilling Food Coloring.** Put a teaspoon of food coloring in a spray bottle filled with water and let kids spray designs on snow.

Provide traction on snow-covered driveways and sidewalks with . . .

- **Tidy Cat.** Sprinkle unused Tidy Cat on the snow-covered surface.

Solar-Powered Camping Shower

Make a solar-powered camping shower with . . .

- **Glad Trash Bags.** Fill a Glad Trash Bag with water, tie it to a solid tree branch, and let the sun heat the water. After you lather up with soap, poke a small hole in the bag to rinse off.

The Secret Life of Horseradish

It may sound completely insane, but horseradish can be used to decontaminate industrial wastewater, according to a 1995 study at Pennsylvania State University that received a $450,000 grant from the Environmental Protection Agency.

Mother Earth News explained how it works: "The horseradish is harvested in tons; then the root is separated from the rest of the bushy plant and minced thoroughly. The horseradish and a proportionate amount of hydrogen peroxide are then added to the polluted water. In half an hour, the pollutants are neutralized, forming insoluble polymers which can be easily filtered from the water."

Horseradish is most effective against phenols—toxic by-products of steel and iron manufacturing, paper bleaching, coal conversion, ore mining, and the production of dyes, plastics, and pesticides.

Horseradish's rigid tissue stabilizes the enzyme peroxidase, traps it, and then causes phenols to precipitate, allowing them to be removed by filtration.

Extracting peroxidase from horseradish is expensive, making the cost of purifying 66,000 gallons of wastewater about $2.5 million. Using minced horseradish, which works equally well, costs only $920.

The same horseradish can be used for up to thirty treatments of toxic water. The only by-product is the used horseradish.

Thermos Bottles
(See page 204)

Toilet Paper
Keep toilet paper waterproof while camping with . . .

● **Maxwell House Coffee.** Carry a roll of toilet paper inside an empty Maxwell House Coffee can.

Waterproofing
Waterproof a backpack with . . .

● **Glad Trash Bags.** Cover the backpack with a Glad Trash Bag and cut small slits in the bag for the straps of the backpack.

Waterproof tents, backpacks, and sleeping bags with . . .

● **Scotchgard.** Stay dry during a camping trip by spraying your gear with Scotchgard.

Windbreakers
Improvise a windbreaker with . . .

● **Glad Trash Bags.** Cut holes in a Glad Trash Bag for your head and arms, and wear it under your coat.

Zippers
(See page 87)

Paint Your House

with Carnation Nonfat Dry Milk

Buckets

Make a paint bucket with . . .

● **Clorox.** Cut a hole in the side of an empty, clean Clorox Bleach jug opposite the handle.

Cleaning

Prevent spray paint from sticking in your hair with . . .

● **Alberto VO5 Conditioning Hairdressing.** Before spray painting, slick a dab of Alberto VO5 Conditioning Hairdressing the size of a quarter over your hair so you can wash away the paint more easily.

Make cleaning up after painting easy with . . .

● **Alberto VO5 Conditioning Hairdressing.** Lightly coating your hands with Alberto VO5 Conditioning Hairdressing before painting allows you to clean them off afterward without harsh solvents.

Clean oil-based paint from hands with . . .

- **Baby Oil.** Rub with baby oil to remove paint.
- **Coppertone.** Coppertone removes paint and stain from hands more gently than turpentine.
- **Wesson Corn Oil.** Use Wesson Corn Oil instead of turpentine.

Remove varnish from hands with . . .

- **Spray 'n Wash.** Spray hands with Spray 'n Wash, rub, then wash with soap and water. Spray 'n Wash generally works better than turpentine, without burning the skin.

Remove latex paint from hands with . . .

- **Barbasol Shaving Cream.** The emollients and moisturizers in Barbasol ease latex paint from skin.

Paint

Retouch walls with . . .

- **Kiwi Shoe Polish.** Touch up scratches, scuff marks, and holes from picture hooks with a dab of the appropriate color Kiwi Shoe Polish.

Stain wood with . . .

- **Kiwi Shoe Polish.** Apply Kiwi Shoe Polish with a dry cloth.

Prevent a skin from forming in paint cans with . . .

- **Reynolds Cut-Rite Wax Paper.** Place the paint can lid on a sheet of Reynolds Cut-Rite Wax Paper, trace around the lid, and cut a pattern from the wax paper. Lay the wax paper directly on the surface of the paint in the can and replace the lid. The wax paper will keep the oil- or water-based paints fresh for months.

- **Reynolds Wrap.** To prevent a layer of skin from forming over the paint surface, set the paint can on top of a sheet of Reynolds Wrap, trace around it, cut out a disk of foil, and place it on the paint surface before sealing the can.

- **Saran Wrap.** Place a sheet of Saran Wrap over the open paint can before tapping the lid closed with a hammer.

Paint your house with . . .

- **Carnation Nonfat Dry Milk.** Mix one and a half cups Carnation Nonfat Dry Milk and one-half cup water until it is the consistency of paint. Blend in water-based color to make the desired hue. Thin the paint by adding more water; thicken the paint by adding more powdered milk. Brush on as you would any other paint. Let the first coat dry for at least twenty-four hours before adding a second coat. Let  the second dry for three days. Early American colonists made their milk paint from the milk used to boil berries, resulting in an attractive gray color. This paint is extremely durable. To strip milk paint, apply ammonia, allow it to dry for about four days, then apply bleach. Make sure you are stripping the paint in a well-ventilated area.

Paintbrushes

Store wet paintbrushes with . . .

● **Reynolds Wrap.** Wrap the wet brushes in Reynolds Wrap and store them in your freezer. When you're ready to paint again, defrost the brushes for an hour or more.

Keep paintbrushes soft with . . .

● **Downy Fabric Softener.** Add a drop of Downy Fabric Softener to the final rinse.

Keep paintbrush bristles from bending while soaking in solvent with . . .

● **Maxwell House Coffee.** Put solvent in an empty Maxwell House Coffee can, cut an X in the plastic lid, and push the brush handle up through the slit so the brush is hanging in the can rather than resting on its bristles.

Apply wood stain, varnish, or polyurethane with . . .

● **L'eggs Sheer Energy.** Old L'eggs make great substitutes for paintbrushes. Ball up the panty hose and use it like a sponge, or secure it to a stick with several rubber bands.

Paint crevices with . . .

● **Q-Tips Cotton Swabs.** Dip one end of a Q-Tips Cotton Swab into the paint.

Odor

Eliminate paint odor with . . .

● **McCormick/Schilling Pure Vanilla Extract.** Mix two teaspoons McCormick/Schilling Pure Vanilla Extract per gallon of paint.

Splatters

Protect chandeliers and hanging lamps when painting a ceiling with . . .

- **Glad Trash Bags.** Pull a Glad Trash Bag over the lighting fixture and tie it up as high on the chain as possible.

Avoid splattering paint on windows, hinges, doorknobs, and lock latches with . . .

- **Alberto VO5 Conditioning Hairdressing.** Coat them with Alberto VO5 Conditioning Hairdressing to prevent paint from adhering to the surfaces. After painting, wipe clean with a cloth.
- **Reynolds Wrap.** Mold Reynolds Wrap around doorknobs when painting.
- **Vaseline.** Before painting a room, dip a Q-Tips Cotton Swab in Vaseline Petroleum Jelly and run it around the edges of the glass; coat door hinges, doorknobs, lock latches; and spread a thin coat of Vaseline Petroleum Jelly along a linoleum or tile floor (obviously not carpet) where it meets the wall. Paint smears will wipe off with a cloth.

Spray Paint Cans

Clean clogged spray paint can nozzles with . . .

- **WD-40.** Remove the nozzles from the spray paint can and the WD-40 can, place the nozzle from the spray paint can on the WD-40 can, give it a couple of quick squirts, and replace both nozzles.

Strainers

Strain lumps from paint with . . .

- **L'eggs Sheer Energy.** Stretch a L'eggs Sheer Energy panty hose leg across the paint can and pour.

What's Really in It?

Coca-Cola
Carbonated water, high fructose corn syrup and/or sucrose, caffeine, phosphoric acid, caramel color, glycerin, lemon oil, orange oil, lime oil, cassia oil, nutmeg oil, vanilla extract, coca, and kola

Crayola Crayons
Paraffin wax, stearic acid, colored pigment

Cream of Tartar
Potassium bitartrate ($KHC_4H_4O_6$)

Krazy Glue
Modified ethyl cyanoacrylate

Lea & Perrins Worcestershire Sauce
Water, vinegar, molasses, high-fructose corn syrup, anchovies, hydrolated soy and corn protein, onions, tamarinds, salt, garlic, cloves, chili peppers, natural flavorings, and échalotes

Lubriderm
Water, mineral oil, petrolatum, sorbitol, lanolin, lanolin alcohol, stearic acid, triethanolamine, cetyl alcohol, fragrance, butylparaben, methylparaben, propylparaben, sodium chloride

Miracle Whip
Soybean oil, water, vinegar, sugar, egg yolks, starch, food

starch-modified, salt, mustard flour, spice, paprika, natural flavor

Pam No Stick Cooking Spray
Canola oil, grain alcohol from corn (added for clarity), lecithin from soybeans (prevents sticking), and propellant

Scotchgard
Naphthol spirits, carbon dioxide, heptane, fluoroalkyl polymer, petroleum distillate, trichloroethane

Silly Putty
Boric acid, silicone oil

SPAM
Chopped pork shoulder, chopped pork ham, water, salt, sugar, and sodium nitrate

Tang
Sugar, fructose, citric acid (provides tartness), calcium phosphate (prevents caking), potassium citrate (controls acidity), ascorbic acid (vitamin C), orange juice solids, natural flavor, titanium dioxide (for color), xanthan and cellulose gums (provide body), yellow 5, yellow 6, niacinamide, artificial flavor, vitamin A palmitate, vitamin B_6, riboflavin (vitamin B_2), BHA (preserves freshness), folic acid

Wonder Bread
Enriched wheat flour (barley malt, niacin, iron [ferrous sulfate], thiamin mononitrate, riboflavin), water, high-fructose

corn syrup, yeast, contains 2 percent or less of: salt, vegetable oil (contains one or more of: canola oil, corn oil, cottonseed oil, soybean oil), soy flour, calcium sulfate, sodium stearoyl lactylate, monoglycerides, starch, yeast nutrients (ammonium sulfate), leavenings (monocalcium phosphate), vinegar, wheat gluten

Shave with

Jif Peanut Butter

Acne

Dry up acne pimples with . . .

- **Colgate Toothpaste.** Dab Colgate on pimples.
- **Listerine.** Use a cotton ball to dab Listerine on blemishes.
- **ReaLemon.** Dab ReaLemon on the blemish a few times a day.

Eliminate blackheads with . . .

- **Epsom Salt.** Add one teaspoon Epsom Salt and three drops of iodine to one-half cup boiling water. After the mixture has cooled a bit, dip strips of cotton into the solution and apply to the problem area. Repeat three or four times, reheating the solution if necessary. Then, gently unclog your pores and go over the area with an alcohol-based astringent.
- **ReaLemon.** Rub ReaLemon over blackheads before going to bed. Wait until morning to wash off the juice

with cool water. Repeat for several nights until you see a big improvement in the skin.

Back Scrubber
Scrub your back with . . .

● **L'eggs Sheer Energy.** Place a bar of soap inside one leg of a pair of L'eggs Sheer Energy at the knee, tie knots on both sides of it, hold one end of the stocking in each hand, and seesaw it across your back in the bathtub.

Bangs
(See page 163)

Bathing
Make your own scented bath oil with . . .

● **Baby Oil.** Mix one-quarter cup baby oil with a few drops of your favorite perfume or cologne for an aromatic, moisturizing bath.

Take a soothing bath with . . .

● **Arm & Hammer Baking Soda.** Dissolve one-half cup Arm & Hammer Baking Soda in a tub of warm water for soft, smooth-feeling skin and a relaxing bath.

● **Coppertone.** Add two tablespoons Coppertone to a warm bath as a bath oil.

Take a mustard bath with . . .

● **Gulden's Mustard.** Spoon six tablespoons Gulden's Mustard and a handful of Epsom Salt into the bathtub as it fills.

Take a milk bath with . . .

● **Carnation Nonfat Dry Milk.** Add one-half cup Carnation Nonfat Dry Milk to warm water for a soothing bath.

Breath

Freshen your breath with . . .

● **Dr. Bronner's Peppermint Soap.** Add a dash of Dr. Bronner's Peppermint Soap to a glass of water and rinse your mouth. Dr. Bronner's Peppermint Soap is 100 percent vegetable oil, but be certain not to swallow soap.

Bubble Bath

Make bubble bath with . . .

● **Clairol Herbal Essences.** Pour one capful of Clairol Herbal Essences under a running tap in the bathtub.

● **Ivory Soap.** Hold a bar of Ivory Soap under a running faucet to fill the tub with bubbles.

● **Wesson Corn Oil.** Mix two cups Wesson Corn Oil, three tablespoons liquid shampoo, and one-quarter teaspoon of your favorite perfume. Mix the solution in a blender at high speed.

Conditioner

Condition your hair with . . .

● **Aunt Jemima Original Syrup.** Massage Aunt Jemima Original Syrup into dry hair, cover hair with a shower cap for thirty minutes, then shampoo and rinse thoroughly.

● **Epsom Salt.** Combine three tablespoons deep con-

LOOK, MOM, NO CAVITIES

Poison toothpaste is used by the CIA as a weapon for assassinations, according to Larry Devlin, a CIA agent who was instructed to kill ousted Belgian Congo Prime Minister Patrice Lumumba. "I received instructions to see that Lumumba was removed from the world," Devlin told *Time* magazine in 1993. "I received poison toothpaste, among other devices, but never used them."

Wacky Birth Control

- In ancient Egypt and Greece, women were advised to insert olive oil or honey into their vaginas for contraceptive purposes. Olive oil or honey was thought to prevent sperm from entering the uterus. They don't.

- Shaking up a bottle of Coca-Cola for use as a douche immediately after sexual intercourse has been considered an effective method of contraception among the uneducated. It does not work.

- The word *vanilla* stems from the latin word *vagina*, perhaps because the vanilla fruit pod vaguely resembles a sheath or possibly because vanilla was considered an aphrodisiac.

- Rumor contends that a piece of Saran Wrap can be used as an impromptu condom. It does not work. Plastic film does not withstand the friction of sexual intercourse nor does it provide an adequate barrier against sperm.

ditioner with three tablespoons Epsom Salt. Microwave the mixture for twenty minutes. Work the warm mixture through your hair from scalp to ends and leave on for twenty minutes. Rinse with warm water. Promotes body and life in your hair and restores curl to permed hair.

- **Heinz Vinegar.** Shampoo, then rinse hair with a mixture of one cup Heinz Apple Cider Vinegar and two cups water. Vinegar adds highlights to brunette hair, restores the acid mantel, and removes soap film and sebum oil.

- **Miracle Whip.** Apply one-half cup Miracle Whip to dry hair once a week as a conditioner. Leave on for thirty minutes, then rinse a few times before shampooing thoroughly.
- **Reddi-wip.** Apply one-half cup Reddi-wip to dry hair once a week as a conditioner. Leave on for thirty minutes, then rinse a few times before shampooing thoroughly.
- **Star Olive Oil.** Warm up Star Olive Oil, massage it into your hair and scalp, wrap your head in a towel, and sit under a dryer. Later, shampoo as usual.
- **SueBee Honey.** Mix one tablespoon SueBee Honey and two teaspoons Star Olive Oil. Warm the mixture (but not too hot), dip your fingers into it, and rub it into the strands of hair. Soak a towel in hot water, wring out completely, and wrap around your head for twenty minutes. Then shampoo as usual, lathering well to remove the olive oil.
- **Wesson Corn Oil.** Massage lukewarm Wesson Corn Oil into dry hair, cover hair with a shower cap for thirty minutes, then shampoo and rinse thoroughly.

Contact Lenses
Identify contact lenses quickly with . . .
- **Con-Tact Paper.** Add a colorful dot of

Con-Tact Paper to your contract lens holder to easily identify the left and right lenses.

Cream Rinse
Cream rinse your hair with . . .
- **Downy Fabric Softener.** If you're out of cream rinse, use a drop of Downy Fabric Softener in your final rinse.

Curlers
Set your hair in curlers with . . .
- **Kleenex Tissue.** Use Kleenex Tissues to provide cushioning under hair curlers.

Store hair curlers with . . .
- **Kleenex Tissue.** A decorative Kleenex Tissue box, when empty, makes an excellent container for storing hair curlers.

Dandruff
(See page 230)

Dentures
Clean dentures with . . .
- **Dr. Bronner's Peppermint Soap.** Add a drop of Dr. Bronner's Peppermint Soap to a glass of water, soak the dentures for ten minutes, then scrub clean with cool water.
- **Heinz Vinegar.** Soak dentures overnight in Heinz White Vinegar, then brush away tartar with a toothbrush.
- **L'eggs Sheer Energy.** Cut a small piece of nylon from the L'eggs and polish dentures.

Deodorant

Deodorize with . . .

- **Arm & Hammer Baking Soda.** Dust Arm & Hammer Baking Soda under arms.
- **Dr. Bronner's Peppermint Soap.** Wet your hand and apply a drop of Dr. Bronner's Peppermint Soap under your arms. According to the label, "Peppermint is nature's own unsurpassed fragrant deodorant!"
- **Listerine.** Listerine helps kill the bacteria that cause perspiration odor. Dab it under your arms.

Dry Shampoo

Give your hair a dry shampoo with . . .

- **Kingsford's Corn Starch.** Work Kingsford's Corn Starch into your hair, then brush out.
- **Quaker Oats.** Apply dry Quaker Oats to your hair, work it through with your fingers, and brush it out to remove the oils.

Eyebrows

Groom your eyebrows with . . .

- **ChapStick.** A little ChapStick will keep bushy eyebrow hairs in place.
- **Oral-B Toothbrushes.** Use a clean, old Oral-B Toothbrush.

Eyeglasses

Fix a broken eyeglass lens temporarily with . . .

WORCESTERSHIRE HAIR TONIC?

An advertisement in 1919 falsely claimed that Worcestershire Sauce was "a wonderful liquid tonic that makes your hair grow beautiful."

- **Scotch Transparent Tape.** Use a small piece of Scotch Transparent Tape at the top and bottom of the crack.

Repair broken eyeglasses temporarily with . . .

- **Forster Toothpicks.** If you lose a screw from your eyeglasses, substitute a Forster Toothpick in its place until you can get it fixed properly.
- **Wrigley's Spearmint Gum.** In an emergency, put a small piece of chewed Wrigley's Spearmint Gum in the corner of the lens to hold it in place.

Label your eyeglass case with . . .

- **Avery Laser Labels.** Print your name, address, and phone number on an Avery Laser Label and adhere it inside your eyeglass case.

Facials

Give yourself a moisturizing facial with . . .

- **Quaker Oats.** Make a paste from Quaker Oats, lemon juice, and honey. Apply to face, let sit for ten minutes, then rinse with warm water.
- **Reddi-wip.** Reddi-wip helps moisten dry skin when applied as a face mask. Wait twenty minutes, then wash it off with warm water followed by cold water.
- **SueBee Honey.** Mash a banana and add one tablespoon SueBee

Honey. Cover your face with the mixture, let sit fifteen minutes, then rinse with warm water.

Give yourself a facial and tighten pores with . . .

- **Miracle Whip.** Miracle Whip helps moisten dry skin when applied as a face mask. Wait twenty minutes, then wash it off with warm water followed by cold water.

Give yourself a facial, scalp, and soothing body rub with . . .

- **Dr. Bronner's Peppermint Soap.** Place a hand towel in a sink filled with hot water, and add a dash of Dr. Bronner's Peppermint Soap. Wring out the towel, lay it over your face and scalp, and massage with fingertips. Repeat procedure until you have rubbed your arms, legs, and body. Rinse towel in plain hot water and massage again.

Make a facial mask with . . .

- **Pepto-Bismol.** Spread Pepto-Bismol over your face, wait twenty minutes, then wash with lukewarm water.

Minimize oily skin with . . .

- **Phillips' Milk of Magnesia.** Apply Phillips' Milk of Magnesia as a thin mask over your face, let dry, then rinse off with warm water.

Clean dry skin with . . .

- **Gerber Applesauce.** Rub applesauce over your face, wait thirty minutes, and wash with lukewarm water. Pure applesauce cleans dry skin naturally.

Tighten pores and cleanse skin with . . .

- **Dannon Yogurt.** Spread Dannon Yogurt over your

face, wait twenty minutes, then wash with lukewarm water.

● **Epsom Salt.** To cleanse and exfoliate your skin, massage handfuls of Epsom Salt over your wet skin, starting with your feet and continuing up toward your face. Then pour two cups of Epsom Salt into a bath of warm water. Sit back and relax. The natural action will soften your skin while easing the kinks and stiffness in your muscles.

Feet

Soothe tired feet with . . .

● **Alberto VO5 Conditioning Hairdressing.** Before going to bed, coat your feet with Alberto VO5 Conditioning Hairdressing and put on a pair of socks.

● **Arm & Hammer Baking Soda.** Add three tablespoons Arm & Hammer Baking Soda to a basin of warm water and soak feet in the solution.

● **Gulden's Mustard.** Fill a pan with warm water and mix in three tablespoons Gulden's Mustard.

● **Wesson Corn Oil.** Rub warmed Wesson Corn Oil into your feet, wrap in a damp hot towel, and sit for ten minutes.

Freckles

Minimize freckles with . . .

● **Coppertone.** Freckles can sometimes be minimized by using sunscreen lotions containing para-aminobenzoic acid (PABA). Freckles are caused by an accumulation of the skin pigment melanin, which responds unevenly to sunlight.

Hair Care

Minimize drying out your hair in a chlorinated pool with . . .

- **Alberto VO5 Conditioning Hairdressing.** Rub a long dab of Alberto VO5 Conditioning Hairdressing through your hair before taking a swim.

Remove conditioner and styling gel buildup from hair with . . .

- **Arm & Hammer Baking Soda.** Wash hair once a week with a tablespoon of Arm & Hammer Baking Soda mixed with your regular shampoo; rinse thoroughly, then condition and style as usual.

- **Epsom Salt.** Combine one gallon distilled water, one cup ReaLemon, and one cup Epsom Salt. Cap the mixture and let it sit for twenty-four hours. The next day, pour the mixture into your dry hair and let it sit for twenty minutes. Then shampoo as normal.

Prevent static electricity in your hair with . . .

- **Alberto VO5 Conditioning Hairdressing.** Comb a dab of Alberto VO5 Conditioning Hairdressing through your hair.

Protect your scalp during a permanent with . . .

- **Alberto VO5 Conditioning Hairdressing.** Rub some Alberto VO5 Conditioning Hairdressing into the scalp before giving yourself a perm.

Hair Coloring

Change blond hair dyed green by chlorine back to its original color with . . .

- **Canada Dry Club Soda.** Simply rinse your green hair with Canada Dry Club Soda.

Create blond highlights with . . .

- **ReaLemon.** Rinse your hair with one-quarter cup ReaLemon in three-quarters cup water.

Prevent hair coloring from dyeing your skin with . . .

- **Alberto VO5 Conditioning Hairdressing.** Dab a little Alberto VO5 Conditioning Hairdressing on your forehead and around your hairline and ears to help keep the color from staining your skin.
- **ChapStick.** Rub ChapStick along your hairline before coloring your hair.
- **Vaseline.** Rub Vaseline Petroleum Jelly along hairline before coloring your hair.

Highlight brown or red hair with . . .

- **Lipton Tea Bags.** Rinse red or brown hair with brewed Lipton Tea for golden highlights.
- **Maxwell House Coffee.** Rinse your hair with Maxwell House Coffee for a rich and shiny color.

Hand Cleaner

Clean ink from hands with . . .

- **Crisco All-Vegetable Shortening.** Apply Crisco All-Vegetable Shortening and wipe clean.
- **Colgate Toothpaste.** Squeeze an inch of Colgate into your palm and wash hands under running water.

Lips

(Also see page 227)

Prevent chapped lips with . . .

- **Coppertone.** Coppertone keeps lips moist and healthy.

Razor-Sharp Shaving Facts

● A typical shave will cut about 20,000 to 25,000 facial hairs.

● Shaving in the shower wastes an average of ten to thirty-five gallons of water. To conserve water, fill the sink basin with an inch of water and vigorously rinse your razor often in the water after every second or third stroke.

● A typical razor blade today is good for about ten shaves.

● Nine out of ten men shave. Three of those men use electric razors.

● Shaving daily with a wet razor exfoliates the beard area of the face, loosening and removing the top layer of skin cells, which is believed to help the skin retain its vitality and youthful appearance.

● According to archaeologists, men shaved their faces as far back as the Stone Age—20,000 years ago. Prehistoric men shaved with clam shells, shark teeth, sharpened pieces of flint, and knives.

● Ancient Egyptians shaved their faces and heads before hand-to-hand combat so the enemy had less to grab. Archaeologists have discovered gold and copper razors in Egyptian tombs dating back to the fourth century B.C.

● The longest beard, according to *The Guinness Book of Records,* measured 17.5 feet long and was presented to the Smithsonian Institute in 1967.

● Seventy percent of women rate clean-shaven men as sexy.

Makeup

Apply makeup with . . .

- **Q-Tips Cotton Swabs.** Use a Q-Tips Cotton Swab to apply eyeshadow or remove excess mascara.

Remove makeup with . . .

- **Alberto VO5 Conditioning Hairdressing.** A dab of Alberto VO5 Conditioning Hairdressing on a tissue or cotton ball gently removes makeup.
- **Baby Oil.** Dab on baby oil, wait ten minutes, and remove with cotton balls. Baby oil gently removes mascara, leaving a thin, protective film that moisturizes lids and lashes.
- **Carnation Nonfat Dry Milk.** Mix a teaspoon of Carnation Nonfat Dry Milk with warm water, apply with a cotton ball, wipe clean, and rinse.
- **Reddi-wip.** Wet face with lukewarm water, spread a handful of Reddi-wip on face, rinse clean with lukewarm water, and blot dry.
- **Vaseline.** Vaseline Petroleum Jelly takes off mascara, eyeliner, lipstick, rouge, and powders.

Massages

Enjoy a massage with . . .

- **Coppertone.** Coppertone is an excellent massage oil.

Give yourself a foot massage with . . .

- **Wilson Tennis Balls.** Roll your foot over a Wilson Tennis Ball.

Make a back massager with . . .

- **Wilson Tennis Balls.** Put several Wilson Tennis Balls inside a sock and tie at the end. This is frequently used by a labor coach to massage the back of a woman in labor.

Moisturizers

Moisturize your face with . . .

- **Alberto VO5 Conditioning Hairdressing.** Rub a little Alberto VO5 Conditioning Hairdressing in the lines around your eyes to help prevent dry lines.
- **ChapStick.** Rubbing ChapStick on your face protects the skin from windburn while snow skiing.
- **Vaseline.** Wash your face thoroughly and, while still wet, rub in a small dab of Vaseline Petroleum Jelly. Keep wetting face until the Vaseline Petroleum Jelly is spread evenly and does not appear greasy. Health spas use this secret treatment.

Moisturize your hands with . . .

- **Coppertone.** The emollients in Coppertone rejuvenate dry skin.

Moisturize skin with . . .

- **Wesson Corn Oil.** Massage Wesson Corn Oil into your skin, wait fifteen minutes, remove the excess oil with Viva Paper Towels, then take a hot bath.

Prevent dry skin in a steam-heated or air-conditioned room with . . .

- **Lubriderm.** Use extra Lubriderm. Steam heat and air-conditioning dry skin.

Mousse

Mousse your hair with . . .

- **Jell-O.** A teaspoon of Jell-O dissolved in a cup of warm water makes an inexpensive setting lotion. Or use prepared Jell-O as you would any hair gel product.

- **Miller High Life.** Miller High Life works as a setting lotion. Shampoo your hair, towel dry, and then spray beer onto your hair using a pump bottle before setting. Excellent for oily hair.

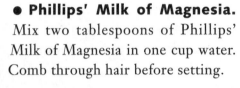

- **Phillips' Milk of Magnesia.** Mix two tablespoons of Phillips' Milk of Magnesia in one cup water. Comb through hair before setting.

Mouthwash
Wash your mouth with . . .
- **Arm & Hammer Baking Soda.** Add one teaspoon Arm & Hammer Baking Soda to one-half glass warm water, and swish through teeth for a refreshing mouthwash.

Mustaches
Groom a mustache with . . .
- **ChapStick.** A little ChapStick will keep the ends of a mustache waxed together.
- **Oral-B Toothbrushes.** Use a clean Oral-B Toothbrush.

Nails
Dry nail polish with . . .
- **Pam No Stick Cooking Spray.** After polishing your nails, spray with Pam No Stick Cooking Spray.

Fix a broken fingernail with . . .
- **Krazy Glue.** Use a small drop of Krazy Glue to secure the nail in place, then coat with nail polish.
- **Lipton Tea Bags.** Cut a piece of gauze paper from a

Lipton Flo-Thru Tea Bag to fit the nail, coat with Maybelline Crystal Clear Nail Polish, and press gently against the break. Then cover with colored nail polish.

Give a manicure or pedicure with . . .

- **Oral-B Toothbrushes.** A clean Oral-B Toothbrush dipped in soapy water is both gentle and effective for cleaning fingernails and toenails.

Prevent hangnails with . . .

- **Lubriderm.** Moisturize your cuticles daily. Rub Lubriderm into the flesh surrounding your nails to keep the area soft.

Prevent the cap from sticking shut on nail polish bottles with . . .

- **Vaseline.** Put a thin coat of Vaseline Petroleum Jelly around the rim of the bottle.

Soften fingernails with . . .

- **Coppertone.** Warm Coppertone and use as a hot oil treatment to soften nails.

Soften dry cuticles with . . .

- **Alberto VO5 Conditioning Hairdressing.** Rub on a dab of Alberto VO5 Conditioning Hairdressing.

Soften brittle fingernails with . . .

- **Baby Oil.** Warm a few tablespoons of baby oil and soak your nails for ten minutes.

THE JOYS OF DRÃNO

According to Shelly Lavigne, author of *Boy or Girl: 50 Fun Ways to Find Out*, a pregnant woman can use Drãno to determine whether she is carrying a boy or a girl. "Add one tablespoon of crystal Drãno to a small amount of your first-of-the-morning urine," explains Lavigne. "Wait a bit. If the mixture turns a bluish-yellow color, that signals a boy. If it turns greenish-brown, count on a baby girl."

Whiten, brighten, and strengthen fingernails with . . .

- **ReaLemon.** Soak fingernails in ReaLemon for ten minutes, then brush with a mixture of equal parts white vinegar and warm water. Rinse well.

Nursing Pads
Improvise nursing pads with . . .

- **Kleenex Tissue.** Nursing mothers can fold a Kleenex Tissue in quarters and secure it inside a bra as an impromptu absorbent pad.

Panty Liners
Improvise panty liners with . . .

- **Kleenex Tissue.** In a pinch, a couple of folded Kleenex Tissues can be used as an impromptu panty liner.

Perfume
Perfume yourself with . . .

- **McCormick/Schilling Vanilla Extract.** A dab of vanilla extract behind each ear makes a delightful fragrance. (Incidentally, vanilla is considered to be an aphrodisiac.)

Personal Items
Identify your camera with . . .

- **Avery Laser Labels.** Print your name on an Avery Laser Label and adhere it to the back of your camera so you can easily identify it at family get-togethers or parties where many people bring the same type of camera.

Sex

Improve marital relations with . . .

- **Bosco.** Everyone knows Bosco chocolate syrup is a seductive temptation that's hard to resist.
- **Reddi-wip.** Give new meaning to the phrase "dessert topping."

Shampoo

Wash your hair with . . .

- **Dr. Bronner's Peppermint Soap.** Fill an empty shampoo bottle with water and two teaspoons of Dr. Bronner's Peppermint Soap, shake, and use the solution like shampoo. Or simply get wet in the shower and squirt a few drops from the bottle into your hair.
- **Epsom Salt.** Add three tablespoons Epsom Salt to one-half cup liquid shampoo made for oily hair. The Epsom Salt acts like a magnet to soak up the oil from hair. Apply one tablespoon of this mixture to dry hair. Massage in well, then rinse with cold water. Next, add the juice of one lemon to a cup of lukewarm water. Pour on your hair and leave it for ten minutes. Finally, rinse thoroughly with cool water.
- **Kingsford's Corn Starch.** Kingsford's Corn Starch can be used as a dry shampoo. Work into your hair, then brush out.

From the Peanut Gallery

- A twenty-eight-ounce jar of Jif contains 1,218 peanuts.
- Peanut butter sticks to the roof of your mouth because its high protein content draws moisture from your mouth.
- Peanut butter is the most commonly used form of the peanut. Half of America's 1.6-million ton annual peanut crop is used to make peanut butter.
- Pound for pound, peanuts have more protein, minerals, and vitamins than beef liver.
- The Adults Only Peanut-Butter Lovers Fan Club publishes a newsletter called *Spread the News*, hosts annual conventions for peanut butter fanatics, and distributes peanut butter recipes.

- **Miller High Life.** Miller High Life is a terrific shampoo for oily hair, although shampooing your hair too frequently with beer can eventually dry out your scalp and lead to dandruff.
- **Palmolive.** In a pinch, Palmolive cleans hair just like many shampoos.
- **Tang.** The citric acid in Tang cuts through sebum oil in hair.

Shaving

Shave with . . .

- **Baby Oil.** Slathering on baby oil raises hair stubs for a clean shave, lubricates the razor, and moisturizes sensitive skin.

- **Bosco.** If you run out of shaving cream, in a pinch slather Bosco chocolate syrup on wet skin.
- **Clairol Herbal Essences.** Apply Clairol Herbal Essences to wet skin as a substitute for shaving cream.
- **Dr. Bronner's Peppermint Soap.** Add two squirts of Dr. Bronner's Peppermint Soap in a sink full of water, slather on your face or legs, and shave.
- **Jif Peanut Butter.** Former senator Barry Goldwater of Arizona once shaved with peanut butter while on a camping trip. (For best results, avoid shaving with Jif Extra Crunchy.)
- **Lubriderm.** If you run out of shaving cream, slather on Lubriderm.
- **Reddi-wip.** Apply Reddi-wip to wet skin as a substitute for shaving cream.
- **Star Olive Oil.** If you run out of shaving cream, try Star Olive Oil.

Prevent friction burns when shaving your legs with an electric razor with . . .

- **Kingsford's Corn Starch.** Dust legs lightly with Kingsford's Corn Starch before shaving.

Soothe your legs after shaving with . . .

- **Alberto VO5 Conditioning Hairdressing.** Rub some Alberto

VO5 Conditioning Hairdressing into your skin after shaving to make your legs feel velvety smooth.

Stop a shaving nick from bleeding with . . .

- **ChapStick.** Dab on some ChapStick if you nick yourself.
- **McCormick/Schilling Alum.** Dab on McCormick/Schilling Alum. Alum is the active ingredient in styptic pencils.

Skin

Soften rough hands with . . .

- **Kingsford's Corn Starch.** Apply Kingsford's Corn Starch as you would hand lotion.

Rejuvenate dry skin with . . .

- **Star Olive Oil.** Lubricate with Star Olive Oil.

Relieve rough hands or sore feet with . . .

- **ReaLemon.** Apply ReaLemon, rinse, then massage with olive oil.

Remove tar with . . .

- **Miracle Whip.** Spread a teaspoon of Miracle Whip on tar, rub, and wipe off.

Remove dead skin with . . .

- **Miracle Whip.** Rub a dab of Miracle Whip into your skin and let it dry for a few minutes. While the skin is moist, massage with your fingertips. Dead skin will rub off your feet, knees, elbows, or face.

Static Cling

Eliminate static cling from panty hose with . . .

- **Bounce.** Rub a slightly dampened sheet of Bounce over the hose.

Stress
Calm your nerves with . . .
- **Silly Putty.** Playing with Silly Putty has therapeutic value in reducing emotional pressure and calming nerves.
- **Slinky.** Bounce a Slinky between two hands and tension magically disappears.

Talcum Powder
Substitute for talcum powder with . . .
- **Kingsford's Corn Starch.** Apply Kingsford's Corn Starch sparingly. Corn starch is actually more absorbent than talcum powder, but apply lightly since it does cake more readily.

Teeth
Brush your teeth with . . .
- **Arm & Hammer Baking Soda.** Plain baking soda is a gentle abrasive that cleans like the strongest toothpaste. Apply Arm & Hammer Baking Soda to a damp toothbrush, brush as usual, and rinse. NOTE: Arm & Hammer Baking Soda does not contain fluoride.

Train a Dog to Stop Barking

with ReaLemon

Barking

Train a dog to stop barking with . . .

- **ReaLemon.** Squirt some ReaLemon in the dog's mouth and say "Quiet."

Bathing

Prevent clogged drains when bathing a dog with . . .

- **S.O.S Steel Wool Soap Pads.** Place a ball made from an S.O.S Steel Wool Soap Pad in the drain opening to catch stray hairs.

Bird Cages

Clean a bird cage more easily with . . .

- **Con-Tact Paper.** Line the base of the bird cage with colorful Con-Tact Paper to create a water-resistant surface that's easier to wash clean.

Line a bird cage with . . .

● **Kleenex Tissue.** Use Kleenex Tissues on the bottom of a bird cage to catch foul matter.

Brushes

Clean a dog or cat brush with . . .

● **Forster Toothpicks.** Run a Forster Toothpick through the rows of bristles.

Catnip Balls

Make a catnip ball with . . .

● **L'eggs Sheer Energy.** Stuff the toe of a L'eggs with catnip and knot it.

Coats

Remove burrs, tar, and sticky substances from a dog's hair with . . .

● **Wesson Corn Oil.** Saturate the area with Wesson Corn Oil. Wash with dog shampoo, rinse immediately, and brush clean.

Prevent cat hair balls and static electricity on your cat's coat with . . .

● **Alberto VO5 Conditioning Hairdressing.** Rub in a little Alberto VO5 Conditioning Hairdressing. (Don't worry if your cat licks its fur; Albert VO5 Conditioning Hairdressing is natural and nontoxic.)

Add a shine to your dog's coat with . . .

● **Wesson Corn Oil.** Add a teaspoon of Wesson Corn Oil to each food serving.

Detangle and shine a dog's coat with . . .

- **Alberto VO5 Conditioning Hairdressing.** Comb in a small amount of Alberto VO5 Conditioning Hairdressing.

Cows

Milk cows organically with . . .

- **Heinz Vinegar.** Clean milking equipment with unperfumed dish detergent followed with a Heinz Vinegar rinse. Pipes, hoses, and bulk tank will come out squeaky clean without any odor, lowering the bacteria count.

Deer

Repulse deer with . . .

- **Ivory Soap.** Hang bars of Ivory Soap around crops.

Dry Shampoo

Give your dog a dry shampoo with . . .

- **Kingsford's Corn Starch.** Rub Kingsford's Corn Starch into your dog's fur, then comb and brush out.

Ear Mites

Treat ear mites in cats with . . .

- **Wesson Corn Oil.** Put a few drops of Wesson Corn Oil into your cat's ear and massage. Then clean out all debris with a ball of cotton. Repeat daily for three days, and the mites should be gone. The oil soothes the cat's sensitive skin, smothers the mites, and promotes healing.

Fish Tanks
Color the water in a fish tank with . . .

- **McCormick/Schilling Food Coloring.** Adding a few drops of food coloring will make a colorful environment without harming the fish.

Fleas
Repel fleas with . . .

- **Morton Salt.** Since salt repels fleas, wash your dog's doghouse with salt water to keep them away.

Furniture
Keep dogs and cats off furniture with . . .

- **Reynolds Wrap.** Place pieces of Reynolds Wrap on the furniture. The sound of rustling foil frightens pets.

Prevent cats from scratching dark woodwork with . . .

- **Tabasco Pepper Sauce.** Rub the area with Tabasco sauce and buff thoroughly. The faint smell of Tabasco Pepper Sauce repels cats.

Hair
Prevent cat hair balls with . . .

- **Wesson Corn Oil.** Add a teaspoon of Wesson Corn Oil to one cat meal daily.

Remove pet hair from furniture with . . .

- **Alberto VO5 Hair Spray.** Spray a tissue with Alberto VO5 Hair Spray and, while sticky, pick up those hairs.
- **Bounce.** Rubbing the area with a sheet of Bounce will magnetically attract all the loose hairs.
- **Scotch Packaging Tape.** Wrap a strip of Scotch Pack-

aging Tape around your hand, adhesive side out, and pat.
● **Silly Putty.** Flatten the Silly Putty into a pancake and pat the surface.

Hens

Prevent hens from eating their own eggs with . . .

● **Gulden's Mustard.** Paint a little mustard on the eggshell.

Horses

Detangle a horse's mane and tail with . . .

● **Alberto VO5 Conditioning Hairdressing.** Brush in a little Alberto VO5 Conditioning Hairdressing.

Prevent a leather saddle from drying out with . . .

● **Alberto VO5 Conditioning Hairdressing.** Rub in a little Alberto VO5 Conditioning Hairdressing.

Prevent shaved horse hair from growing back white with . . .

● **Preparation H.** Apply Preparation H to the shaved skin of the horse every day.

Prevent snow from balling up under a horse's hooves with . . .

● **Pam No Stick Cooking Spray.** Spray Pam No Stick Cooking Spray on the bottom of the horse's hooves before going out for a winter ride.

Shine a horse's hooves with . . .

● **Alberto VO5 Conditioning Hairdressing.** Rub in a little Alberto VO5 Conditioning Hairdressing.

Litter Boxes

Deodorize a cat litter box with . . .

- **Arm & Hammer Baking Soda.** Cover the bottom of the litter box with one-quarter inch Arm & Hammer Baking Soda, then add the litter.
- **20 Mule Team Borax.** Mix one and a half cups 20 Mule Team Borax to every five pounds of cat filler to reduce and control odor in the cat box.

Mange

Cure Mange with . . .

- **WD-40.** While spraying a dog with WD-40 gets rid of parasitic mites, according to *USA Today*, the WD-40 Company, feeling that the potential misuse of the product is too great, refuses to condone using WD-40 to cure mange on animals.

Paw Pads

Protect your dog's or cat's paw pads with . . .

- **Alberto VO5 Conditioning Hairdressing.** Rub in a little Alberto VO5 Conditioning Hairdressing before sending your pet outdoors.

Pet Dishes

Improvise a pet dish with a . . .

- **Frisbee.** When camping or hiking, an upside-down Frisbee works well as a food or water dish for your dog.

Pooper Scoopers

Make a pooper scooper with . . .

- **Clorox.** Cut an empty, clean Clorox Bleach jug in half. Use the half with the handle to scoop.

Shedding

Slow a dog from shedding with . . .

- **Star Olive Oil.** Pour one table-spoon Star Olive Oil on your dog's food while a dog is shedding.

Decrease pet shedding in the house with . . .

- **Velcro.** Adhere strips of Velcro around your pet's flexible door so your dog or cat brushes against the strips, keeping loose hair behind.

Skunk

Eliminate skunk odor on pets with . . .

- **Campbell's Tomato Juice.** Using rubber gloves to avoid getting the skunk odor on yourself, pour Campbell's Tomato Juice over your pet and rub it in. Sponge it over the pet's face. Rinse and repeat.

Stains

Eliminate animal urine stains from carpets with . . .

- **Heinz Vinegar.** Blot up urine, flush several times with lukewarm water, then apply a mixture of equal parts Heinz White Vinegar and cool water. Blot up, rinse, and let dry. The vinegar deodorizes the spot and prevents the animal from urinating in that spot again.

Clean up pet accidents with . . .

- **Arm & Hammer Baking Soda.** Clean with club soda, let dry thoroughly, then sprinkle on Arm & Hammer Baking Soda, allow to sit for fifteen minutes, then vacuum up.

Neutralize pet urine with . . .

- **20 Mule Team Borax.** Dampen the spot, rub in 20 Mule Team Borax, let dry, then vacuum or brush clean.

Ticks

Remove ticks from inside the ear of a horse, dog, or cat with . . .

- **Krazy Glue.** Put a drop of Krazy Glue on a broom straw, apply it to the tick, and pull the tick right out.

Who Are They?

Aunt Jemima

In 1889, while seeking a name and a package design for the world's first self-rising pancake mix, Chris L. Rutt, a newspaperman in St. Joseph, Missouri, saw a vaudeville team know as Baker and Farrell. In their act, Baker sang the catchy song "Aunt Jemima" dressed as a southern mammy. Inspired by the wholesome name and image, Rutt appropriated them both to market his new pancake mix.

Unable to raise the money to promote Aunt Jemima pancake mix, Rutt and his associates sold their company to R. T. Davis Mill and Manufacturing Company, which promoted the new product at the World's Columbian Exposition in Chicago in 1893. The company hired Nancy Green, a famous African-American cook born in Montgomery County, Kentucky, to play the part of Aunt Jemima and demonstrate the pancake mix.

As Aunt Jemima, Nancy Green made and served over a million pancakes by the time the fair closed, prompting buyers to place over fifty thousand orders for Aunt Jemima pancake mix. For the next thirty years, Green played the part of Aunt Jemima at expositions all over the country.

A caricature of Nancy Green as a black mammy was pictured on packages of Aunt Jemima pancake mix. In 1917, Aunt Jemima was redrawn as a smiling, heavyset black housekeeper with a bandanna wrapped around her head. In 1923, Nancy Green died in an automobile accident at the age of eighty-nine.

In 1989, the company modernized Aunt Jemima, making her thinner, eliminating her bandanna, and giving her a perm and a pair of pearl earrings.

Betty Crocker

In 1921, the Washburn Crosby Company, maker of Gold Medal Flour, was inundated with letters from customers responding to an offer for a free floursack pincushion and asking for recipes. Sam Gale, head of the company's advertising department, created a fictional spokeswoman, Betty Crocker (named in honor of a retired company director, William G. Crocker), so that correspondence to housewives could go out with a single spokeswoman's signature. An employee named Florence Lindeberg provided Betty's signature. Employees in the Washburn Crosby test kitchens provided recipes. In 1924, Blanche Ingersoll provided Betty Crocker's voice on the radio. In 1936, fifteen years after Betty Crocker was first created, artist Neysa McMein painted Betty Crocker's first formal portrait. Betty is now in her seventh incarnation.

The Campbell Soup Kids

In 1904, Philadelphia illustrator Grace Wiederseim drew the cherubic cartoon children, modeling the chubby-faced kids after herself. Like the Campbell Soup Kids, Wiederseim had a round face, wide eyes, and a turned-up nose. Over the years, the Campbell Soup Kids grew taller and lost a little baby fat.

Dr. Bronner

Born in Germany to a soap-making family, Emanuel H. Bronner immigrated to Wisconsin as a young man and worked for a soap maker until his public speeches for peace and against fluoridation landed him in a Milwaukee jail. After being transferred to a mental institution in Elgin, Illinois, Bronner escaped and relocated to Los Angeles in 1947. Two years later, he started making and selling Dr. Bronner's Peppermint Soap, which became a favorite of natural food devotees, backpackers, and hippies. Bronner printed his "Moral ABC"—his 3,000-word philosophy—on the label of his liquid soap bottle. In the 1960s, Bronner moved his company to Escondido, California. Although he only relied on word of mouth to advertise his liquid soap, it sells 1.5 million bottles annually. Bronner died in 1997.

Elsie the Cow

In 1936, Borden launched a series of advertisements featuring cartoon cows, including Elsie, the spokescow for Borden dairy products. In 1940, compelled by Elsie's popularity, Borden dressed up "You'll Do Lobelia," a seven-year-old, 950-pound Jersey cow from Brookfield, Massachusetts, as Elsie for an exhibit at the World's Fair. She stood in a barn boudoir decorated with whimsical props including churns used as tables, lamps made from milk bottles, a wheelbarrow for a chaise lounge, and oil paintings of Elsie's ancestors—among them Great Aunt Bess in her bridal gown and Uncle Bosworth, the noted Spanish-American War admiral. This attracted the attention of RKO Pictures, which hired Elsie to star with Jack Oakie and Kay Francis in the movie *Little Men*. Borden needed to find a replacement for Elsie for the World's Fair exhibit. Elsie's husband, Elmer, was chosen, and the boudoir was converted overnight into a bachelor apartment, complete with every conceivable prop to suggest a series of nightly poker parties. In 1951, Borden chose Elmer to be the marketing symbol for all of Borden's glue and adhesive products. Elsie the Cow and her husband, Elmer, have two calves, Beulah and Beauregard.

The Gerber Baby

In 1928, after Gerber baby food was introduced, a number of artists were invited to submit illustrations for the first advertising campaign. Among the entries was a small unfinished charcoal sketch of a neighbor's baby submitted by artist Dorothy Hope Smith. Smith planned to complete the sketch if the age and size of the baby were suitable. The unfinished little sketch won the hearts of all who saw it. The illustration's popularity prompted Gerber to adopt it as its official trademark in 1931. Since that time, the Gerber Baby has appeared on all Gerber packaging and in every Gerber advertisement, making the Gerber Baby the best-known baby in the world.

Over the years several people have claimed to have been the model for the Gerber Baby. A persistent rumor holds that the model was Humphrey Bogart. In reality, the actual baby sketched by Dorothy Hope Smith was Ann Turner. Turner grew up, married James E. Cook, raised four children, taught high school English, and, after serving as chairperson of the English department at a Florida high school, retired in 1990.

The original charcoal sketch of the Gerber Baby is kept under glass in the company vault.

The Lipton Tea Man

A portrait of company founder, Sir Thomas Lipton, dressed in nautical atire, adorns all Lipton Tea packages. Born in 1850 in Glasgow, Scotland, Sir Thomas Lipton sold cured meats, eggs, butter, and cheeses from a small store that grew into a chain of stores throughout Scotland and England. In 1888, Lipton entered the tea trade, and two years later he entered the American market, pioneering packaged tea with the famous Flo-Thru Bag. He was knighted in 1898 and was made a baronet in 1902. A yachting enthusiast, Lipton made five unsuccessful attempts to win the Americas Cup. He died at the age of eighty-one in 1931.

The Man From Glad

The Man from Glad, seen in television commercials during the 1970s, was a take-off on *The Man from U.N.C.L.E.*

The Morton Salt Girl

An advertising agency developed the famous trademark depicting a little girl standing in the rain with an umbrella over her head and holding a package of salt tilted backward with the spout open and the salt running out. The timeless Morton Umbrella Girl has been updated with new dresses and hairstyles five times (in 1921, 1933, 1941, 1956, and 1968) since she first appeared in 1914.

Orville Redenbacher

Born in 1907, Orville Redenbacher started his popcorn career selling home-grown popcorn from bushel baskets in stores near his father's Indiana farm. He began wearing bow

ties while in high school. He became the first county agricul-
tural agent to broadcast radio interviews direct from the corn-
fields. With his clean-cut hairstyle, bow tie, and spectacles,
he became trusted as the man who would spend forty years
crossbreeding thirty thousand popcorn hybrids in search of
the perfect kernel—which popped up twice as fluffy as the
competition's. When Hunt-Wesson bought the brand in 1976,
the company kept Redenbacher as spokesperson.
Redenbacher died in 1995 at the age of eighty-eight.

Rosie

Comedienne Nancy Walker starred as Rosie, a down-to-earth
waitress who extolled the virtues of Bounty, "the quicker
picker upper," in television commercials. She also played
housekeeper Emily Turner on *Family Affair*, Ida Morgenstern
on *The Mary Tyler Moore Show* and *Rhoda*, and the housekeeper Mildred on *McMillan & Wife*.

The Quaker Oats Man

Portrait artist Haddon Sundblom painted the picture of the
Quaker Oats man, printed on all canisters of Quaker Oats.
The trustworthy face with gleaming blue eyes and friendly
smile might have been inspired by William Penn, the famous
English Quaker who founded Pennsylvania.

Speedy Alka-Seltzer

Early promotions for Alka-Seltzer featured Speedy Alka-Seltzer, created in 1951 as a baby-faced puppet with red hair
and a tablet-shaped hat. Stop-motion animation brought
Speedy to life in 212 television commercials between 1954

and 1964, requiring nineteen plaster heads with various lip positions, two sets of legs and arms, and as many as 1,440 adjustments for a single sixty-second commercial. Voice-over talent Dick Beals provided Speedy's voice. Speedy Alka-Seltzer co-starred with Buster Keaton, Martha Tilton, Sammy Davis Jr., and the Flintstones. Speedy Alka-Seltzer celebrated America's Bicentennial, participated in the 1980 Winter Olympics, attended thousands of holiday dinners, and has helped Santa Claus. The original six-inch-high Speedy Alka-Seltzer working model became so famous that it was insured for $100,000 and is kept in the vault of a Beverly Hills bank.

Suzi Chapstick

Suzi Chaffey, a member of the United States Olympic Women's Alpine Skiing Team, became a spokesperson for ChapStick in the 1970s, using the nickname Suzi Chapstick.

Uncle Ben

The orginal Uncle Ben was a black rice farmer known to rice millers in and around Houston in the 1940s for consistently delivering the highest quality rice for milling. Uncle Ben harvested his rice with such care that he purportedly received several honors for full-kernel yields and quality. Legend holds that other rice growers proudly claimed their rice was "as good as Uncle Ben's." Unfortunately, further details of Uncle Ben's life (including his last name) were lost to history. Frank Brown, a maître d' in a Houston restaurant, posed for the portrait of Uncle Ben.

Clean Your Typewriter Keys

with Silly Putty

Backpacks

Keep school books and supplies dry inside a student backpack with . . .

- **Scotchgard.** Spray the outside of a student backpack with Scotchgard.

Bills

Hold mail and bills with . . .

- **Kleenex Tissue.** A decorative Kleenex Tissue box, when empty, makes an excellent container for storing mail and bills.

Book Covers

Hide the title of a paperback book with . . .

- **Con-Tact Paper.** Give the book a mystery cover made from Con-Tact Paper.

Make book covers with . . .

- **Con-Tact Paper.** Use clear Con-Tact Paper to cover and protect school books.

Protect a book cover with . . .

- **Saran Wrap.** Use a sheet of Saran Wrap to protect a dust jacket.

Repair torn book covers with . . .

- **Scotch Packaging Tape.** Adhere the cover back to the binding with Scotch Packaging Tape.

Book Labels

Label your books with . . .

- **Avery Laser Labels.** Print your name, address, and phone number on Avery Laser Labels and adhere them to books.

Bookmarks

Improvise a bookmark with . . .

- **Forster Toothpicks.** Keep your place with a Forster Toothpick.

Books

Prevent or kill mildew in damp books with . . .

- **Kingsford's Corn Starch.** Sprinkle Kingsford's Corn Starch throughout the book to absorb the moisture from damp pages, wait several hours, then brush clean. If the pages are mildewed, brush the corn starch off outdoors to keep mildew spores out of the house.

Prevent the wet pages of a book from wrinkling with . . .

- **Viva Paper Towels.** Place sheets of Viva Paper Towels between every wet page, close the book, place a heavy book on top, and let sit overnight.

Calculators and Cameras

Remind yourself to turn off your calculator or camera flash attachment with . . .

- **Cover Girl NailSlicks Classic Red.** Paint the off button with Cover Girl NailSlicks Classic Red Nail Polish.

Computer Disks

Label computer disks with . . .

- **Avery Laser Labels.** Use an Avery Laser Label. Avery Dennison also makes diskette labels.

Envelopes

Seal an envelope with . . .

- **Cover Girl NailSlicks Classic Red.** Use Cover Girl NailSlicks Classic Red Nail Polish to seal a letter as you would use wax.
- **Crayola Crayons.** Melt Crayola Crayons as sealing wax for envelopes.

Are Erasers a Mistake?

Eberhard Faber was the first company to put erasers on pencils. The idea caught on in the United States immediately, but it has never caught on in Europe. Europeans claim they shun erasers because they encourage schoolchildren to be careless. Students (and just about everyone else in Europe) use separate erasers.

The Monkees and Liquid Paper

In 1966, two Hollywood producers chose four un-known boys—Davy Jones, Peter Tork, Michael Nesmith, and Micky Dolenz—to star as the Monkees, a caricature of the Beatles, in their own television series to promote their albums.

When the Monkees broke up, Michael Nesmith re-corded a few solo albums, but most rock critics contin-ued making a Monkee of him. Eventually, through lavish spending and poor tax planning, Nesmith lost most of the million dollars he had made with the Monkees.

Then his mother died and made him a millionaire all over again. In 1951, after toiling for years as a secretary, Bette Nesmith Graham came up with something she first called Mistake Out, then Liquid Paper. In 1979, two years before she died, she sold her company to Gillette for more than $47 million. Nesmith inherited approximately $25 million, and he earns a royalty on every bottle of Liquid Paper sold.

Erasers

Erase pencil marks from paper with . . .

- **Wonder Bread.** Ball up a small piece of Wonder Bread (without the crust) and use it as you would an eraser.

Filing Cabinets

Organize your filing cabinets with . . .

- **Con-Tact Paper.** Use different patterns of Con-Tact Paper to coordinate your files.

Finger Grip
Make a finger grip for sorting through papers with . . .
- **Playtex Living Gloves.** When your Playtex Living Gloves wear out, cut off a fingertip and slip it over your index or middle finger to sort through papers.

Mail
Protect valuables in packages to be mailed with . . .
- **Kleenex Tissue.** Use tissues as filler to pack a box.

Memo Board
Make a memo board with . . .
- **Con-Tact Paper.** Create an instant memo board by covering a sheet of cardboard with Con-Tact Paper, adhering to an office wall or refrigerator door with Velcro, and using an erasable marker.

Packing
Pack fragile packages with . . .
- **Orville Redenbacher's Gourmet Popping Corn.** Use popped Orville Redenbacher's Gourmet Popping Corn as environmentally friendly packing material.

Pencil Holder
Make a pencil holder with . . .

● **Con-Tact Paper.** Wrap an clean, empty tin can with your favorite Con-Tact Paper.

School Supplies
Label your child's school supplies with . . .

● **Avery Laser Labels.** Print your child's name on Avery Laser Labels and adhere them to rulers, crayon boxes, lunch boxes, and Thermos bottles, then cover with transparent tape.

Stamps
Keep stamps with . . .

● **Reynolds Cut-Rite Wax Paper.** Keep stamps between sheets of Reynolds Cut-Rite Wax Paper to prevent them from sticking together.

Tape
Mark the starting point of a roll of masking tape or packaging tape with . . .

● **Forster Toothpicks.** Stick a Forster Toothpick under the loose end of the tape so you can find it easily the next time you use the tape.

Typewriters
Clean typewriter keys with . . .

● **Oral-B Toothbrushes.** Scrub the keys with a clean, old Oral-B Toothbrush dipped in alcohol.

● **Silly Putty.** Roll the Silly Putty into a ball and press into the typewriter keys.

Videotapes
Organize home videotapes with . . .

● **Con-Tact Paper.** Decorating home videos with unique labels made from Con-Tact Paper makes them easy to find.

Fix a Hem with
Wrigley's Spearmint Gum

Baseball Caps

Replace broken plastic straps on baseball caps with . . .

- **Velcro.** When the plastic strap breaks, replace it with strips of Velcro.

Buttons

Store buttons in your sewing basket with . . .

- **Gerber Applesauce.** Fill a clean, empty Gerber baby food jar with your buttons.

Sew buttons on heavy coats with . . .

- **Oral-B Mint Waxed Floss.** Use Oral-B Mint Waxed Floss as a durable thread.

Replace troublesome buttons with . . .

- **Velcro.** Attach Velcro in place of buttons.

Dye

(See page 211)

Fraying

Prevent cut fabric from fraying with . . .

- **Maybelline Crystal Clear Nail Polish.** Apply a thin coat of Maybelline Crystal Clear Nail Polish along seam edges to prevent unraveling.

Guide Strip

Make sewing simple with . . .

- **Con-Tact Paper.** Cut a strip of brightly colored Con-Tact Paper and adhere it to your sewing machine as a guide strip.

Hems

Fix a hem temporarily with . . .

- **Wrigley's Spearmint Gum.** Reattach a drooping hem with a dab of chewed Wrigley's Spearmint Gum.

Knitting

Mark a stitch when knitting with . . .

- **Glad Flexible Straws.** Cut a one-eighth-inch length from a Glad Flexible Straw and use as a ring to mark a stitch on needles up to size ten.

Needles

Thread a needle with ease with . . .

- **Alberto VO5 Hair Spray.** Stiffen the end of the thread with Alberto VO5 Hair Spray so it can be easily poked through the eye of a needle.
- **Maybelline Crystal Clear Nail Polish.** Dip the

end of the thread in Maybelline Crystal Clear Nail Polish. Let dry, then thread.

Needlepoint

Create unique needlepoint patterns on pillows with . . .

- **Con-Tact Paper.** Use the Con-Tact Paper pattern as a guide for your needlepoint.

SCOTCH TAPE: A FASHION STATEMENT?

The Scottish tartans used to designate Scotch Tape were exclusively designed for the 3M Company by New York color consultant Arthur Allen in the 1940s.

Patterns

Attach a sewing pattern to fabric with . . .

- **Scotch Transparent Tape.** Use Scotch Transparent Tape to attach the pattern to the material, then cut the pattern, leaving a reinforced edge.

Preserve sewing patterns with . . .

- **Scotchgard.** Spray a new pattern with Scotchgard to prevent rips, tears, and wrinkles.

Pincushions

Make a pincushion with . . .

- **Ivory Soap.** Using a wrapped bar of Ivory Soap as a pincushion makes needles glide through fabric.
- **Pink Pearl Erasers.** Keep needles, pins, and safety pins stuck in a Pink Pearl Eraser.
- **S.O.S Steel Wool Soap Pads.** Stuff a homemade pincushion with a clean, dry, used S.O.S Steel Wool Soap Pad. The steel wool will help keep pins and needles sharp.

Sewing Machines

Push fabrics through the presser foot of a sewing machine with . . .

- **Forster Toothpicks.** Use a Forster Toothpick to free fabric that gets stuck under the presser foot.

Rewind a bobbin with . . .

- **Crayola Crayons.** Mark the thread with a contrasting color Crayola Crayon a few yards after starting to wind it onto the bobbin. The crayon mark will alert you when the thread is coming to the end.

Absorb excess oil from a sewing machine with . . .

- **Viva Paper Towels.** After oiling your sewing machine, stitch several rows on a sheet of Viva Paper Towels before sewing any fabric.

Extend the spout of an oil can with . . .

- **Glad Flexible Straws.** Put a Glad Flexible Straw over the end of the spout of an oil can to reach tight spots.

Help vinyl glide through a sewing machine with . . .

- **Baby Oil.** Wipe the seam line with a cotton ball dipped in baby oil before stitching.

Snaps

Make sewing snaps on clothing a snap with . . .

- **Scotch Transparent Tape.** Tape the snaps, hooks, and eyes to the garment, sew them on right along with the Scotch Transparent Tape, then pull off the tape.

Thread

Prevent thread from tangling with . . .

- **Bounce.** Run a threaded needle through a sheet of Bounce to eliminate the static cling on the thread before sewing.

The Moon and Back

- If all the Coca-Cola ever produced were in regular-size bottles and laid end to end, they would reach to the moon and back 1,045 times. That is one trip per day for two years, ten months, and eleven days.
- Dannon sells over 2 million cups of yogurt every day. That's enough to feed every citizen of Botswanna every day.
- In 1991, Kraft sold enough Miracle Whip to make 3.8 billion servings of potato salad.
- Over 3 billion denture cleanser tablets were sold in the United States in 1993. That's enough to clean one pair of dentures every day for the next 8 million years.
- Over 10 billion Mr. Coffee paper filters are sold every year. That's enough to make two pots of coffee for nearly every person on earth.
- Americans currently drink nearly 35 billion glasses of iced tea every year, according to Nestea spokesperson Andrea Cook. That's seven gallons per person.
- Americans buy more than 2 million eggs of Silly Putty every year. That's enough to completely cover the White House lawn in plastic eggs.
- On March 22, 1994, Hormel Foods Corporation celebrated the production of its five-billionth can of SPAM.

If laid end to end, five billion cans of SPAM would circle the earth 12.5 times. Five billion cans of SPAM would feed a family of four, three meals a day, for 4,566,210 years.

● Binney & Smith produces 2 billion Crayola Crayons a year, which, if placed end to end, would circle the earth 4.5 times.

● Americans charged a total of $480 billion on credit cards in 1990. That's equal to $1 million every minute.

● Each year, Reynolds Metals sells enough Cut-Rite Wax Paper to circle the globe more than fifteen times.

● More than 50 million bottles of Tabasco Pepper Sauce are sold every year. Laid end to end, they would reach from New York to Los Angeles and back again.

● Today it would take more than 250 mule teams to transport the borax ore processed in just one day at Borax's modern facility in the Mojave Desert.

● In the United States, more Frisbees are sold each year than baseballs, basketballs, and footballs *combined*.

● Consumers purchase more than 3.5 billion yards of dental floss every year. That's enough to wrap around the earth 250 times.

● In 1996, Eberhard Faber sold more than 4.7 million Pink Pearl Erasers. Laid end to end, that's enough erasers to reach from Washington, D.C., to Philadelphia.

● According to *The Great American Chewing Gum Book* by Robert Hendrickson, if all the sticks of gum chewed in America each year were laid end to end, they would equal a stick of gum 5 million miles long. That's long enough to reach the moon and back ten times.

Zippers

Sew in a zipper with . . .

● **Scotch Transparent Tape.** Baste the seam closed, press open, tape the zipper face down along the basted seam on the wrong side of the fabric (allowing the tape to hold the zipper flat). Sew on a machine, then remove tape and basting.

Replace a zipper with . . .

● **Velcro.** Instead of sewing in a new zipper, attach strips of Velcro.

Make Ski Pants
with Scotchgard

Baseball Mitts
Break in a new baseball mitt with . . .

● **Alberto VO5 Conditioning Hairdressing.** Rub the center of the glove with Alberto VO5 Conditioning Hairdressing, place a baseball in the glove, fold the mitt around it, and secure with rubber bands. Tuck the glove under a mattress overnight.

● **Barbasol Shaving Cream.** Rub the center of the glove with Barbasol, then follow the above directions.

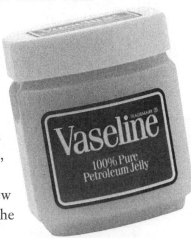

● **Vaseline.** Vaseline Petroleum Jelly, rubbed into a baseball glove, softens the leather.

● **Wesson Corn Oil.** Rub a few drops of Wesson Corn Oil into the palm of the glove, then follow the directions above for Alberto VO5 Conditioning Hairdressing.

Basket Tennis
Play "basket tennis" with . . .
- **Wilson Tennis Balls.** Remove the bottom from an empty coffee can and nail the can above the garage door. Use a Wilson Tennis Ball to play basketball.

Bicycling
Add racing stripes to a bicycle with . . .
- **Con-Tact Paper.** Cut racing stripes from Con-Tact Paper and adhere to your bicycle.
  Lubricate bicycle chains with . . .
  - **Alberto VO5 Conditioning Hairdressing.** Use a dab of Alberto VO5 Conditioning Hairdressing.
    - **Pam No Stick Cooking Spray.** Spray the bicycle chain with Pam No Stick Cooking Spray.
      Prevent mud and clay buildup on bicycles with . . .
    - **WD-40.** Spray the bicycle with a thin coat of WD-40.
    Find a puncture in a bicycle tire with . . .
    - **Palmolive.** Mix a few drops of Palmolive with water and brush on a leaky tire. The bubbles will indicate the exact location of the puncture.

Boating
Bail a boat with . . .

- **Clorox.** Cap an empty, clean Clorox Bleach bottle, cut diagonally across the bottom, and scoop out the water.

Make an anchor with . . .

- **Clorox.** Fill an empty, clean Clorox Bleach bottle with cement.

Make a boating buoy with . . .

- **Clorox.** Cap an empty, clean Clorox Bleach jug tightly, tie a rope to the handle, and tie a weight to the other end of the rope. These buoys can also be strung together to mark swimming and boating areas.

Cards

Clean a deck of playing cards with . . .

- **Gold Medal Flour.** Place the deck of cards into a paper bag, add four tablespoons Gold Medal Flour, and shake briskly. Remove the cards from the bag and wipe clean.
- **Kingsford's Corn Starch.** Place the deck of cards into a paper bag, add four tablespoons Kingsford's Corn Starch, and shake briskly. Remove the cards from the bag and wipe clean.

Prevent playing cards from sticking together with . . .

- **Turtle Wax.** Wax the backs of the cards with Turtle Wax and rub with a soft cloth.

Croquet

Make croquet wickets visible on the lawn with . . .

- **Glad Flexible Straws.** Run the wickets through Glad Flexible Straws before sticking them into the ground.

Fishing

Lure fish with . . .

- **SPAM.** SPAM makes excellent bait, according to Ann Kondo Corum, author of *Hawaii's SPAM Cookbook*.
- **Vaseline.** Coat small pieces of sponge with Vaseline Petroleum Jelly to simulate fish egg bait and lure trout.
- **WD-40.** When sprayed on fishing bait, WD-40 covers up the scent of human hands so the bait will better lure fish, according to *USA Today*. The WD-40 Company receives hundreds of letters from consumers confirming this use but prefers not to promote WD-40 as a fishing lure since the petroleum-based product could potentially pollute rivers and streams, damaging the ecosystem.

Lure crabs with . . .

- **Wrigley's Spearmint Gum.** Chew a piece of Wrigley's Spearmint Gum briefly and use it as bait on a fishing line.

Clean fishing reels with . . .

- **Q-Tips Cotton Swabs.** Use a Q-Tips Cotton Swab to reach small crevices and hard-to-reach places when cleaning a fishing reel.

Transport live fishing bait with . . .

- **Maxwell House Coffee.** Keep worms in a Maxwell House Coffee can filled with moist coffee grounds.

THE MAN WITH THE GOLDEN TOOTHPICK

In November 1993, Leland's, a premier auctioneer of sports memorabilia, auctioned off Tom Seaver's chewed-up toothpick for $440.

The First Frisbee?

In May 1989, Middlebury College in Vermont unveiled a bronze statue of a dog jumping to catch a Frisbee to commemorate the alleged fiftieth anniversary of the Frisbee. According to Middlebury legend, five undergraduates driving through Nebraska in 1939 suffered a flat tire. As two boys changed the tire, a third found a discarded pie tin from the Frisbie Pie Company near a cornfield and threw the circular disk into the air. Middlebury President Olin Robison told *Time* magazine, "Our version of the story is that it happened all over America, but it started here."

Frisbee Golf
Play Frisbee golf with a . . .

● **Frisbee.** Designate a tee-off spot and choose a tree, pole, or other landmark as the "hole." Toss a Frisbee toward the hole, pick it up wherever it lands, and continue tossing until you hit the hole. Keep score. The player with the fewest tosses to hit all the holes wins.

Golf
Make golf clubs shine with . . .

● **Alberto VO5 Conditioning Hairdressing.** Clean the shafts with a dab of Alberto VO5 Conditioning Hairdressing on a clean cloth.

Label golf balls with . . .

- **Cover Girl NailSlicks Classic Red.** Paint a small mark with Cover Girl NailSlicks Classic Red Nail Polish so you can easily identify sports equipment.

Clean golf balls with . . .

- **Pink Pearl Erasers.** Pack a Pink Pearl Eraser in your golf bag.
- **S.O.S Steel Wool Soap Pads.** Rub the golf club gently with a dry S.O.S Steel Wool Soap Pad.

TRUE LOVE

In 1930, a can of three Wilson Tennis Balls sold for $1.50 in the Sears and Roebuck catalog. In 1990, that same can of balls sold for less than $2.00.

Helmets

Make a helmet easy to identify with . . .

- **Con-Tact Paper.** Add shapes and designs cut from Con-Tact Paper.

Megaphone

Make a megaphone with . . .

- **Clorox.** Remove the cap and cut off the bottom of an empty, clean Clorox Bleach bottle.

Roller-skating and Skateboarding

Give a skateboard personality with . . .

- **Con-Tact Paper.** Cut racing stripes or other funky shapes from Con-Tact Paper and adhere to the skateboard.

Lubricate wheels with . . .

- **Alberto VO5 Conditioning Hairdressing.** Use a dab of Alberto VO5 Conditioning Hairdressing.
- **Pam No Stick Cooking Spray.** Spray with Pam No Stick Cooking Spray.

● **Vaseline.** Smear Vaseline Petroleum Jelly around the cylinders on the wheels so they roll faster.

Sailing

Prevent a sailboat's spinnaker pole fittings from jamming or sticking with . . .

● **Alberto VO5 Conditioning Hairdressing.** Lubricate with Alberto VO5 Conditioning Hairdressing.

● **Vaseline.** Lubricate with Vaseline Petroleum Jelly.

Skiing

Prevent ski goggles from fogging up with . . .

● **Barbasol Shaving Cream.** Spray with Barbasol, then wipe clean.

● **Endust.** Spray the inside of the goggles with Endust, then wipe clean.

Make ski pants with . . .

● **Scotchgard.** Spray a pair of old jeans with Scotchgard. Be sure to wear long underwear for warmth.

Sledding

Speed up a sled with . . .

● **Pam No Stick Cooking Spray.** Spray Pam No Stick Cooking Spray on the bottom of a sled or an inner tube before taking it out in the snow.

Sled down a snow-covered hill with . . .

● **Glad Trash Bags.** Tie a Glad Trash Bag around your bottom like a diaper, and slide down the hill.

Tennis

Label tennis balls with . . .

- **Cover Girl NailSlicks Classic Red.** Paint a small mark with Cover Girl NailSlicks Classic Red Nail Polish so you can easily identify sports equipment.

Weight Lifting

Make dumbbells with . . .

- **Clorox.** Fill two empty, clean Clorox Bleach bottles with sand.

Working Out

Strengthen your grip with . . .

- **Silly Putty.** Squeeze Silly Putty for ten minutes every day in each hand.
- **Wilson Tennis Balls.** Squeeze a Wilson Tennis Ball in each hand.

Wrestling

Wrestle in . . .

- **Jell-O.** Pour 2,347 boxes of Jell-O into an eight-foot-square padded box, add boiling water, and chill for two days.

Remove Gum From Hair
with Miracle Whip

Bowls
Improvise a bowl with a . . .
- **Frisbee.** In an emergency, an upside-down Frisbee can be used as a bowl or plate.

Burned Mouth
Soothe the burn on the roof of your mouth from hot pizza with . . .
- **Reddi-wip.** Fill your mouth with Reddi-wip to coat the lesion.

Clothing Repair
Repair clothes in an emergency with . . .
- **Scotch Packaging Tape.** Scotch Packaging Tape will hold fabric together until you can find a needle and thread.

Contact Lenses
Find a contact lens on the floor or carpet with . . .

The Trouble With Jell-O

In July 1950, the FBI arrested thirty-two-year-old electrical engineer Julius Rosenberg as a spy for the Soviet Union. According to the FBI, Rosenberg had torn a Jell-O box top in half, given a piece to his brother-in-law, David Greenglass, and told him that his contact at Los Alamos would produce the other half. The contact turned out to be spy courier Harry Gold, who received atomic energy data from Greenglass and paid him $500, allegedly giving the Soviet Union the secret of the atomic bomb. Although Rosenberg insisted on his innocence, he and his wife Ethel were sentenced to death in 1951, and after several appeals, in June 1953, the Rosenbergs became the first Americans ever executed for using Jell-O.

● **L'eggs Sheer Energy.** Cover your vacuum hose nozzle carefully with a piece of L'eggs hose and a rubber band to keep the lens from being sucked in. Gently move the nozzle over the floor.

Crooks
Detain crooks with . . .

● **Scotch Packaging Tape.** Wrap a captured thief or burglar securely to a chair with Scotch Packaging Tape, call 911, and wait for the police.

Down the Drain

Retrieve a coin or piece of jewelry that has fallen down a drain with . . .

- **Wrigley's Spearmint Gum.** Tie a fishing weight to a long string, chew a piece of Wrigley's Spearmint Gum briefly, stick it on the bottom of the weight, dangle it down the drain, let it take hold, then pull up.

Frozen Tongue

Free a tongue stuck to frozen metal in winter with . . .

- **WD-40.** Spray WD-40 on the metal around the tongue.

Gum

Remove bubble gum from hair with . . .

- **Miracle Whip.** Rub a dollop of Miracle Whip into the bubble gum.
- **Jif Peanut Butter.** Rub a dollop of Jif Peanut Butter into the bubble gum until it slides out.
- **Spray 'n Wash.** Spray the gum with Spray 'n Wash, rub between fingers, comb out, then shampoo hair.
- **Vaseline.** Apply Vaseline Petroleum Jelly and work into the hair until the gum slides off.

Insect in Ear

Remove an insect from your ear with . . .

- **Baby Oil.** Gently pour a little baby oil into your ear and float the insect out.

Knots
Detangle knots with . . .
- **Kingsford's Corn Starch.** Sprinkle a stubborn knot with a little Kingsford's Corn Starch.

Photographs
Free a snapshot stuck in a magnetic photo album with a . . .
- **Conair Pro Style 1600.** Blow warm air from a Conair Pro Style 1600 underneath the plastic page.

Snoring
Prevent snoring with . . .
- **Wilson Tennis Balls.** Sew a Wilson Tennis Ball inside a pocket on the back of your pajama top to prevent you from sleeping on your back.

Stuck Ring
Remove a ring stuck on a finger with . . .
- **Alberto VO5 Conditioning Hairdressing.** Rub on a little Alberto VO5 Conditioning Hairdressing, then hold your hand up toward the ceiling to drain the blood from the area, and slide off the ring.
- **ChapStick.** Coat finger with ChapStick, and slide the ring off.
- **Lubriderm.** Apply Lubriderm around the ring band

Don't Have a Manic Episode Without It

During her highly publicized disappearance for four days in April 1996, Margot Kidder, who costarred with Christopher Reeve as Lois Lane in the *Superman* movies, lived inside a cardboard box with a homeless person in downtown Los Angeles while suffering a manic-depressive episode. According to *People* magazine, "Kidder had lost some caps on her front teeth that sometimes fell out and which she cemented back in place with Krazy Glue. 'When you're having a manic episode,' she says, 'you don't always remember to pack the Krazy Glue.'"

and slide the ring off.

● **Miracle Whip.** Smear on some Miracle Whip and slide the ring off.

● **Vaseline.** Coat finger with Vaseline Petroleum Jelly and slide the ring off.

● **WD-40.** Several medical journals claim that WD-40 is the perfect cure for a toe stuck in the bathtub faucet, a finger stuck in a soda bottle, or a ring stuck on a finger.

Clean Rust from Tools

with Heinz Vinegar

Batteries

Fix battery-operated toys or appliances with . . .

● **Reynolds Wrap.** If the batteries in a Walkman or a toy are loose as the result of a broken spring, wedge a small piece of Reynolds Wrap between the battery and the spring.

Boom Box Speakers

Attach loose speakers to a boom box with . . .

● **Scotch Packaging Tape.** Use Scotch Packaging Tape.

Box Springs

Take squeaks out of a box spring mattress with . . .

● **WD-40.** Remove the fabric covering the bottom of the box spring mattress (by simply removing the staples), and spray the springs with WD-40. Staple the fabric covering back in place with a staple gun.

Caulking

Improvise caulking compound with . . .

- **Wrigley's Spearmint Gum.** Use a piece of well-chewed Wrigley's Spearmint Gum to seal holes.

Clean-Up

Clean dirt, grime, and oil from hands with . . .

- **Arm & Hammer Baking Soda.** Sprinkle Arm & Hammer Baking Soda onto wet hands with liquid soap, rub vigorously, rinse, and dry.
- **Barbasol Shaving Cream.** Rubbing Barbasol between your hands will dissolve grime without water. Keep a can of it at the workbench.
- **Clairol Herbal Essences.** A dab of Clairol Herbal Essences cuts through the grime on your hands.
- **Coppertone.** Rub Coppertone into the skin and wash clean with water.
- **Crisco All-Vegetable Shortening.** Rub in Crisco All-Vegetable Shortening before using soap.
- **Domino Sugar.** Sprinkle a little Domino Sugar on your hands, then lather with soap and water.
- **Pam No Stick Cooking Spray.** Spray your hands with Pam No Stick Cooking Spray, then wash clean.

Con-Tact Paper

Remove Con-Tact Paper with a . . .

- **Conair Pro Style 1600.** Set a Conair Pro Style 1600 on warm, work one section, and gently pull the edges.

Door Hinges

Prevent squeaky door hinges with . . .

- **Alberto VO5 Conditioning Hairdressing.** Apply

a little bit of Alberto VO5 Conditioning Hairdressing.

- **Barbasol Shaving Cream.** Spray the joint with Barbasol.
- **Endust.** Lubricate the hinges with Endust.
- **Pam No Stick Cooking Spray.** Spray with Pam No Stick Cooking Spray.
- **Vaseline.** Rub a dab of Vaseline into the hinges.
- **WD-40.** Spray the hinge with WD-40.

Drill Bits

Store small drill bits with . . .

- **Pink Pearl Erasers.** Twist the bits point-first into a large Pink Pearl Eraser.

Ducting

Make flex tubing for conduits with . . .

- **Slinky.** Stretch a Slinky from one duct to another and secure it in place, then wrap plastic trash bags around the coils, securing them in place with duct tape (or clear packaging tape) to make excellent ducting in a pinch.

Files

Clean a metal file with . . .

- **Scotch Packaging Tape.** Put a piece of Scotch Packaging Tape over the length of the file, press firmly, then peel off. The shavings will stick to the tape.

Funnels

(See page 195)

Furniture
Paint small crevices in furniture with . . .

- **Forster Toothpicks.** Dip a Forster Toothpick in paint to retouch fine scratches or reach small nooks and crannies.

Glue
Apply glue with . . .

- **Forster Toothpicks.** Dip one end of a Forster Toothpick into the glue to apply small drops.
- **Q-Tips Cotton Swabs.** A Q-Tips Cotton Swab doubles as an excellent brush for dabbing on glue.

Gutters
Keep leaves out of your rain gutters with . . .

- **Slinky.** Place a Slinky in your rain rugger and stretch if from one end to the next, keeping it in place by simply clipping the Slinky to each end.

Joint Compound
Dry joint compound with a . . .

- **Conair Pro Style 1600.** Use a Conair Pro Style 1600 to speed up the drying process.

Keys
Prevent a key from sticking in a lock with . . .

- **Pam No Stick Cooking Spray.** Spray with Pam No Stick Cooking Spray.

Motors
Clean a motor with . . .

- **Oral-B Toothbrushes.** Dip a clean, old Oral-B

Toothbrush in kerosene or mineral spirits to remove gunk from crevices.

Nails and Screws

Caddy nails with . . .

- **Scotch Transparent Tape.** Place nails between layers of Scotch Transparent Tape so they're readily available.

Lubricate nails and screws with . . .

- **ChapStick.** Nails and screws rubbed with ChapStick will go into wood more easily.
- **Ivory Soap.** Nails and screws rubbed with Ivory Soap will go in easier.

Store nails, screws, bolts, and washers with . . .

- **Gerber Applesauce.** Fill clean, empty Gerber baby food jars with leftover nails, screws, nuts, and bolts. You can also nail the caps of the food jars under a wooden shelf and screw the jars in place.
- **Huggies Baby Wipes.** Use empty Huggies Baby Wipes boxes in the workshop to hold loose screws, bolts, nuts, nails, drill bits, and spare parts.

- **Maxwell House Coffee.** Maxwell House Coffee cans make perfect storage containers.
- **Ziploc Storage Bags.** Organize nuts, bolts, drill bits, nails, washers, and screws in the workshop.

Oil

Extend the spout of an oil can with . . .

- **Glad Flexible Straws.** Put a Glad Flexible Straw over the end of the spout of an oil can to reach tight spots.

Apply oil to tools and machine parts with . . .

- **Q-Tips Cotton Swabs.** Dip a Q-Tips Cotton Swab in machine oil to lubricate tools and precision machine parts.

Paint

(See page 266)

Paintings and Pictures

Prevent framed pictures from tilting or scratching the wall with . . .

- **Pink Pearl Erasers.** Glue at least two Pink Pearl Erasers to the bottom edge of the back of the frame.

Paper

Remove paper stuck to a wood surface with . . .

- **Wesson Corn Oil.** Saturate the paper with Wesson Corn Oil, let sit for a while, and gently peel the paper off.

Pipes

Stop pipes from freezing or thaw frozen pipes with . . .

- **Morton Salt.** Sprinkle Morton Salt down waste pipes in cold weather.

Defrost frozen pipes with a . . .

- **Conair Pro Style 1600.** Set a Conair Pro Style 1600 on hot and aim at the pipes.

Pipe Joints

Lubricate pipe joints with . . .

- **Alberto VO5 Conditioning Hairdressing.** A thin layer of Alberto VO5 Conditioning Hairdressing on pipe connections will make them fit together more easily.
- **Coppertone.** Coppertone works as an oil lubricant for fitting pipe joints together.
- **Vaseline.** Dab a little Vaseline on the ends of the pipes so they fit together smoothly.

Plaster

Remove excess plaster after filling a hole with . . .

- **L'eggs Sheer Energy.** Scrub with a balled-up pair of L'eggs.

Retard patching plaster from drying with . . .

- **Heinz Vinegar.** Add one tablespoon Heinz White Vinegar to the water when mixing plaster to slow the drying time.

Plaster Walls

Prevent a plaster wall from crumbling when driving a nail into it with . . .

- **Scotch Transparent Tape.** Make a small *X* over the spot with two strips of Scotch Transparent Tape, then drive the nail.

Pliers

Prevent pliers from leaving marks with . . .

- **Playtex Living Gloves.** When your Playtex Living Gloves wear out, cut off two fingers and slip them over the jaws of pliers as protective padding.

Plumbing

Stop a faucet from screeching with . . .

- **Alberto VO5 Conditioning Hairdressing.** Remove the handle and stem, coat both sets of metal threads with Alberto VO5 Conditioning Hairdressing, and replace.
- **Vaseline.** Coat the threads on the handle and stem of your faucet with Vaseline Petroleum Jelly.

Rattling Machinery

Stop a small machine part from rattling with . . .

- **Silly Putty.** Wrap Silly Putty as a buffer between two pieces of rattling metal.

Rust

(Also see Tools, page 354)

Remove rust with . . .

- **Canada Dry Club Soda.** Loosen rusty nuts and bolts by pouring Canada Dry Club Soda over them.
- **Coca-Cola.** Household-hints columnist Mary Ellen suggests applying a cloth soaked in a carbonated soda to the rusted bolt for several minutes.
- **Heinz Vinegar.** Soak the rusted tool, bolt, or spigot in undiluted Heinz White Vinegar overnight.

Prevent rust on outdoor machinery with . . .

- **Vaseline.** Apply a generous coat of Vaseline Petroleum Jelly.

Prevent nuts and bolts from rusting together with . . .

- **Alberto VO5 Conditioning Hairdressing.** Lubricate the nuts and bolts with a dab of Alberto VO5 Conditioning Hairdressing before screwing them together.

Sawdust
Wipe up sawdust from drilling or sandpapering with . . .

- **Bounce.** A used sheet of Bounce will collect sawdust just like a tack cloth.

Saws
Lubricate a handsaw blade with . . .

- **Ivory Soap.** Rub Ivory Soap across the sides and teeth of the saw to help the blade glide through wood.

Scooper
Make a scooper with . . .

- **Clorox.** Cap an empty, clean Clorox Bleach bottle, cut diagonally across the bottom, and use it to scoop up flour, sugar, rice, dog food, sand, fertilizer, or snow.

Screwdrivers
Prevent a screwdriver from slipping with . . .

- **Crayola Chalk.** Rub Crayola Chalk on the blade.

Screws
(Also see Nails and Screws, page 347)
Tighten a loose screw with . . .

- **Elmer's Glue-All.** When a screw hole is too worn out to hold a screw, soak a cotton ball in Elmer's Glue-All, stuff it into the hole, and let it dry for twenty-four hours. Use a screwdriver to put a new screw into the hole.

● **Forster Toothpicks.** Insert a Forster Toothpick into the screw hole, break it off at the surface, and rescrew the screw.

● **S.O.S Steel Wool Soap Pads.** Wrap a few steel strands from an S.O.S Steel Wool Soap Pad around the threads of a screw.

Hold a screw in position with . . .

● **Saran Wrap.** Push the screw through a small piece of Saran Wrap, fit the screwdriver into the groove in the head, hold the Saran Wrap back over the blade of the screwdriver, and screw.

Shop Aprons

Make a shop apron with . . .

● **Glad Trash Bags.** Cut open the bottom of a Glad Trash Bag, put it over your head, and slip your arms through the handles.

Small Parts

Avoid losing small parts when fixing an appliance with . . .

● **Scotch Transparent Tape.** Before dismantling the item, tape a strip of Scotch tape, adhesive side up, on your worktable. Place the parts on the tape in the order you remove them, so they are ready to be reassembled.

Soldering

Hold wires in place while soldering with . . .

● **Scotch Packaging Tape.** Use Scotch Packaging Tape.

Spackle

Fix small holes in walls with . . .

- **Colgate Toothpaste.** Use a small dab of Colgate as emergency spackling to fill in small holes in plaster walls. Let dry before painting.
- **Crayola Chalk.** Insert a piece of Crayola Chalk into the hole, cut it off even with the wall, then plaster.
- **Elmer's Glue-All.** Small nail holes can be filled by squirting in a drop of Elmer's Glue-All before painting.
- **Ivory Soap.** Rub a bar of Ivory Soap over the hole until it looks flat and even, then paint.
- **S.O.S Steel Wool Soap Pads.** Fill cracks with pieces of an S.O.S Steel Wool Soap Pad, then plaster.
- **Wrigley's Spearmint Gum.** Use a well-chewed stick of Wrigley's Spearmint Gum.

Tape

Mark the starting point of a roll of masking tape or packaging tape with . . .

- **Forster Toothpicks.** Stick a Forster Toothpick under the loose end of the tape so you can find it easily the next time you use the tape.

Tile

Re-adhere a linoleum floor tile with . . .

- **Reynolds Wrap.** Put a piece of Reynolds Wrap on top of the tile and run a hot iron over it several times to melt the glue underneath. Place several books on top of the tile until the glue dries completely.

Tools

Prevent tools from rusting with . . .

- **Alberto VO5 Conditioning Hairdressing.** Give your tools a light coat of Alberto VO5 Conditioning Hairdressing.
- **Crayola Chalk.** Place a few pieces of Crayola Chalk in your toolbox to absorb moisture.
- **Kingsford Charcoal Briquets.** Placing a charcoal briquet in a toolbox will absorb moisture, according to household hints columnist Mary Ellen.
- **Turtle Wax.** Coat tools with a light coat of Turtle Wax.

Hang any item on a pegboard with . . .

- **Scotch Packaging Tape.** Fold a piece of Scotch Packaging Tape over the edge of any small object, punch a hole in the tape, and hang on a peg.

Remove rust from household tools with . . .

- **Heinz Vinegar.** Soak the rusted tool in undiluted Heinz White Vinegar overnight.
- **Morton Salt.** Make a paste using two tablespoon Morton Salt and one tablespoon lemon juice. Apply the paste to rust with a dry cloth and rub.

Wallpaper

Remove wallpaper with . . .

- **Heinz Vinegar.** Mix equal parts Heinz Vinegar and hot water. Use a paint roller to wet the paper thoroughly with the mixture. Repeat. Paper should peel off in sheets.
- **Downy Fabric Softener.** Mix one capful Downy Fabric Softener with one quart hot water in a plastic bucket, sponge the wallpaper, wait twenty minutes, and peel off the paper.

Tint wallpaper paste with . . .

- **McCormick/Schilling Food Coloring.** Add a few drops of food coloring to wallpaper paste so you can see how well you're covering the wallpaper.

Windows

Repair a small dent in a window with . . .

- **Maybelline Crystal Clear Nail Polish.** Fill hole with a few drops of Maybelline Crystal Clear Nail Polish, let it dry, then add a few more drops until full.

Repair a loose pane of glass temporarily with . . .

- **Wrigley's Spearmint Gum.** Use a wad of chewed Wrigley's Spearmint Gum as window putty.

Lubricate windows with . . .

- **Alberto VO5 Conditioning Hairdressing.** Lubricate the tracks with a little Alberto VO5 Conditioning Hairdressing.
- **ChapStick.** Rub ChapStick on the tracks so the windows slide open and shut easily.
- **Ivory Soap.** Rub the tracks with a bar of Ivory Soap.
- **Vaseline.** Lubricate the tracks with a dollop of Vaseline Petroleum Jelly.
- **WD-40.** Spray WD-40 along the tracks to make the window slide easier.

Determine which windows are leaking heat with a . . .

- **Conair Pro Style 1600.** Hold a lit candle just inside a window,

while someone else goes outside with a Conair Pro Style 1600 and blows air along the frame. If the flame flickers, the window needs caulking.

Thaw frozen windows with a . . .

- **Conair Pro Style 1600.** Use a Conair Pro Style 1600 to thaw windows that are frozen shut.

Remove a broken windowpane with . . .

- **Scotch Packaging Tape.** Wearing gloves, crisscross Scotch Packaging Tape on both sides of the broken glass, tap the inside edges with a hammer until the pane breaks free, then peel off the tape to remove any shards.

Temporarily repair a window with . . .

- **Saran Wrap.** Tape Saran Wrap over a small hole to keep out wind, rain, or snow.

Wiring

Thread electrical wire through conduits with . . .

- **WD-40.** Spray WD-40 on the electrical wire to help it glide through winding conduits.

Woodwork

Repair scratched woodwork with . . .

- **Lea & Perrins Worcestershire Sauce.** Use a cotton ball to apply Worcestershire Sauce to the scratched surface.
- **Maxwell House Coffee.** Mix one teaspoon instant Maxwell House Coffee with two teaspoons water. Apply to the scratch with a cotton ball.
- **Nestea.** Mix a level teaspoon of Nestea with two teaspoons of water. Use a cotton ball to apply the paste to the scratched surface.

Patch woodwork with . . .

- **Maxwell House Coffee.** Mix dry instant Maxwell

The Name Game: Part 3

Pam No Stick Cooking Spray

Pam is believed to be named after the daughter of company cofounder Arthur Meyerhoff. Coincidentally, the archaic meaning of the word *pamper* is "to indulge with rich food."

Playtex

Playtex is a hybrid of the words *plastic* and *latex*.

Pringles

Pringles seems to be a combination of the words *prince*, meaning regal, and *shingles*, denoting chips.

Q-Tips Cotton Swabs

The Q stands for *quality* and the word *tip* describes the cotton swab on the end of the stick. Q-Tips Cotton Swabs were originally called Baby Gays.

Quaker Oats

In 1887, Henry D. Seymour, one of the founders of a new American oatmeal milling company, purportedly came across an article on the Quakers in an encyclopedia and was struck by the similarity between the religious group's qualities and the image he desired for oatmeal.

A second story contends that Seymour's partner, William Heston, a descendant of Quakers, was walking in Cincinnati one day and saw a picture of William Penn, the English Quaker, and was similarly struck by the parallels in quality.

Revlon

The word *Revlon* is derived from the last name of company founder Charles Revson, who changed the letter *S* to the letter *L* in honor of one of his partners, Charles Lachman, whose first name was used for the perfume Charlie.

Scotch Transparent Tape

In 1925, the automobile industry, eager to satisfy America's craving for two-tone cars, had difficulty making a clean, sharp edge where one color met another. Richard Drew, a twenty-five-year-old laboratory employee at the Minnesota Mining and Manufacturing Company (better known as 3M), developed a two-inch-wide strip of paper tape coated with a rubber-based adhesive. To cut costs, the tape was coated with only a strip of glue one-quarter-inch wide along the edges, instead of covering the entire two-inch width.

Unfortunately, the tape failed to hold properly, and the painters purportedly told the 3M salesmen, "Take this tape back to those Scotch bosses of yours and tell them to put adhesive all over the tape, not just on the edges." The 3M company complied, but when the salesman returned to the automobile paintshop, a painter derogatorily asked him if he was still selling that "Scotch" tape, launching a trade name based on an ethnic slur denoting stinginess. The name, like the improved tape, stuck.

Silly Putty

Toy store proprietor and former advertising copywriter Paul Hodgson came up with the name Silly Putty off the top of his head while playing with the pink polymer.

S.O.S Steel Wool Soap Pads

Mrs. Edwin Cox, the inventor's wife, named the soap pads S.O.S. for "Save Our Saucepans," convinced that she had cleverly adapted the Morse code international distress signal for "Save Our Ships." In fact, the distress signal S.O.S. doesn't stand for anything. It's simply a combination of three letters represented by three identical marks (the *S* is three dots, the *O* is three dashes). The period after the last *S* was deleted from the brand name in order to obtain a trademark for what would otherwise be an international distress symbol.

SPAM

SPAM, possibly a contraction of *sp*iced h*am*, was named by actor Kenneth Daigneau, the brother of R. H. Daigneau, a former Hormel Foods vice president. When other meat packers started introducing similar products, Jay C. Hormel decided to create a catchy brand name to give his spiced ham an unforgettable identity, offering a $100 prize to the person who came up with a new name. At a New Year's Eve party in 1936, Daigneau suggested the name SPAM.

SueBee Honey

SueBee is a combination of the misspelled word *Sioux*, the Indian tribe for which Sioux City, Iowa, is named, and the word *bee*, the insect that makes honey.

Tabasco Pepper Sauce

Tabasco, a word of Central American Indian origin, was chosen by creator Edmund McIlhenny because he liked the sound of the word.

Tidy Cat

Ed Lowe coined the name Kitty Litter and sold his first cat box filler exclusively through pet stores beginning in 1947. Twenty years later, when grocery stores finally agreed to carry Kitty Litter, Lowe repackaged his product as Tidy Cat (so the grocery stores could charge a lower price for the cat box filler, while the pet stores could continue charging a premium price for Kitty Litter).

Turtle Wax

While driving from Beloit, Wisconsin, company founder Benjamin Hirsch, the developer of Plastone car polish, stopped at a place named Turtle Creek, rested by a stream, and was struck by his reflection in the water. Realizing that his car polish provided a wax coating as tough as a turtle shell and as reflective as Turtle Creek, he renamed his product Turtle Wax.

20 Mule Team Borax

20 Mule Team Borax is named for the twenty-mule teams used to transport borax from the mines in Death Valley during the late nineteenth century. The word *borax* derives from the Arabic *buraq* or *baurach*, which means "to glitter or shine."

Vaseline

Robert Augustus Chesebrough combined the German word *wasser* (water) with the Greek word *elaion* (olive oil).

Velcro

Inventor George de Mestral combined *vel* (from *velvet*) with *cro* (from the French *crochet*, which means "hook").

WD-40

Norman Larsen, president and head chemist at the Rocket Chemical Company, developed a *water-d*isplacement formula on his fortieth try, naming it WD-40.

Wilson Tennis Balls

When the Ashland Manufacturing Company was forced into receivership in 1914, a group of bankers decided to rename the company Wilson and Company to capitalize on President Woodrow Wilson's popularity at the time.

Wonder Bread

Elmer Cline, the Taggart Baking Company vice president appointed to merchandise a new one-and-a-half-pound loaf of bread, was awed by the sight of the sky filled with hundreds of colorful hot-air balloons at the International Balloon Race at the Indianapolis Speedway. The wonder of that sight prompted Cline to name the new bread Wonder Bread, and colorful balloons have been featured on Wonder Bread wrappers ever since.

House Coffee with spackling paste until you achieve the desired brown tone, fill the crack or hole, and smooth with a damp cloth.

Plug small nail or thumbtack holes in wood with . . .

● **Forster Toothpicks.** Dip the end of a Forster Toothpick in glue, insert into the hole, slice flush with a single-edge razor blade, sand smooth, and refinish the wood.

For more offbeat uses for brand-name products, visit Joey Green on the internet at:
www.wackyuses.com

Acknowledgments

My extraordinary editor, Laurie Abkemeier, made working on this book a pleasure. As always, I am grateful for her enthusiasm, passion, and keen sense of humor.

I am also indebted to Claudyne Bedell, Samantha Miller, Marianne Magid, Erica Keating, Bob Miller, Liz Kessler, Mark Rifkin, Victor Weaver, Adrian James, Jeremy Solomon, Judianne Jaffe, Kim from L.A., Bob Baskinsherry, and Tim Nyberg, and a battalion of proof-readers and copy-editors.

In the corporate world, I take my hat off to Daniel Stone at Alberto-Culver USA, Inc. (makers of Alberto VO5 products), Carol Alberti at Bayer (makers of Alka-Seltzer, Bayer Aspirin, and Phillips' Milk of Magnesia), David Worrell at Church & Dwight Co., Inc. (makers of Arm & Hammer Baking Soda), Janet Silverberg at Quaker Oats Company (makers of Aunt Jemima Original Syrup and Quaker Oats), Arthur Moore and Martha Erickson at Avery Dennison Corporation (makers of Avery Labels), Dean Siegel at Block Drug Company, Inc. (makers of Balmex), Richard Cahill at Pfizer Inc. (makers of Barbasol), Pam Becker at General Mills (makers of Betty Crocker Potato Buds and Gold Medal Flour), Steven Sanders at Bosco Products, Inc. (makers of Bosco chocolate syrup), Mary Jon Dunham at Procter &

Gamble (makers of Bounce, Cascade, Crisco, Dawn, Downy, Ivory, Jif, Pampers, Pepto-Bismol, and Vicks VapoRub), Lucy Billhime at Campbell Soup Company, Andrew Bridge at Dr. Pepper/Seven Up, Inc. (makers of Canada Dry Club Soda), Rita Henderson and Terry Haywood at Nestlé Food Company (makers of Carnation Nonfat Dry Milk and Nestea), Steven Flynn and Ronald Alice at American Home Products Corporation (makers of ChapStick), Karen Johnston at Hunt-Wesson, Inc. (makers of Chun King Soy Sauce, Hunt's Tomato Paste, Orville Redenbacher's Gourmet and Popping Corn, and Wesson Corn Oil), Peter Sanders at Bristol-Myers Squibb Company (makers of Clairol Herbal Essences), Sandy Sullivan at the Clorox Company (makers of Clorox, Kingsford Charcoal Briquets, and S.O.S), Norman Mandel at the Coca-Cola Company, Scott Thompson at Colgate-Palmolive (makers of Colgate, Murphy's Oil Soap, and Palmolive), Charles Oppenheimer at Schering-Plough Corporation (makers of Coppertone), Richard O'Planick at Rubbermaid, Incorporated. (makers of Con-Tact Paper), Frank Lindsey at Conair Corporation (makers of the Conair Pro Style 1600), Georgianna Mandelos at Marina Maher (public relations firm for Cover Girl), Debi Lindaberry at Binney & Smith Inc. (makers of Crayola Crayons and chalk, and Silly Putty), Bonny Beetham and Anna Moses at the Dannon Company, Robert Alexander at James River Corporation (makers of Dixie Cups), Josephine Anguili at Domino Sugar Corporation, Ralph Bronner at All-One-God-Faith, Inc. (makers of Dr. Bronner's Peppermint Soap), John O'Shea at Warner-Lambert (makers of Efferdent, Listerine, and Lubriderm), Colleen Nissi at Borden Inc. (makers of Elmer's Glue-All and ReaLemon), Arthur DeBaugh and Susan Meyer at Sara Lee Corporation (makers of Endust, Kiwi Shoe Polish, and L'eggs Sheer Energy), Tom Knuesel at Diamond Brands (makers of Forster Toothpicks), Benton Spayd at Mattel (makers of Frisbee), Mack Jenks at Gerber Products Company (makers of Gerber baby foods), Nancy Lovre at SmithKline Beecham (makers of Geritol), Gary Wamer at First Brands Corporation (makers of Glad products), Marc Gold at Gold's Horseradish, Harriet Grabus at International Home Products, Inc. (makers of Gulden's Mustard), William Perlberg at Hartz Mountain Corporation, Deb Magness at H. J. Heinz Company (makers of Heinz Vinegar and Heinz Ketchup), Nancy Lee Carter and Boyd Tracy at Kimberly-Clark Corporation (makers of Huggie's Baby Wipes, Kleenex Tissues, and Viva Paper Towels), Sharon Ptak-Miles at Kraft Foods, Inc. (makers of Jell-O, Kool-Aid, Maxwell House Coffee, Miracle Whip, and Tang), Mitchell Frank at CPC International Inc. (makers of Kingsford's Corn Starch), Wendy Schwimmer and Tom Boyden at GCI Group (public relations firm for Krazy-Glue), Jan Belowich and Micke Schwartzman at Lea & Perrins (makers of Lea & Perrins Worcestershire Sauce), Peter Mendelson at the Thomas J. Lipton Company (makers of Lipton Tea), Danielle Frizzi at Gillette (makers of Liquid Paper), Lisa Gigliotti at Maybelline, Inc. (makers of Maybelline Crystal Clear Nail Polish), Diane Hamel at McCormick & Company, Inc. (makers of McCormick and Schilling Alum, Black Pepper, Cream of Tartar, Food Coloring, Garlic Powder, Meat Tenderizer, and Vanilla Extract), James Koester at Anheuser-Busch, Inc. (makers of Miller High Life), E.C. Thorne at Morton International, Inc. (makers of Morton Salt), Kathy Vanderwist at Signature Brands, Inc. (makers of Mr. Coffee Filters), Kerry Gleeson at Oral-B Laboratories, Ellen Ciuzio at International Home Foods (makers of Pam No Stick Cooking Spray), Bob Parker at Sanford Corporation (makers of Pink Pearl Erasers), Trish O'Connell at Playtex Products, Inc. (makers of Playtex Living Gloves), Karen Brown at Whitehall-Robbins (makers of Preparation H), Robert Phillips and Melvin Kurtz at Chesebrough-Pond's USA Co. (makers of Q-Tips and Vaseline), Leslie Tripp at Beatrice Cheese, Inc. (makers of Reddi-wip), Alan McDonald at Reynolds Metals Company (makers of Reynolds Wrap and Cut-Rite Wax Paper), Lauren Cislak at DowBrands, Inc. (makers of Saran Wrap, Spray 'n Wash, and Ziploc Storage Bags), Judy Schuster at 3M (makers of Scotch Transparent Tape, Scotch Packaging Tape, and Scotchgard), Cheryl Sprangler at Star Fine Foods (makers of Star Olive Oil), Gary Evans at Sioux Honey Association (makers of SueBee Honey), Betty James at James Industries (makers of Slinky), Kevin Jones at Hormel Foods Corporation (makers of SPAM luncheon meat), Jo Osborn at Sunshine Biscuits, Inc. (makers of Sunshine Krispy Original Saltine Crackers), Paul McIlhenny at McIlhenny Company (makers of Tabasco Pepper Sauce), Barbara Gargiulo at Tambrands Inc. (makers of Tampax Tampons), Donna Frazier and Stacy Banes at Ralston Purina Company (makers of Tidy Cat), Charles Tornabene at Turtle Wax Inc. (makers of Turtle Wax), Kurt Ganderup at U.S. Borax Inc. and Rebecca Nittle at The Dial Corporation (makers of 20 Mule Team Borax), Bertille Glass and Marlene Machut at Uncle Ben's, Inc. (makers of Uncle Ben's Converted Brand Rice), Pauwla van Sambeek-Ronde and Sari Ann Starsburg at Velcro Industries (makers of Velcro), Paige Perdue at the WD-40 Company (makers of WD-40), Ray Berens at Wilson Sporting Goods Co. (makers of Wilson Tennis Balls), Mark Dirkes at Interstate Brands Corporation (makers of Wonder Bread), and Christopher Perille at Wm. Wrigley Jr. Company (makers of Wrigley's Spearmint Gum).

Upstanding Americans who shared their ingenuity include Robert and Barbara Green, Dr. Jeffrey Gorodetsky, Lora and Barry Schwartzberg, Amy and Robin Robinson, Leonard Sherman, Mindy Staley, Adam Turteltaub, Allan and Andrea Brum, Cindy Press, Howard Gershen, Robin Rouda, Bill Aitchison, Kathy McMahon, Anne Allen McGrath, John Fiorre Pucci, Gretchen Van Pelt, Jeffrey Combs, Dr. Richard Swatt, Betty Jeffress, and the dancing feet of Chris Spear.

Above all, all my love to Debbie, Ashley, and Julia for putting up with me.

The Fine Print

Sources

● *All-New Hints* from Heloise by Heloise (New York: Perigee, 1989)

● *Another Use For* by Vicki Lansky (Deephaven, MN: Book Peddlers, 1991)

● *Ask Anne & Nan* by Anne Adams and Nancy Walker (Brattleboro, VT: Whetstone, 1989)

● "Baking Soda's Star Rises" by Bruce Horovitz (*Los Angeles Times*, August 16, 1994)

● *Can You Trust a Tomato in January?* by Vince Staten (New York: Simon & Schuster, 1993)

● *Chicken Soup & Other Folk Remedies* by Joan Wilen and Lydia Wilen (New York: Fawcett Columbine, 1984)

● *Coca-Cola: An Illustrated History* by Pat Watters (New York: Doubleday & Company, Inc., 1978)

● *A Dash of Mustard* by Katy Holder and Jane Newdick (London: Chartwell Books, 1995)

● *Dictionary of Trade Name Origins* by Adrian Room (London: Routledge & Kegan Paul, 1982)

● *The Doctors Book of Home Remedies* by Editors of Prevention Magazine (Emmaus, PA: Rodale Press, 1990)

● *The Doctors Book of Home Remedies II* by Sid Kirchheimer

and the Editors of Prevention Magazine (Emmaus, PA: Rodale Press, 1993)

● *The Duct Tape Book* by Jim and Tim (Duluth, MN: Pfeifer-Hamilton, 1995)

● *Encyclopedia of Pop Culture* by Jane & Michael Stern (New York: HarperCollins, 1992)

● *Famous American Trademarks* by Arnold B. Barach (Washington, D.C.: Public Affairs Press, 1971)

● *From Beer to Eternity* by Will Anderson (Lexington, MA: Stephen Greene Press, 1987)

● "Have a Problem? Chances Are Vinegar Can Help Solve It" by Caleb Solomon (*Wall Street Journal*, September 30, 1992)

● *Hints from Heloise* by Heloise (New York: Arbor House, 1980)

● *Hoover's Handbook of World Business 1993* (Austin: Reference Press, 1993)

● *Hoover's Handbook of American Business 1994* (Austin: Reference Press, 1994)

● *Hoover's Company Profile Database* (Austin: The Reference Press, 1996)

● *Household Hints & Formulas* by Erik Bruun (New York: Black Dog and Leventhal, 1994)

● *Household Hints for Upstairs, Downstairs, and All Around the House* by Carol Reese (New York: Henry Holt and Company, 1982)

● *Household Hints & Handy Tips* by Reader's Digest (Pleasantville, NY: Reader's Digest Association, 1988)

● *How the Cadillac Got Its Fins* by Jack Mingo (New York: HarperCollins, 1994)

● *I'll Buy That!* by the Editors of Consumer Reports (Mount Vernon, NY: Consumers Union, 1986)

- "Is There Anything Vinegar Is Not Good For?" by Lora Rader (*Country Stock & Small Stock Journal*, March-April 1993)
- *Kitchen Medicines* by Ben Charles Harris (Barre, MA: Barre, 1968)
- *Make It Yourself* by Dolores Riccio and Joan Bingham (Radnor, PA: Chilton, 1978)
- *Mary Ellen's Best of Helpful Hints* by Mary Ellen Pinkham (New York: Warner/B. Lansky, 1979)
- *Mary Ellen's Greatest Hints* by Mary Ellen Pinkham (New York: Fawcett Crest, 1990)
- "More Than You Want to Know About SPAM" by Judith Stone (*New York Times Magazine*, July 3, 1994)
- "A Most Favored Food" by Alice M. Geffen and Carole Berglie (*Americana*, May-June 1989)
- *The New Our Bodies, Ourselves* by the Boston Women's Health Book Collective (New York: Touchstone, 1992)
- *Our Story So Far* (St. Paul, MN: 3M, 1977)
- *Panati's Extraordinary Origins of Everyday Things* by Charles Panati (New York: HarperCollins, 1987)
- *Practical Problem Solver* by Reader's Digest (Pleasantville, NY: Reader's Digest, 1991)
- *Rodale's Book of Hints, Tips & Everyday Wisdom* by Carol Hupping, Cheryl Winters Tetreau, and Roger B. Yepsen Jr. (Emmaus, PA: Rodale Press, 1985)
- *Steal This Book* by Abbie Hoffman (New York: Pirate Press, 1972)
- *Symbols of America* by Hal Morgan (New York: Viking, 1986)
- *The Tabasco Cookbook* by Paul McIlhenny with Barbara Hunter (New York: Clarkson Potter, 1993)
- "WD-40," *USA Today*, 1993

- *The Woman's Day Help Book* by Geraldine Rhoads and Edna Paradis (New York: Viking, 1988)
- *Why Did They Name It . . . ?* by Hannah Campbell (New York: Fleet, 1964)

Trademarks and Disclaimers

All photographs used with permission of the trademark holders:

"Alberto VO5" is a registered trademark of Alberto-Culver USA, Inc.

"Alka-Seltzer" is a registered trademark of Miles, Inc. "Bayer" and "Phillips" are registered trademarks of Bayer Corporation. Bayer Corporation does not endorse any use for Alka-Seltzer, Bayer Aspirin, or Phillips' Milk of Magnesia other than those indicated on the package label.

"Arm & Hammer" is a registered trademark of Church & Dwight Co, Inc. Church & Dwight Co., Inc. does not recommend uses of Arm & Hammer Baking Soda not described on the package or in current company brochures.

"Aunt Jemima" is a registered trademark of the Quaker Oats Company.

"Avery" is a registered trademark of Avery Dennison Corporation.

"Balmex" is a registered trademark of Block Drug Company, Inc.

"Barbasol" and "Beard Buster" are registered trademarks of Pfizer Inc. Pfizer Inc. does not recommend or endorse any use of Barbarsol Shaving Cream beyond those indicated on the usage instructions on the package label.

"Betty Crocker" and "Potato Buds" are registered trademarks of General Mills, Inc.

"Bosco" is a registered trademark of Bosco Products, Inc.

"Bounce," "Cascade," "Crisco," "Dawn," "Downy," "Ivory," "Jif," "Pampers," "Pepto-Bismol," "Vicks," and "VapoRub" are registered trademarks of Procter & Gamble. Procter & Gamble does not recommend or endorse any use of Bounce, Cascade, Crisco, Dawn, Downy, Ivory soap, Jif, Pampers, Pepto-Bismol, or Vicks VapoRub beyond those for which these products have been tested as indicated on the usage instructions on each package label.

"Campbell" is a registered trademark of Campbell Soup Company. Campbell Soup Company does not endorse or recommend any use of Campbell's tomato juice beyond those for which the product has been tested as indicated on the usage instructions on the label or in product promotion material distributed by or on behalf of the company.

"Canada Dry" and the shield are registered trademarks of Cadbury Beverages Inc.

"Carnation" is a registered trademark of Nestlé Food Company.

"ChapStick" is a registered trademark of A. H. Robbins Company.

"Chun King" is a registered trademark of Hunt-Wesson, Inc.

"Clairol" and "Herbal Essences" are registered trademarks of Clairol.

"Clorox" is a registered trademark of the Clorox Company.

"Coca-Cola" and "Coke" are registered trademarks of the Coca-Cola Company. The Coca-Cola Company does not endorse any use of Coca-Cola other than as a soft drink.

"Colgate," "Palmolive," and "Murphy" are registered trademarks of Colgate-Palmolive. Colgate-Palmolive Company does not recommend or endorse any use of Colgate toothpaste, Palmolive dish washing liquid, or Murphy Oil Soap surface cleaning product other than those uses indicated on the package label.

"Con-Tact" is a registered trademark of Rubbermaid, Incorporated.

"Conair" and "Pro Style" are registered trademarks of Conair Corporation. The Conair Corporation does not endorse the use of a hair dryer for other than drying hair.

"Coppertone" is a registered trademark of Schering-Plough HealthCare Products, Inc.

"Cover Girl" and "NailSlicks" are registered trademarks of Noxell, Inc.

"Crayola" is a registered trademark of Binney & Smith Inc.

"Dannon" is a registered trademark of the Dannon Company. The Dannon Company, Inc. does not support usage of its yogurt products in any manner other than for normal daily food and dairy consumption.

"Dixie" is a registered trademark of James River Corporation.

"Domino" is a registered trademark of Domino Sugar Corporation.

"Dr. Bronner's" is a registered trademark of All-One-God-Faith, Inc.

"Efferdent," "Listerine," and "Lubriderm" are registered trademarks of Warner-Lambert Co. Warner-Lambert Company does not endorse any use of Efferdent denture cleanser, Listerine mouthwash, and Lubriderm lotion other than those indicated in the usage instructions on the package label.

"Elmer's Glue-All," Elmer the Bull, and Elsie the Cow are registered trademarks of Borden, Inc.

"Endust" is a registered trademark of Sara Lee Corporation.

"Forster" is a registered trademark of Forster Manufacturing Company, Inc.

"Frisbee" is a registered trademark of Mattel.

"Gerber" is a registered trademark of Gerber Products Company. Gerber Products Company does not endorse the use of its baby food jars for any purpose other than the use of baby food.

"Geritol" is a registered trademark of Beecham, Inc.

"Glad" is a registered trademark of First Brands Corporation.

"Gold Medal" is a registered trademark of General Mills, Inc.

"Gulden's" is a registered trademark of International Home Products, Inc.

"Hartz" is a registered trademark of Hartz Mountain Corporation.

"Heinz" is a registered trademark of H. J. Heinz Company.

"Huggies" is a registered trademark of Kimberly-Clark Corporation.

"Hunt's" is a registered trademark of Hunt-Wesson, Inc.

"Jell-O," "Kool-Aid," "Maxwell House," "Good to the Last Drop," "Miracle Whip," and "Tang" are registered trademarks of Kraft Foods, Inc. Kraft Foods, Inc. does not endorse any use of its products mentioned in this book other than the intended use of each product which is indicated on the packaging labels for each product.

"Kingsford's" and the Kingsford logo are registered trademarks of CPC International Inc.

"Kingsford" is a registered trademark of the Kingsford Products Company.

"Kiwi" is a registered trademark of Sara Lee Corporation.

"Kleenex" is a registered trademark of Kimberly-Clark Corporation.

"Krazy" is a registered trademark of Borden, Inc. Elmer's Products, Inc. accepts no liability for any mentioned use for Krazy Glue that is not specifically endorsed in the product's packaging and labeling.

"L'eggs" and "Sheer Energy" are registered trademarks of Sara Lee Corporation.

"Lea & Perrins" is a registered trademark of Lea & Perrins. Lea & Perrins does not endorse any use of Lea & Perrins Worcestershire Sauce other than as a table sauce or sauce for specific food recipes or marinades.

"Lipton," "The 'Brisk' Tea," and "Flo-Thru" are registered trademarks of Lipton.

"Liquid Paper" is a registered trademark of Liquid Paper Corporation.

"Maybelline" is a registered trademark of Maybelline, Inc. Maybelline Cosmetics Corporation does not recommend or endorse any use of Maybelline Crystal Clear Nail Polish other than as a nail polish.

"McCormick" and "Schilling" are registered trademarks of McCormick & Company, Inc. McCormick & Company, Inc. does not endorse any use of meat tenderizer, alum, garlic powder, vanilla extract, cream of tartar, food coloring, or black pepper other than as a seasoning in foods.

"Miller" and "High Life" are registered trademarks of Anheuser-Busch, Inc.

"Morton" and the Morton Umbrella Girl are registered trademarks of Morton International, Inc.

"Mr. Coffee" is a registered trademark of Signature Brands, Inc.

"Nestea" is a registered trademark of Nestlé.

"Oral-B," "Indicator," and "Mint Waxed Floss" are registered trademarks of Oral-B Laboratories.

"Orville Redenbacher's Gourmet" and "Popping Corn" are registered trademarks of Hunt-Wesson, Inc.

"Pam" is a registered trademark of International Home Foods, Inc. International Home Foods, Inc. does not endorse any use of Pam No Stick Cooking Spray other than those indicated on the label.

"Pink Pearl" is a registered trademark of Sanford.

"Playtex," "Living" and "Made Strong to Last Long" are registered trademarks of Playtex Products, Inc.

"Preparation H" is a registered trademark of Whitehall-Robbins.

"Q-Tips" is a registered trademark of Chesebrough-Pond's USA Co.

"Quaker Oats" is a registered trademark of the Quaker Oats Company.

"ReaLemon" is a registered trademark of Borden, Inc.

"Reddi-wip" is a registered trademark of Beatrice Cheese, Inc. Beatrice Cheese, Inc. does not recommend or accept liability for any use of Reddi-wip whipped topping other than for food topping.

"Reynolds," "Reynolds Wrap," and "Cut-Rite" are registered trademarks of Reynolds Metals Company.

"S.O.S" is a registered trademark of the Clorox Company.

"Saran Wrap" is a registered trademark of DowBrands, Inc.

"Scotch," "3M," "Scotchgard," and the plaid design are registered trademarks of 3M.

"Silly Putty" is a registered trademark of Binney & Smith Inc.

"Slinky" is a registered trademark of James Industries.

"SPAM" and "SPAMBURGER" are registered trademarks of Hormel Foods Corporation.

"Spray 'n Wash" is a registered trademark of DowBrands L.P.

"Star" is a registered trademark of Star Fine Foods.

"SueBee" is a registered trademark of Soiux Honey Association.

"Sunshine" and "Krispy" are registered trademarks of Sunshine Biscuits, Inc.

"Tabasco" is a registered trademark of McIlhenny Company.

"Tampax" is a registered trademark of Tambrands Inc.

"Tidy Cat" is a registered trademark of the Ralston Purina Company.

"Turtle Wax" and "Super Hard Shell" are registered trademarks of Turtle Wax, Inc.

"20 Mule Team" is a registered trademark of Dial Corp.

"Uncle Ben's" and "Converted" are registered trademarks of Uncle Ben's, Inc.

"Vaseline" is a registered trademark of the Chesebrough-Pond's USA.

"Velcro" is a registered trademark of Velcro Industries B.V.

"Vicks" and "VapoRub" are registered trademarks of Procter & Gamble.

"Viva" is a registered trademark of Kimberly-Clark Corporation.

"WD-40" is a registered trademark of the WD-40 Company.

"Wesson" is a registered trademark of Hunt-Wesson, Inc.

"Wilson" is a registered trademark of Wilson Sporting Goods Co.

"Wonder" is a registered trademark of Interstate Brands Corporation.

"Wrigley" and "Wrigley's Spearmint" are registered trademarks of Wm. Wrigley Jr. Company.

"Ziploc" is a registered trademark of DowBrands.

Index

About the Author

Joey Green, author of *Polish Your Furniture with Panty Hose, Paint Your House with Powdered Milk*, and *Wash Your Hair with Whipped Cream*, got Jay Leno to shave with Jif Peanut Butter on *The Tonight Show*, Rosie O'Donnell to mousse her hair with Jell-O on *The Rosie O'Donnell Show*, and Katie Couric to drop her diamond engagement ring in a glass of Efferdent on *Today*. He has been seen polishing furniture with SPAM on *CNN Headline News*, cleaning a toilet with Coca-Cola in the *New York Times*, and washing his hair with Reddi-wip in *People*. Green, a former contributing editor to *National Lampoon* and a former advertising copywriter at J. Walter Thompson, is the author of a dozen books, including *The Zen of Oz: Ten Spiritual Lessons from Over the Rainbow, Selling Out: If Famous Authors Wrote Advertising*, and *The Bubble Wrap Book*. A native of Miami, Florida, and a graduate of Cornell University, he wrote television commercials for Burger King and Walt Disney World, and won a Clio Award for a print ad he created for Eastman Kodak. He backpacked around the world for two years on his honeymoon, and lives in Los Angeles with his wife, Debbie, and their two daughters, Ashley and Julia.

- Dry nail polish with Pam® No Stick Cooking Spray
- Relieve a toothache with Tabasco® Pepper Sauce
- Kill slugs with Miller® High Life®
- Fertilize a lawn with Maxwell House® Coffee
- Lure crabs with Wrigley's Spearmint® Gum

Wash Your Hair with Whipped Cream

The third hilarious book in the series will have you dancing in the supermarket aisles, as you discover how to:

- Clean a toilet bowl with Alka Seltzer®
- Mousse your hair with Jell-O®
- Clean wallpaper with Wonder® Bread
- Give yourself a facial with Miracle Whip®
- Make ski pants with Scotchgard®
- Clean your dishwasher with Tang®

Dubbed a "modern day Heloise" by the *New York Times* and the "pantry professor" by *People*, Joey Green—the guru of weird uses for brand-name products—has been seen on *The Tonight Show with Jay Leno*, *The Rosie O'Donnell Show*, *Today*, and *Good Morning America.*

In Bookstores Everywhere from Hyperion